diabetic LIVING Everyday COOKING

VOLUME 4

DIABETIC LIVING® EVERYDAY COOKING
IS PART OF A BOOK SERIES PUBLISHED BY
BETTER HOMES AND GARDENS SPECIAL
INTEREST MEDIA, DES MOINES, IOWA

Tasty, nutritional meals may be as simple as toasted panini sandwiches, artfully arranged salads, fresh-from-the-oven casseroles, and slow-simmering soups.

Mediterranean
Chicken Panini
recipe on page 77

Letter from the Editor

When the seasons change here in the Midwest, so do my cooking methods and food preferences. On cold winter nights, there's nothing better than preparing and savoring a warm, flavorful soup or a comforting casserole. As the trees begin to bud and flowers burst into bloom, I'm ready to hit the deck for some grilling and outdoor meals. Summertime means enjoying dishes that contain garden-fresh ingredients and require minimal prep time.

As a person with type 1 diabetes, I know that eating nutritious food every day is an important component of my health. That's why I'm excited about this new collection of delicious recipes that will help me follow my meal plan and please my family at the same time. There are hearty one-pot meals to simmer on days we have time to spend at home, 30-minute dinners when we need to dash off to evening activities, flavor-packed salads to toss together when it's too hot to cook, health-conscious yet satisfying desserts, and lots more.

Because the recipes have been perfected by the home economists and registered dietitians in the Better Homes and Gardens® Test Kitchen, I know that each dish will turn out well and taste great. I also know each recipe contains healthful amounts of calories, carbs, and sodium. Some of the recipes even use wholesome, time-saving convenience products.

Keep this collection of breakfast, lunch, dinner, and snack recipes handy. You'll discover you can cook the way you want and eat the way you like every day.

Kelly Rawlings

Kelly Rawlings, PWD type 1
Editor, *Diabetic Living*® magazine

ON THE COVER:
Banana Split Ice Cream Pie
recipe on page 139

Photographer: Alison Miksch

Editorial
Advisory Board

Connie Crawley, M.S., R.D., L.D., is a nutrition and health specialist for the University of Georgia Cooperative Extension Service in Athens, specializing in diabetes and weight loss. Connie is a member of the American Dietetic Association Diabetes Care and Education practice group.

Marion J. Franz, M.S., R.D., L.D., CDE, has authored more than 200 publications on diabetes, nutrition, and exercise, including core-curriculum materials for diabetes educators. Marion is a member of the American Dietetic Association Diabetes Care and Education practice group.

Joanne Gallivan, M.S., R.D., is executive director of the National Diabetes Education Program at the National Institutes of Health. Joanne is a member of the American Dietetic Association Diabetes Care and Education practice group.

Marty Irons, R.Ph., CDE, practices at a community pharmacy and also served in industry and the military.

Jeannette Jordan, M.S., R.D., CDE, works for the Medical University of South Carolina in Charleston and consults with the Centers for Disease Control and Prevention.

Irene B. Lewis-McCormick, M.S., CSCS, is a fitness presenter and educator. Certified by the nation's leading fitness organizations, she is a faculty member of the American Council on Exercise.

Chris Smith, The Diabetic Chef®, is the president of Health Range, Inc., and a professionally trained chef. He is a food consultant and cookbook author and conducts healthy-cooking classes.

Hope S. Warshaw, M.S., R.D., CDE, BC-ADM, is a writer specializing in diabetes care. She has authored several American Diabetes Association books. Hope is a member of the American Dietetic Association Diabetes Care and Education practice group.

Fred Williams, Jr., M.D., FACP, FACE, practices endocrinology and specializes in diabetes. He is an active member of the American Association of Clinical Endocrinologists and serves on the board of directors.

John Zrebiec, M.S.W., CDE, is director of Behavioral Health Services at the Joslin Diabetes Center in Boston and a lecturer in the department of psychiatry at Harvard Medical School.

diabetic LIVING Everyday COOKING
VOLUME 4

CONSUMER MARKETING

Vice President, Consumer Marketing	DAVID BALL
Consumer Product Marketing Director	STEVE SWANSON
Consumer Product Marketing Manager	WENDY MERICAL
Business Director	RON CLINGMAN
Production Manager	AL RODRUCK
Contributing Editorial Director	SHELLI McCONNELL
Contributing Design Director	JILL BUDDEN
Contributing Photographer	JASON DONNELLY
Contributing Copy Editor	GRETCHEN KAUFFMAN
Contributing Proofreader	CARRIE SCHMITZ
Test Kitchen Director	LYNN BLANCHARD
Test Kitchen Product Supervisor	ELIZABETH BURT, MPH, R.D.
Editorial Assistants	LORI EGGERS, MARLENE TODD

SPECIAL INTEREST MEDIA

Editorial Director	GREGORY H. KAYKO
Art Director	TIM ALEXANDER
Executive Editor, Food and Health	JENNIFER DARLING
Managing Editor	DOUG KOUMA

DIABETIC LIVING® MAGAZINE

Editorial Manager	KELLY RAWLINGS
Art Director, Health	MICHELLE BILYEU
Assistant Editor	JESSIE SHAFER

MEREDITH NATIONAL MEDIA GROUP

President TOM HARTY

Executive Vice President ANDY SAREYAN

Vice President, Production BRUCE HESTON

Chairman and Chief Executive Officer STEPHEN M. LACY

Vice Chairman MELL MEREDITH FRAZIER

In Memoriam — E.T. MEREDITH III (1933-2003)

Diabetic Living® Everyday Cooking is part of a series published by Meredith Corp., 1716 Locust St., Des Moines, IA 50309-3023.

If you have comments or questions about the editorial material in *Diabetic Living® Everyday Cooking*, write to the editor of *Diabetic Living* magazine, Meredith Corp., 1716 Locust St., Des Moines, IA 50309-3023. Send an e-mail to diabeticlivingmeredith.com or call 800/678-2651. *Diabetic Living* magazine is available by subscription or on the newsstand. To order a subscription to *Diabetic Living* magazine, go to *DiabeticLivingOnline.com.*

© Meredith Corporation 2011. All rights reserved.

First edition. Printed in U.S.A.

ISSN 1943-2887   ISBN 978-0-696-30029-5

contents

Curried Chicken with
Cabbage, Apple, and Onion

recipe on page 8

family-pleasing dinners

Whether you are in a hurry or have time to enjoy the pleasures of cooking, preparing a healthful dinner is easy with a just-right recipe. From quick stir-fries and simple simmers to grilled specialties and bubbly casseroles, here's a collection of delicious dishes made with ingredients that are good for you.

Crisp Chicken Parmesan

A crumb coating made with whole grains and low-salt spices adds great flavor and crispness without a lot of sodium and unhealthful fats.

SERVINGS 4 (2 to 3 chicken pieces, ½ cup sauce, and ½ cup pasta each)
CARB. PER SERVING 35 g

Olive oil nonstick cooking spray
¼ cup refrigerated or frozen egg product, thawed, or 2 egg whites, lightly beaten
1 clove garlic, minced
1 cup bran cereal flakes, crushed (about ½ cup crushed)
¼ cup grated Parmesan cheese
1 teaspoon dried Italian seasoning, crushed
1 pound chicken breast tenderloins
4 ounces dried multigrain or whole grain spaghetti
1 cup 1-inch pieces eggplant, peeled if desired
1½ cups no-sugar-added light tomato-basil pasta sauce
1 cup torn fresh spinach leaves
½ cup chopped roma tomatoes

1. Preheat oven to 425°F. Line a 15×10×1-inch baking pan with foil; lightly coat foil with cooking spray. Set aside. In a shallow dish, combine egg, garlic, and 1 tablespoon *water*. In another dish, combine bran flakes, Parmesan cheese, and Italian seasoning.
2. Dip chicken pieces, one at a time, in egg mixture, turning to coat evenly and allowing excess to drip off. Dip chicken in cereal mixture, turning to coat evenly. Place chicken in a single layer in the prepared baking pan. Coat tops of chicken with cooking spray. Bake for 15 to 20 minutes or until chicken is no longer pink (170°F).
3. Meanwhile, cook spaghetti according to package directions; drain and keep warm. Coat an unheated medium saucepan with cooking spray. Preheat saucepan over medium heat. Add eggplant; cook about 5 minutes or until tender, stirring occasionally. Add pasta sauce; heat through. Stir in spinach and tomatoes.
4. Divide spaghetti among four plates. Top with sauce and chicken. If desired, garnish with *fresh basil leaves*.
PER SERVING: 236 cal., 5 g total fat (1 g sat. fat), 70 mg chol., 520 mg sodium, 35 g carb., 6 g fiber, 37 g pro. Exchanges: 1 vegetable, 2 starch, 4 lean meat. Carb choices: 2.
EGGPLANT PARMESAN: Prepare as above, except substitute eight ½-inch-thick slices eggplant for the chicken. Bake 15 to 20 minutes or until eggplant is tender and golden.
PER SERVING: 240 cal., 4 g total fat (1 g sat. fat), 4 mg chol., 464 mg sodium, 42 g carb., 10 g fiber, 13 g pro. Exchanges: 2 vegetable, 2 starch, 0.5 lean meat, 0.5 fat. Carb choices: 3.

Curried Chicken with Cabbage, Apple, and Onion

Curry powder brings out the best in both the chicken and the warm cabbage-and-apple slaw.

SERVINGS 4 (1 chicken breast half and 1 cup cabbage mixture each)

CARB. PER SERVING 19 g

- 1 teaspoon curry powder
- ¼ teaspoon salt
- ¼ teaspoon black pepper
- 4 small skinless, boneless chicken breast halves (1 to 1¼ pounds total)
- 2 teaspoons olive oil
- 2 teaspoons butter
- 1 medium onion, sliced and separated into rings
- 3 cups shredded cabbage
- 2 red-skin cooking apples (such as Rome or Jonathan), cored and thinly sliced
- ½ cup apple juice

1. In a small bowl, combine ½ teaspoon of the curry powder, the salt, and pepper. Sprinkle spice mixture evenly over chicken; rub in with your fingers.

2. In a large nonstick skillet, heat oil over medium-high heat. Add chicken. Cook for 8 to 12 minutes or until no longer pink (170°F), turning once. Transfer chicken to a platter. Cover to keep warm.

3. Melt butter in the hot skillet. Add onion. Cook about 5 minutes or until onion is tender, stirring occasionally. Stir in cabbage, apples, and apple juice. Sprinkle with the remaining ½ teaspoon curry powder. Cook for 3 to 4 minutes or just until apples and vegetables are tender, stirring occasionally.

4. To serve, divide chicken and cabbage mixture among four dinner plates.

PER SERVING: 237 cal., 6 g total fat (2 g sat. fat), 71 mg chol., 231 mg sodium, 19 g carb., 4 g fiber, 27 g pro. Exchanges: 1 vegetable, 1 fruit, 3.5 lean meat. Carb choices: 1.

Poblano Chicken Bundles

Cut into these cornmeal-coated chicken rolls and discover a luscously gooey mix of cheese, cilantro, and chile pepper.

SERVINGS 4 (1 chicken breast portion and 2 tablespoons pico de gallo each)
CARB. PER SERVING 15 g

- 4 6-ounce skinless, boneless chicken breast halves
- 2 tablespoons snipped fresh cilantro
- 4 2½x½-inch sticks reduced-fat Monterey Jack cheese (1½ to 2 ounces total)
- 12 2½x½-inch strips fresh poblano chile pepper (1 large pepper) or 3 large fresh jalapeño chile peppers, quartered and seeded*
- ⅓ cup yellow cornmeal
- 1 teaspoon chili powder
- ¼ teaspoon salt
- 2 tablespoons refrigerated or frozen egg product, thawed
- 1 tablespoon water
- 1 tablespoon canola oil or olive oil
- ½ cup bottled pico de gallo or salsa

1. Place each chicken breast half between two pieces of plastic wrap. Using the flat side of a meat mallet, pound chicken until ⅛ inch thick. Remove plastic wrap.
2. Divide the 2 tablespoons cilantro evenly among chicken pieces. Place a cheese stick and three poblano strips or jalapeño quarters across the center of each chicken piece. Fold in sides; roll up from bottom. Secure with wooden toothpicks.
3. In a shallow dish, combine cornmeal, chili powder, and salt. In another shallow dish, combine egg product and the water. Dip chicken bundles into egg mixture and then into cornmeal mixture, turning to coat.
4. In a large nonstick skillet, heat oil over medium heat. Add chicken bundles, seam sides down. Cook about 10 minutes or until browned on all sides, turning occasionally. Reduce heat to medium-low. Cover and cook for 10 to 12 minutes more or until no longer pink (170°F), turning once. Serve with pico de gallo and, if desired, sprinkle with additional snipped cilantro.
***TEST KITCHEN TIP:** Because chile peppers contain volatile oils that can burn your skin and eyes, avoid direct contact with chiles as much as possible. When working with chile peppers, wear plastic or rubber gloves. If your bare hands do touch the peppers, wash your hands and nails well with soap and warm water.
PER SERVING: 315 cal., 8 g total fat (2 g sat. fat), 106 mg chol., 501 mg sodium, 15 g carb., 1 g fiber, 44 g pro. Exchanges: 1 starch, 6 lean meat. Carb choices: 1.

Chicken and Pepper Sauté

A zesty, low-calorie tomato, sweet pepper, and garlic sauce dresses up succulent quick-fried chicken.

SERVINGS 4 (1 chicken breast half and ½ cup vegetable mixture each)
CARB. PER SERVING 12 g

- ¼ cup all-purpose flour
- ¼ teaspoon salt
- ¼ teaspoon black pepper
- 4 small skinless, boneless chicken beast halves (1 to 1¼ pounds total)
- 1 tablespoon canola oil or olive oil
- 2 small red and/or green sweet peppers, cut into bite-size strips
- 1 small onion, halved and sliced
- 2 cloves garlic, minced
- 3 roma tomatoes, seeded and chopped (1 cup)
- ⅔ cup dry white wine or reduced-sodium chicken broth
- 1 tablespoon lemon juice
- 2 tablespoons snipped fresh flat-leaf parsley

1. In a shallow dish, combine flour, salt, and black pepper. Dip chicken breast halves in flour mixture, turning to coat both sides.
2. In a large skillet, heat oil over medium heat. Add chicken to skillet. Cook for 8 to 12 minutes or until chicken is no longer pink (170°F), turning once. Remove chicken from skillet; cut up if desired. Cover to keep warm.
3. Add sweet peppers, onion, and garlic to skillet. Cook and stir for 2 minutes. Remove skillet from heat. Add tomatoes, wine, and lemon juice to skillet. Return to heat. Bring to boiling; reduce heat. Boil gently about 4 minutes more or until liquid is slightly thickened. Stir in parsley.
4. Serve pepper mixture and chicken in shallow bowls.
PER SERVING: 236 cal., 5 g total fat (1 g sat. fat), 66 mg chol., 138 mg sodium, 12 g carb., 2 g fiber, 28 g pro. Exchanges: 1 vegetable, 0.5 starch, 3.5 lean meat, 0.5 fat. Carb choices: 1.

Perfect for a potluck, this kid-friendly dish is delish down to the last spoon. If toting, place the tomatoes in a resealable plastic bag and cut the fresh avocado just before serving.

Chicken Taco Casserole

Sweet pepper and spinach bring lots of vitamins A and C to this Tex-Mex layered meal-in-a-dish.

SERVINGS 6 (about 1 cup each)
CARB. PER SERVING 18 g

Nonstick cooking spray
12 ounces chicken breast strips for stir-frying
2 cloves garlic, minced
1 teaspoon chili powder
2 teaspoons canola oil
1 medium onion, halved and thinly sliced
1 medium red or green sweet pepper, chopped
1 10-ounce package frozen chopped spinach, thawed and squeezed dry
1½ cups purchased salsa
4 6-inch corn tortillas, coarsely torn
¾ cup shredded reduced-fat Monterey Jack cheese (3 ounces)
½ cup cherry tomatoes, chopped
½ of an avocado, seeded, peeled, and chopped
Fresh cilantro leaves (optional)

1. Preheat oven to 350°F. Coat an unheated large nonstick skillet with cooking spray. Preheat skillet over medium-high heat. In a medium bowl, toss together chicken, garlic, and chili powder. Add to hot skillet. Cook for 4 to 6 minutes or until chicken is no longer pink, stirring frequently. Remove chicken from skillet; set aside.
2. Pour oil into hot skillet. Add onion and sweet pepper. Cook over medium heat about 5 minutes or until tender, stirring occasionally. Stir in spinach.
3. Coat a 2-quart square baking dish with cooking spray. Spread about ½ cup of the salsa into the bottom of the baking dish. Top with half of the tortilla pieces, half of the chicken mixture, and half of the vegetable mixture. Pour half of the remaining salsa over the vegetables and top with half of the cheese. Repeat layers once, except do not top with the remaining cheese.
4. Bake, covered, for 30 to 35 minutes or until heated through. Sprinkle with remaining cheese. Let stand for 5 minutes before serving. Garnish with cherry tomatoes, chopped avocado, and, if desired, fresh cilantro.

PER SERVING: 223 cal., 8 g total fat (2 g sat. fat), 43 mg chol., 550 mg sodium, 18 g carb., 4 g fiber, 20 g pro. Exchanges: 1 vegetable, 1 starch, 2 lean meat, 1 fat. Carb choices: 1.

Chicken Taco Casserole

Curry-Lime Chicken Kabobs

Thanks to a yogurt-base marinade, these kabobs are especially tender.

SERVINGS 4 (2 skewers each)
CARB. PER SERVING 15 g

- 1 pound skinless, boneless chicken breast halves, cut into 1½-inch pieces
- 1 6-ounce carton plain yogurt
- ¼ cup snipped fresh cilantro
- 1 teaspoon finely shredded lime peel
- 2 tablespoons lime juice
- 2 tablespoons olive oil or vegetable oil
- 1 tablespoon honey
- 1 tablespoon Dijon-style mustard
- 2 cloves garlic, minced
- ½ teaspoon curry powder
- ¼ teaspoon salt
- ¼ teaspoon black pepper
- 2 medium green and/or red sweet peppers, cut into 1-inch pieces
- 1 medium zucchini, cut into ½-inch slices
- 8 yellow and/or red cherry tomatoes

1. Place chicken in a resealable plastic bag set in a large bowl. For marinade: In a small bowl, combine yogurt, cilantro, lime peel, lime juice, oil, honey, mustard, garlic, curry powder, salt, and black pepper. Pour marinade over chicken. Seal bag; turn to coat chicken. Marinate in the refrigerator for 4 to 24 hours, turning bag occasionally. Drain chicken, reserving marinade.

2. On eight metal skewers, alternately thread chicken, sweet peppers, and zucchini, leaving ¼ inch between pieces. Brush vegetables with reserved marinade.

3. For a charcoal grill, arrange medium-hot coals around a drip pan. Test for medium heat above pan. Place chicken skewers on grill rack over drip pan. Grill, covered, for 18 to 20 minutes or until chicken is no longer pink, turning once halfway through grilling and threading a tomato onto each skewer during the last 1 minute of grilling. (For a gas grill, preheat grill. Reduce heat to medium. Adjust for indirect cooking. Grill as above.)

PER SERVING: 263 cal., 9 g total fat (2 g sat. fat), 68 mg chol., 336 mg sodium, 15 g carb., 2 g fiber, 30 g pro. Exchanges: 1 vegetable, 0.5 starch, 4 lean meat, 0.5 fat. Carb choices: 1.

Oven Cassoulet

Cooking your own dried beans rather than using canned beans saves you money and loads of sodium.

SERVINGS 6 (1 chicken thigh and about ¾ cup bean mixture each)

CARB. PER SERVING 32 g

8 ounces dried Great Northern beans (1¼ cups)
1 tablespoon canola oil or olive oil
6 chicken thighs (about 2¼ pounds total), skinned
1 cup thinly sliced carrots (2 medium)
1 medium onion, cut into thin wedges
½ cup sliced celery (1 stalk)

Oven Cassoulet

2 cloves garlic, minced
1 14.5-ounce can no-salt-added diced tomatoes, undrained
6 ounces light cooked smoked sausage, cut into bite-size pieces
½ teaspoon dried thyme, crushed
¼ teaspoon salt
⅛ to ¼ teaspoon cayenne pepper (optional)

1. Rinse beans. In a large saucepan, combine beans and 4 cups cold *water*. Bring to boiling; reduce heat. Simmer, uncovered, for 2 minutes. Remove from heat. Cover; let stand for 1 hour. (Or soak beans in water overnight in a covered pan.) Drain beans and rinse. In the same saucepan, combine beans and 4 cups cold *water*. Bring to boiling; reduce heat. Cover and simmer for 1 to 1½ hours or until tender. Drain beans.
2. Preheat oven to 350°F. In a large skillet, heat oil over medium-high heat. Add chicken; reduce heat to medium-low. Brown chicken about 10 minutes, turning once to brown both sides. Remove chicken from skillet. Drain all but 1 tablespoon of drippings from the skillet.
3. Add carrots, onion, celery, and garlic to drippings in skillet. Cover and cook about 10 minutes or until vegetables are just tender, stirring occasionally. Stir in beans, tomatoes, sausage, thyme, salt, and, if desired, cayenne pepper. Bring to boiling. Transfer mixture to a 2-quart rectangular baking dish. Arrange chicken thighs on top.
4. Bake, uncovered, about 25 minutes or until chicken is no longer pink (180°F).
PER SERVING: 347 cal., 10 g total fat (3 g sat. fat), 98 mg chol., 481 mg sodium, 32 g carb., 10 g fiber, 33 g pro. Exchanges: 1 vegetable, 1.5 starch, 4 lean meat, 0.5 fat. Carb choices: 2.

Chimichurri Chicken

Chimichurri Chicken

The herb-base sauce gives grilled chicken a flavor upgrade.
SERVINGS 4 (1 chicken breast half, ⅔ cup green beans, and 1 tablespoon sauce each)
CARB. PER SERVING 10 g

4 small skinless, boneless chicken breast halves
1 tablespoon olive oil or canola oil
¼ teaspoon salt
¼ teaspoon black pepper
12 ounces fresh young green beans
1 recipe Chimichurri Sauce (right)
1 lemon (peel and juice)

1. Brush chicken with the oil; sprinkle with salt and pepper. For a charcoal grill, place chicken on grill rack directly over medium coals. Grill, uncovered, for 12 to 15 minutes or until no longer pink (170°F), turning once halfway through grilling time. (For a gas grill, preheat grill. Reduce heat to medium. Place chicken over heat. Cover and grill as above.)
2. Meanwhile, place beans in a 1½-quart microwave-safe dish. Add 1 tablespoon *water*. Cover with vented plastic wrap. Microwave on 100 percent power (high) for 3 minutes; drain.
3. Serve chicken and beans topped with Chimichurri Sauce, lemon peel, and lemon juice.
CHIMICHURRI SAUCE: In small food processor, combine ¾ cup packed flat-leaf parsley; 2 tablespoons olive oil or canola oil; 1 tablespoon cider vinegar; 2 cloves garlic, halved; ¼ teaspoon salt; and ¼ teaspoon crushed red pepper. Process until nearly smooth.
PER SERVING: 253 cal., 12 g total fat (2 g sat. fat), 66 mg chol., 232 mg sodium, 10 g carb., 5 g fiber, 28 g pro. Exchanges: 1.5 vegetable, 3.5 lean meat, 1 fat. Carb choices: 0.5.

Lemon-Thyme
Roasted Chicken
with Fingerlings

3. Carefully stir broth and blended tomatoes into mixture in skillet. Return to boiling; reduce heat. Boil gently, uncovered, for 2 minutes. Stir in evaporated milk; boil gently about 3 minutes more or until sauce thickens slightly.

4. Drain noodles and peas; transfer to a warm serving dish. Spoon sauce over noodles and peas; toss gently. Top with Parmigiano-Reggiano cheese.

PER SERVING: 329 cal., 6 g total fat (1 g sat. fat), 71 mg chol., 419 mg sodium, 44 g carb., 5 g fiber, 25 g pro. Exchanges: 1.5 vegetable, 2.5 starch, 2 lean meat. Carb choices: 3.

Lemon-Thyme Roasted Chicken with Fingerlings

Fingerling potatoes are small, long, knobby spuds that are shaped like fingers. Look for them in the produce departments of larger supermarkets or at farmers' markets.

SERVINGS 4 (1 chicken breast half and ¾ cup potatoes each)

CARB. PER SERVING 23 g

    4   teaspoons canola oil or olive oil
    1   teaspoon dried thyme, crushed
    ¼   teaspoon salt
    ¼   teaspoon freshly ground black pepper
    1   pound fingerling potatoes, halved lengthwise, or tiny new red or white potatoes, halved
    4   small skinless, boneless chicken breast halves (1 to 1¼ pounds total)
    2   cloves garlic, minced
    1   lemon, thinly sliced

1. In a very large skillet, heat 2 teaspoons of the oil over medium heat. Stir in ½ teaspoon of the thyme, the salt, and pepper. Add potatoes; toss to coat. Cover and cook for 12 minutes, stirring twice.

2. Stir potatoes; push to one side of the skillet. Add the remaining 2 teaspoons oil. Arrange chicken breast halves on the other side of the skillet. Cook, uncovered, for 5 minutes.

3. Turn chicken. Spread garlic over chicken breast halves; sprinkle with the remaining ½ teaspoon thyme. Arrange lemon slices on top of chicken. Cover and cook for 7 to 10 minutes more or until chicken is no longer pink (170°F) and potatoes are tender.

PER SERVING: 259 cal., 6 g total fat (1 g sat. fat), 66 mg chol., 212 mg sodium, 23 g carb., 4 g fiber, 29 g pro. Exchanges: 1.5 starch, 3.5 lean meat. Carb choices: 1.5.

Pappardelle with Chicken and Peas

Evaporated fat-free milk makes the pasta sauce rich and creamy without any cream.

SERVINGS 4 (1¼ cups each)

CARB. PER SERVING 44 g

    6   ounces dried pappardelle or other wide egg noodles
    1½ cups shelled sweet peas or loose-pack frozen peas
    ½   of a 14.5-ounce can Italian-style stewed tomatoes, undrained
    2   teaspoons olive oil
    8   ounces skinless, boneless chicken breast halves, cut into large bite-size pieces
    1   small onion, cut into thin wedges
    ¼   teaspoon coarsely ground black pepper
    ¼   cup reduced-sodium chicken broth
    ¼   cup evaporated fat-free milk
    2   tablespoons freshly grated Parmigiano-Reggiano cheese

1. Cook noodles according to package directions, adding peas during the last 3 minutes of cooking. Meanwhile, place undrained tomatoes in a blender or food processor. Cover and blend until smooth; set aside.

2. In a large skillet, heat oil over medium-high heat. Add chicken, onion, and pepper. Cook for 2 to 4 minutes or until chicken is no longer pink.

QUICK TIP
You can substitute turkey breast tenderloins for the chicken breast halves in this one-dish dinner.

Pappardelle with Chicken and Peas

Creamy Turkey
and Spinach Pie
recipe on page 18

Spicy Egg-Stuffed Peppers

Turkey and Black Bean
Chimichangas

Sodium on the Menu

To avoid salt land mines when dining out, check restaurant websites before you go. If that's not an option, follow these guidelines.

1. **Skip the soup.** Even a healthful-sounding vegetable soup is likely loaded with sodium.

2. **Control condiments.** Assume salad dressings, sauces, and other toppers are high in sodium. Request condiments on the side so you can limit the amount you eat.

3. **Eat a half portion.** Automatically cut your sodium (and calorie) intake in half by putting half of your entrée in a to-go container as soon as the server delivers it to your table.

4. **Watch menu clues.** Titles or descriptions including barbecued, marinated, seasoned, and smoked are signs of sodium.

5. **Keep it simple.** Order simply prepared, plain lean meats.

Spicy Egg-Stuffed Peppers

Sweet peppers make tasty edible bowls to corral the zucchini and chicken sausage filling.

SERVINGS 4 (1 stuffed pepper each)
CARB. PER SERVING 12 g

- 4 medium yellow, red, and/or green sweet peppers and/or medium fresh poblano chile peppers (see tip, page 9)
- 2 teaspoons olive oil
- 1 cup chopped zucchini
- ½ cup chopped onion
- 1 3-ounce link cooked habeñero-chile chicken sausage or sweet Italian chicken sausage* or 3 ounces cooked smoked turkey sausage,* chopped
- 1 cup refrigerated or frozen egg product, thawed, or 1 egg, lightly beaten
- 2 tablespoons fat-free milk
- ¼ cup shredded reduced-fat Monterey Jack cheese (1 ounce)

1. Preheat oven to 325°F. Slice tops from sweet peppers; remove and discard seeds. (Or if using poblano peppers, cut off a thin slice from the side of each and discard seeds.) In a large saucepan or pot, cook peppers in a large amount of boiling water for 3 to 5 minutes or just until tender. Invert peppers onto paper towels to drain.
2. In a large skillet, heat oil over medium heat. Add zucchini, onion, and sausage. Cook for 3 minutes or just until zucchini is tender, stirring occasionally. Remove zucchini mixture from skillet; set aside.
3. In a medium bowl, whisk together egg and milk. Add egg mixture to hot skillet. Cook over medium heat, without stirring, until mixture begins to set on the bottom and around the edge. With a spatula or large spoon, lift and fold the partially cooked egg mixture so the uncooked portion flows underneath. Continue cooking over medium heat for 2 to 3 minutes or until egg mixture is cooked through but still glossy and moist. Fold in zucchini mixture.
4. In a 2-quart rectangular baking dish, arrange peppers open sides up. Spoon egg mixture into peppers. Sprinkle with cheese. Bake, uncovered, for 10 to 15 minutes or until cheese melts and egg mixture is heated through.
*TEST KITCHEN TIP: If using Italian chicken sausage or turkey sausage, add 1 fresh jalapeño chile pepper, seeded and finely chopped (see tip, page 9) to skillet with sausage.
PER SERVING: 149 cal., 5 g total fat (1 g sat. fat), 23 mg chol., 352 mg sodium, 12 g carb., 3 g fiber, 14 g pro. Exchanges: 1 vegetable, 0.5 starch, 1.5 lean meat, 0.5 fat. Carb choices: 1.

Turkey and Black Bean Chimichangas

Traditionally fried, this healthful baked version of the Mexican classic is filled with beans and bursting with protein, fiber, and potassium.

SERVINGS 6 (1 chimichanga each)
CARB. PER SERVING 33 g

- Nonstick cooking spray
- 6 10-inch low-carb whole wheat flour tortillas
- 8 ounces ground turkey breast
- ½ cup chopped onion
- 1 15-ounce can no-salt-added black beans, rinsed and drained, or 1¾ cups cooked black beans
- 1 14.5-ounce can no-salt-added diced tomatoes, drained
- ¼ cup bottled salsa
- ¼ cup snipped fresh cilantro
- 1 tablespoon lime juice
- ½ teaspoon ground cumin
- ½ cup shredded reduced-fat Monterey Jack cheese (2 ounces)
- ¼ cup light sour cream
- 2 tablespoons fresh cilantro leaves

1. Preheat oven to 425°F. Coat a baking sheet with cooking spray; set aside. Wrap the tortillas in foil. Heat in the oven for 5 minutes.
2. Meanwhile, in a large skillet, cook turkey and onion until turkey is no longer pink and onion is softened, stirring to break up turkey as it cooks. Add black beans. Using a fork or potato masher, mash beans slightly. Stir in tomatoes, salsa, snipped cilantro, lime juice, and cumin. Heat through.
3. To assemble, spoon about ½ cup of the filling onto each tortilla just below the center. Fold bottom edge of each tortilla up and over filling. Fold opposite sides in and over filling. Roll up from the bottom. If necessary, secure rolled tortillas with wooden toothpicks. Place filled tortillas on prepared baking sheet, seam sides down. Lightly coat tops and sides of the filled tortillas with cooking spray.
4. Bake for 10 to 12 minutes or until tortillas are golden brown. Sprinkle chimichangas with cheese, sour cream, and cilantro sprigs.
PER SERVING: 217 cal., 5 g total fat (1 g sat. fat), 28 mg chol., 430 mg sodium, 33 g carb., 18 g fiber, 23 g pro. Exchanges: 1 vegetable, 2 starch, 2 lean meat. Carb choices: 2.

Creamy Turkey and Spinach Pie

Using turkey breast, light sour cream, and fat-free cream cheese lowers calories and keeps the fat in check.
Pictured on page 16.

SERVINGS 8 (1 wedge each)
CARB. PER SERVING 15 g

Nonstick cooking spray
4 ounces dried multigrain or plain angel hair pasta, broken
1 8-ounce package fat-free cream cheese, softened
¾ cup refrigerated or frozen egg product, thawed, or 3 eggs
½ cup light sour cream
¼ cup snipped fresh basil or 2 teaspoons dried basil, crushed
¼ teaspoon salt
¼ teaspoon garlic powder
¼ teaspoon crushed red pepper
2 cups chopped cooked turkey breast (10 ounces)*
1 10-ounce package frozen chopped spinach, thawed and well drained
1 cup shredded part-skim mozzarella cheese (4 ounces)
⅓ cup chopped bottled roasted red sweet pepper

1. Preheat oven to 350°F. Coat a 9-inch deep-dish pie plate or a 2-quart square baking dish with cooking spray; set aside. Cook pasta according to package directions; drain well.
2. Meanwhile, in a large bowl, beat cream cheese with an electric mixer on low to medium speed until smooth. Gradually beat in eggs and sour cream. Stir in basil, salt, garlic powder, and crushed red pepper. Stir in cooked pasta, turkey, spinach, mozzarella cheese, and roasted red pepper. Spread mixture in prepared plate or dish.
3. Bake, uncovered, for 40 to 45 minutes or until edges are slightly puffed and golden and center is heated through. Let stand on a wire rack for 10 minutes before serving. Cut into wedges or rectangles to serve.
*TEST KITCHEN TIP: Cook turkey breast tenderloin rather than using purchased cooked turkey breast to keep sodium down. To cook turkey breast tenderloin, heat water in a skillet to boiling. Cut 1 turkey breast tenderloin in half lengthwise and add to skillet. Return to boiling; reduce heat. Simmer, covered, 10 to 12 minutes or until no longer pink. Drain, cool slightly, and chop. Makes 2 cups.
PER SERVING: 207 cal., 4 g total fat (2 g sat. fat), 46 mg chol., 488 mg sodium, 15 g carb., 2 g fiber, 25 g pro. Exchanges: 0.5 vegetable, 1 starch, 3 lean meat. Carb choices: 1.

Taco Pizza

Topped with chopped tomatoes, this lightened-up version of classic taco pizza offers antioxidant benefits.

SERVINGS 8 (1 slice each)
CARB. PER SERVING 34 g

Nonstick cooking spray
1 1-pound loaf frozen whole wheat bread dough, thawed
12 ounces lean ground beef
½ cup chopped onion (1 medium)
½ cup bottled salsa
1½ cups chopped tomatoes (2 medium)
½ cup shredded reduced-fat cheddar cheese (2 ounces)
½ to 1 cup shredded lettuce and/or spinach
1 cup baked tortilla chips, coarsely crushed
¼ cup light sour cream

1. Preheat oven to 425°F. Lightly coat a 12- to 13-inch pizza pan with cooking spray. Pat dough evenly into prepared pan, building up edge slightly. (If dough is hard to pat out, allow to rest for 10 minutes.) Prick dough all over with a fork. Bake for 12 minutes.
2. Meanwhile, in a large skillet, cook the ground beef and onion until meat is browned and onion is tender. Drain off fat. Stir in salsa. Top partially baked crust with meat mixture. Bake for 5 minutes more. Sprinkle with tomatoes and cheese. Bake for 2 to 3 minutes more or until cheese melts.
3. To serve, top with lettuce and tortilla chips. Serve with sour cream.
PER SERVING: 281 cal., 9 g total fat (3 g sat. fat), 35 mg chol., 531 mg sodium, 34 g carb., 3 g fiber, 18 g pro. Exchanges: 0.5 vegetable, 2 starch, 1.5 lean meat, 1 fat. Carb choices: 2.
STUFFED-CRUST PIZZA: Lightly coat a 12- to 13-inch pizza pan with cooking spray. Pat dough evenly into prepared pan, extending edge over pan slightly. (If dough is hard to pat out, allow to rest for 10 minutes.) Sprinkle 2 ounces shredded reduced-fat cheddar cheese in a thin strip around the edge of the dough. Moisten edge of dough. Fold down edge over cheese and seal tightly to enclose the cheese. Prick dough all over with a fork. Bake as above.
PER SERVING: 303 cal., 10 g total fat (4 g sat. fat), 40 mg chol., 592 mg sodium, 34 g carb., 3 g fiber, 20 g pro. Exchanges: 2 starch, 0.5 vegetable, 2 lean meat, 1 fat. Carb choices: 2.

Mexican Beef Bake with Cilantro-Lime Cream

Use hot salsa if you like your foods spicy.

SERVINGS 6 (about 1 cup each)

CARB. PER SERVING 29 g

- 4 ounces dried multigrain or regular rotini or elbow macaroni (1⅓ cups)
- 12 ounces lean ground beef
- 2 cloves garlic, minced
- 1 15-ounce can black beans or pinto beans, rinsed and drained
- 1 14.5-ounce can no-salt-added diced tomatoes, undrained
- ¾ cup bottled picante sauce or salsa
- 1 teaspoon dried oregano, crushed
- ½ teaspoon ground cumin
- ½ teaspoon chili powder
- ½ cup shredded reduced-fat Colby and Monterey Jack cheese (2 ounces)
- 1 recipe Cilantro-Lime Cream (right)
- 1 tablespoon sliced green onion

1. Preheat oven to 350°F. In a large saucepan, cook pasta according to package directions; drain. Return pasta to hot saucepan; set aside.

2. Meanwhile, in a large skillet, cook the ground beef and garlic until meat is browned, stirring to break up meat as it cooks. Drain off fat.

3. Stir the cooked meat into pasta in saucepan. Stir in beans, undrained tomatoes, picante sauce, oregano, cumin, and chili powder. Transfer mixture to a 1½- to 2-quart casserole or baking dish.

4. Bake, covered, about 30 minutes or until heated through. Uncover and sprinkle with cheese. Bake, uncovered, about 3 minutes more or until cheese melts.

5. To serve, top each serving with a spoonful of Cilantro-Lime Cream. Sprinkle with green onion.

CILANTRO-LIME CREAM: In a small bowl, stir together ⅓ cup light sour cream, 2 tablespoons green onion, 2 teaspoons coarsely chopped fresh cilantro, and ½ teaspoon finely shredded lime peel.

PER SERVING: 261 cal., 7 g total fat (3 g sat. fat), 43 mg chol., 520 mg sodium, 29 g carb., 7 g fiber, 23 g pro. Exchanges: 1 vegetable, 1.5 starch, 2.5 lean meat, 0.5 fat. Carb choices: 2.

Southern Beefy Skillet

Easy and tasty—it's the perfect weeknight supper.
SERVINGS 4 (1¼ cups each)
CARB. PER SERVING 33 g

- 1 pound lean ground beef
- 1 cup chopped celery (2 stalks)
- ½ cup chopped onion (1 medium)
- 2 cloves garlic, minced
- 1 15.5- to 16-ounce can butter beans, rinsed and drained
- 1 14.5-ounce can no-salt-added diced tomatoes
- 1 8-ounce can no-salt-added tomato sauce
- 1 medium green sweet pepper, cut into bite-size strips
- 1 fresh jalapeño chile pepper, seeded and finely chopped*
- 2 teaspoons Worcestershire sauce
- 1 teaspoon dried basil, crushed
- 1 teaspoon dried oregano, crushed
- ½ teaspoon bottled hot pepper sauce
- ¼ teaspoon black pepper

1. In a large skillet, cook ground beef, celery, onion, and garlic over medium heat until browned. Drain off fat.

2. Add butter beans, undrained tomatoes, tomato sauce, sweet pepper, jalapeño pepper, Worcestershire sauce, basil, oregano, hot pepper sauce, and black pepper. Bring to boiling. Reduce heat and simmer, uncovered, for 10 to 15 minutes or until desired consistency.

***TEST KITCHEN TIP:** Because chile peppers contain volatile oils that can burn your skin and eyes, avoid direct contact with chiles as much as possible. When working with chile peppers, wear plastic or rubber gloves. If your bare hands do touch the chile peppers, wash your hands and nails well with soap and warm water.

PER SERVING: 342 cal., 12 g total fat (5 g sat. fat), 74 mg chol., 499 mg sodium, 33 g carb., 9 g fiber, 30 g pro. Exchanges: 2 vegetable, 1.5 starch, 3 lean meat, 1 fat. Carb choices: 2.

Grilled Beef Tenderloin with Mediterranean Relish

Grilled Beef Tenderloin with Mediterranean Relish

Make sure to let the roast stand for 15 minutes before slicing. This helps to set the juices, making each slice supremo!
SERVINGS 12 (3 ounces cooked beef and ⅓ cup relish each)
CARB. PER SERVING 6 g

- 1 3- to 4-pound center-cut beef tenderloin roast
- 2 teaspoons dried oregano, crushed
- 2 teaspoons cracked black pepper
- 1½ teaspoons finely shredded lemon peel
- ½ teaspoon salt
- 3 cloves garlic, minced
- 2 Japanese eggplants, halved lengthwise, or 1 small eggplant, sliced
- 2 red and/or yellow sweet peppers, halved lengthwise and seeded
- 1 sweet onion (such as Walla Walla or Vidalia), cut into ½-inch slices
- 1 tablespoon olive oil
- ⅔ cup chopped roma tomatoes (2 medium)
- 2 tablespoons chopped pitted Kalamata olives
- 2 tablespoons snipped fresh basil
- 1 tablespoon balsamic vinegar
- ¼ teaspoon salt
- ⅛ teaspoon black pepper

1. Trim fat from meat. For rub: In a small bowl, stir together oregano, cracked black pepper, lemon peel, 1/2 teaspoon salt, and 2 of the garlic cloves. Sprinkle mixture evenly over meat; rub in with your fingers. Brush eggplants, sweet peppers, and onion with oil.
2. For a charcoal grill, arrange hot coals around a drip pan. Test for medium-high heat above pan. Place meat on grill rack over drip pan. Place vegetables around edge of grill rack directly over coals. Grill, covered, for 10 to 12 minutes or until vegetables are tender, turning once halfway through grilling. Remove vegetables from grill. Cover and continue grilling meat for 30 to 40 minutes more or until medium-rare (140°F). (For a gas grill, preheat grill. Reduce heat to medium-high. Adjust for indirect cooking. Grill as above.)
3. Remove meat from grill. Cover with foil; let stand for 15 minutes. (The meat's temperature will rise 5°F during standing.)
4. Meanwhile, for relish: Coarsely chop grilled vegetables. In a medium bowl, combine grilled vegetables, the remaining garlic clove, tomatoes, olives, basil, vinegar, 1/4 teaspoon salt, and 1/8 teaspoon black pepper. Slice meat. Serve meat with relish.
PER SERVING: 232 cal., 12 g total fat (4 g sat. fat), 70 mg chol., 227 mg sodium, 6 g carb., 2 g fiber, 25 g pro. Exchanges: 1 vegetable, 3 lean meat, 1.5 fat. Carb choices: 0.5.

Korean Barbecued
Flank Steak

Korean Barbecued Flank Steak

One of the most popular Korean dishes is grilled steak known as bulgogi. The marinade ingredients lend a traditional spiced flavor. And don't forget the final sprinkling of sesame seeds and green onion.

SERVINGS 6 (3 ounces steak and 1/2 cup bok choy leaves each)
CARB. PER SERVING 4 g

- 1 1 1/2-pound beef flank steak
- 1/4 cup soy sauce
- 2 tablespoons packed brown sugar
- 1 tablespoon toasted sesame oil
- 1 tablespoon grated fresh ginger
- 3 cloves garlic, minced
- 3 cups baby bok choy leaves
- 1 tablespoon sesame seeds, toasted
- 2 tablespoons chopped green onion

1. Trim fat from steak. Place steak in a resealable plastic bag set in a shallow dish. For marinade: In a small bowl, combine soy sauce, brown sugar, oil, ginger, and garlic. Pour marinade over steak. Seal bag; turn to coat steak. Marinate in the refrigerator for 6 to 24 hours, turning bag occasionally. Drain steak, discarding marinade.
2. For a charcoal grill, place steak on the grill rack directly over medium coals. Grill, uncovered, for 17 to 21 minutes for medium (160°F), turning once halfway through grilling. (For a gas grill, preheat grill. Reduce heat to medium. Place steak on grill rack over heat. Cover and grill as above.)
3. To serve, thinly slice steak diagonally across the grain. Arrange steak slices on top of bok choy leaves and sprinkle with sesame seeds and green onion.
PER SERVING: 193 cal., 8 g total fat (3 g sat. fat), 39 mg chol., 276 mg sodium, 4 g carb., 1 g fiber, 26 g pro. Exchanges: 0.5 vegetable, 3.5 lean meat, 0.5 fat. Carb choices: 0.

Sesame Ginger
Beef Stir-Fry

Sesame Ginger Beef Stir-Fry

*If you have time, place the beef in the freezer about
30 minutes before slicing. It makes it easier to cut.*

SERVINGS 4 (1 cup stir-fry and ⅓ cup rice each)
CARB. PER SERVING 25 g

- 12 ounces boneless beef sirloin steak
- 1 cup reduced-sodium chicken broth
- 1 tablespoon grated fresh ginger or 1 teaspoon ground ginger
- 1 tablespoon cornstarch
- 2 cloves garlic, minced
- 1 teaspoon ground coriander
- ⅛ to ¼ teaspoon crushed red pepper
- 2 teaspoons sesame oil
- 1 medium onion, halved and sliced
- 2 cups broccoli florets
- 1 medium red sweet pepper, cut into bite-size strips
- 1⅓ cups hot cooked brown rice
- 1 teaspoon sesame seeds, toasted (optional)

1. Thinly slice meat across the grain into bite-size strips. Set aside.

2. For sauce: In a small bowl, stir together chicken broth, ginger, cornstarch, garlic, coriander, and crushed red pepper; set aside.

3. In a wok or large skillet, heat sesame oil over medium-high heat. Add onion; cook and stir for 2 minutes. Add broccoli and sweet pepper; cook and stir for 1 to 2 minutes more or until vegetables are crisp-tender. Remove from wok.

4. Add beef strips to hot wok (lightly coat wok with nonstick cooking spray, if needed). Cook and stir for 2 to 3 minutes or until meat is slightly pink in center. Push meat from center of wok.

5. Stir sauce. Add sauce to center of wok. Cook and stir until thickened and bubbly. Return cooked vegetables to wok; stir to coat all ingredients with sauce. Cook and stir for 1 to 2 minutes more or until heated through. Serve immediately with rice. If desired, sprinkle with sesame seeds.

PER SERVING: 255 cal., 7 g total fat (2 g sat. fat), 36 mg chol., 212 mg sodium, 25 g carb., 4 g fiber, 23 g pro. Exchanges: 1 vegetable, 1.5 starch, 2.5 lean meat, 0.5 fat. Carb choices: 1.5.

Southwestern Skirt Steak

This fajita-style steak gets its tantalizing flavor from a delightful mix of citrus, cilantro, cumin, and garlic.

SERVINGS 2 (3 ounces cooked beef each)

CARB. PER SERVING 3 g

- ⅓ cup orange juice
- 2 tablespoons snipped fresh cilantro
- 2 tablespoons lime juice
- 1 teaspoon ground cumin
- ¼ teaspoon salt
- ¼ teaspoon black pepper
- 1 clove garlic, minced
- 8 ounces beef skirt steak or flank steak

1. For marinade: In a large resealable plastic bag set in a shallow dish, combine orange juice, cilantro, lime juice, cumin, salt, pepper, and garlic. Trim fat from steak. Score both sides of steak in a diamond pattern by making shallow diagonal cuts at 1-inch intervals. Add steak to orange juice mixture. Seal bag; turn to coat steak. Marinate in the refrigerator for 1 to 4 hours, turning bag occasionally.

2. Drain steak, discarding marinade. For a charcoal grill, place steak on the grill rack directly over medium coals. Grill, uncovered, until desired doneness, turning once halfway through grilling. For skirt steak, allow 8 to 10 minutes. For flank steak, allow 10 to 12 minutes for medium-rare doneness (145°F) or 12 to 14 minutes for medium doneness (160°F). (For a gas grill, preheat grill. Reduce heat to medium. Place steak on grill rack over heat. Cover and grill as above.)

3. To serve, thinly slice steak across the grain.

PER SERVING: 181 cal., 8 g total fat (3 g sat. fat), 58 mg chol., 215 mg sodium, 3 g carb., 0 g fiber, 22 g pro. Exchanges: 3 lean meat, 0.5 fat. Carb choices: 0.

Pork Tenderloin with Green Olive Tapenade

Thanks to zesty tapenade, juicy tenderloin takes a tasty trip to Provence. If you don't have a meat mallet, lightly pound the pork with the bottom of a wide, heavy saucepan.

SERVINGS 6 (⅓ of 1 stuffed pork tenderloin each)

CARB. PER SERVING 1 g

- 1 cup pitted green olives
- 1 tablespoon capers, drained
- 1 tablespoon Dijon-style mustard
- 1 tablespoon olive oil
- 1 tablespoon lemon juice
- 2 teaspoons anchovy paste
- 1 teaspoon snipped fresh thyme
- 1 clove garlic, minced
- 2 12- to 16-ounce pork tenderloins

1. For tapenade: In a food processor or blender, combine olives, capers, mustard, oil, lemon juice, anchovy paste, thyme, and garlic. Cover and process until nearly smooth, scraping down sides as necessary. If desired, cover and chill for up to 24 hours.

2. Trim fat from tenderloins. Make a lengthwise cut down the center of each tenderloin, cutting almost to, but not through, the opposite side. Spread meat open. Place tenderloins between two pieces of plastic wrap, overlapping tenderloins about 2 inches along one long side. Using the flat side of a meat mallet, pound meat lightly into a 12×10-inch rectangle. Remove plastic wrap.

3. Spread tapenade over meat to within 1 inch of the edges. Fold in long sides just to cover edges of tapenade. Starting at one of the short sides, roll up meat. To secure, tie at 1-inch intervals with 100-percent-cotton kitchen string.

4. For a charcoal grill, arrange medium-hot coals around a drip pan. Test for medium heat above pan. Place meat on grill rack over drip pan. Grill, covered, for 45 to 50 minutes or until an instant-read thermometer inserted in meat registers 155°F. (For a gas grill, preheat grill. Reduce heat to medium. Adjust for indirect cooking. Grill as above, except place meat on a rack in a roasting pan; place pan on grill rack.)

5. Remove meat from grill. Cover with foil; let stand for 10 minutes before slicing. (The meat's temperature will rise 5°F during standing.) Remove and discard strings. Slice meat.

PER SERVING: 201 cal., 10 g total fat (2 g sat. fat), 83 mg chol., 347 mg sodium, 1 g carb., 0 g fiber, 27 g pro. Exchanges: 4 lean meat, 1 fat. Carb choices: 0.

Pork Tenderloin Medaillons with Plum Sauce

Pork tenderloin is often sold with two per package. If yours come this way, freeze the extra for another use.

SERVINGS 4 (2 to 3 slices pork, ⅔ cup bok choy, and ¼ cup sauce each)
CARB. PER SERVING 12 g

- ¼ cup chopped onion
- 1 clove garlic, minced
- 1 teaspoon sesame oil
- 2 medium plums, pitted and chopped (1½ cups)
- 1½ teaspoons rice vinegar
- 1½ teaspoons grated fresh ginger or ¼ teaspoon ground ginger
- 1 teaspoon reduced-sodium soy sauce
- 1 teaspoon honey
- ¼ teaspoon ground coriander
- ⅛ teaspoon salt
- 1 1-pound pork tenderloin
- ⅛ teaspoon salt
- Nonstick cooking spray
- 7 cups chopped bok choy (1 head)
- ¼ cup chopped green onions (2)

1. In a small saucepan, cook onion and garlic in hot sesame oil over medium heat about 4 minutes or until tender. Stir in plums, vinegar, ginger, soy sauce, honey, coriander, and ⅛ teaspoon salt. Bring to boiling; reduce heat. Simmer, covered, about 5 minutes or until plums are tender. Transfer mixture to a blender or food processor. Cover and blend or process until smooth; set aside.

2. Trim fat from meat. Cut meat crosswise into 1-inch slices. Press cut side of each piece with the palm of your hand to make an even thickness. Sprinkle meat with ⅛ teaspoon salt. Coat a large skillet with cooking spray. Heat over medium-high heat. Add pork and cook for 2 to 3 minutes per side or until juices run clear. Remove from skillet and keep warm.

3. Add bok choy to skillet. Cover and cook for 3 minutes or until wilted, stirring occasionally. Place bok choy on a serving platter. Top with pork and some of the plum sauce. Sprinkle with green onions. Pass any remaining plum sauce.

PER SERVING: 191 cal., 4 g total fat (1 g sat. fat), 74 mg chol., 392 mg sodium, 12 g carb., 3 g fiber, 28 g pro. Exchanges: 1.5 vegetable, 1 fruit, 3.5 lean meat. Carb choices: 1.

Pork and Pineapple Tacos

Olé! Two tasty tacos make one great serving.

SERVINGS 8 (2 tacos each)
CARB. PER SERVING 35 g

- ½ of a medium peeled and cored fresh pineapple
- 8 dried pasilla and/or guajillo chile peppers (see tip, page 9)
- ¼ cup orange juice
- ¼ cup vinegar
- 4 cloves garlic, minced
- ½ teaspoon ground cumin
- ⅛ teaspoon ground cloves
- 2 pounds boneless pork loin, trimmed of fat and cut into ½-inch slices
- 16 6-inch corn tortillas
- 1 cup chopped onion (1 large)
- 2 tablespoons snipped fresh cilantro
- 8 lime wedges

1. Cut pineapple into ½-inch-thick slices, reserving juice; cover and chill pineapple and juice separately.

2. Remove stems and seeds from chile peppers. Place peppers in a medium bowl and add enough boiling water to cover. Allow peppers to stand about 30 minutes or until soft; drain, discarding water.

3. In a food processor or blender, combine chile peppers, any juice from the pineapple, the orange juice, vinegar, garlic, ½ teaspoon *salt*, cumin, and cloves. Cover and process or blend until nearly smooth.

4. In a 3-quart baking dish, arrange pork in a single layer, overlapping slices as necessary. Pour chile pepper mixture over pork, spreading evenly. Cover and marinate in the refrigerator for 4 to 24 hours. Remove pork from marinade; discard marinade. Wrap tortillas in foil.

5. For a charcoal grill, place tortilla packet on grill rack directly over medium coals. Place pork and pineapple slices on the grill rack alongside foil packet directly over medium coals. Grill pork and pineapple slices, uncovered, for 6 to 7 minutes or until pork slices are slightly pink in the center and juices run clear (160°F), turning once. Grill tortilla packet for 10 minutes, turning once. (For a gas grill, preheat grill. Reduce heat to medium. Grill tortilla packet, pork, and pineapple as above.)

6. Coarsely chop pork and pineapple and combine. Fill tortillas with pork and pineapple mixture. Sprinkle tacos with onion and cilantro. Serve with lime wedges.

PER SERVING: 321 cal., 7 g total fat (2 g sat. fat), 71 mg chol., 233 mg sodium, 35 g carb., 6 g fiber, 30 g pro. Exchanges: 0.5 fruit, 1.5 starch, 3.5 lean meat. Carb choices: 2.

QUICK TIP

For a family of four, offer tacos one night and serve the remaining pork and pineapple mixture over salad greens the next.

Pork and Pineapple Tacos

Pork Skewers
with Fruit Glaze

Pork Skewers with Fruit Glaze

To make equal-size meatballs, pat the meat mixture into a 6×5-inch rectangle on a piece of waxed paper. Cut into thirty 1-inch squares. Roll each square into a ball.

SERVINGS 6 (1 skewer and 2 tablespoons glaze each)
CARB. PER SERVING 18 g

- 1 egg, lightly beaten
- 1/3 cup finely chopped water chestnuts
- 1/4 cup fine dry bread crumbs
- 2 teaspoons grated fresh ginger
- 1 clove garlic, minced
- 1/4 teaspoon salt
- 1/4 teaspoon black pepper
- 1 pound lean ground pork loin
- 1 large red, yellow, or green sweet pepper, cut into 1-inch pieces
- 1 recipe Fruit Glaze (below)

1. In a large bowl, combine egg, water chestnuts, bread crumbs, ginger, garlic, salt, and pepper. Add ground pork; mix well. Shape pork mixture into 30 meatballs.
2. On six long metal skewers, alternately thread meatballs and sweet pepper pieces, leaving 1/4 inch between pieces.
3. For a charcoal grill, arrange medium-hot coals around a drip pan. Test for medium heat above pan. Place skewers on well-greased grill rack over pan. Grill, covered, for 10 to 12 minutes or until meatballs are no longer pink and juices run clear. Brush with some of the Fruit Glaze. Immediately remove skewers from grill. (For a gas grill, preheat grill. Reduce heat to medium. Adjust for indirect cooking. Grill as above.)
4. Serve skewers with remaining glaze.
FRUIT GLAZE: Place 2/3 cup desired-flavor low-sugar fruit preserves in a small saucepan; snip any large pieces. Stir in 1/4 cup unsweetened pineapple juice, 1 tablespoon lemon juice, and 1/4 teaspoon ground cardamom. Bring to boiling; reduce heat. Simmer, uncovered, for 15 minutes. Cool for 10 minutes (glaze will thicken as it cools)
PER SERVING: 187 cal., 4 g total fat (1 g sat. fat), 85 mg chol., 268 mg sodium, 18 g carb., 1 g fiber, 19 g pro. Exchanges: 1 carb., 2.5 lean meat. Carb choices: 1.

Pork Chops with Braised Red Cabbage

Add a fresh spinach or mixed greens salad to complete your meal.

SERVINGS 4 (1 pork chop and 1 cup cooked cabbage each)
CARB. PER SERVING 20 g

- 1 teaspoon vegetable oil
- 1 medium sweet onion, sliced
- 8 cups shredded red cabbage (about 1/2 of a large head)
- 1/3 cup cider vinegar
- 2 tablespoons coarse ground or spicy brown mustard
- 1 tablespoon sugar
- 1 teaspoon chopped fresh thyme or 1/2 teaspoon dried thyme, crushed
- 1/2 cup reduced-sodium chicken broth
  Nonstick cooking spray
- 4 3/4- to 1-inch-thick pork rib chops (1 1/2 pounds total)
- 1/4 teaspoon black pepper
- 1/8 teaspoon salt

1. For cabbage: In a 4-quart Dutch oven, heat oil over medium heat. Cook onion in hot oil for 8 minutes or until soft. Add cabbage; cook and stir until wilted. Add vinegar, mustard, sugar, and dried thyme (if using). Simmer, covered, for 20 minutes. Uncover and add broth and fresh thyme (if using). Simmer, uncovered, about 5 minutes more or until cabbage is tender.
2. Meanwhile, lightly coat a very large skillet with cooking spray. Heat skillet over medium-high heat until very hot. Sprinkle pork chops with pepper and salt. Add pork chops to skillet. Reduce heat to medium and cook for 8 to 12 minutes or until done (160°F), turning once halfway through cooking time.
3. Serve pork chops with cabbage.
PER SERVING: 245 cal., 6 g total fat (2 g sat. fat), 57 mg chol., 431 mg sodium, 20 g carb., 4 g fiber, 25 g pro. Exchanges: 2 vegetable, 0.5 carb., 3 lean meat, 0.5 fat. Carb choices: 1.

Floribbean Ribs with
Black-Eyed Pea Salsa

Floribbean Ribs with Black-Eyed Pea Salsa

The spiciness of mixed seeds is tamed by the gentle flavors of mango, honey, and lime in the Mango Mojo.

SERVINGS 6 (about 5 ribs, ¼ cup sauce, and ¾ cup salsa each)

CARB. PER SERVING 35 g

- 1 tablespoon whole allspice
- 1 tablespoon cumin seeds
- 2 teaspoons fennel seeds
- 1 teaspoon mustard seeds
- ½ teaspoon salt
- 3½ to 4 pounds meaty pork spareribs or pork loin back ribs
- 2 cups hickory or oak chips
- 1 recipe Mango Mojo (right)
- 1 recipe Black-Eyed Pea Salsa (page 29)

1. Preheat oven to 350°F. Heat a medium skillet over medium heat. Add allspice, cumin seeds, fennel seeds, and mustard seeds to skillet. Toast about 3 minutes or until seeds are fragrant, stirring occasionally. Crush seeds with a mortar and pestle or in a clean coffee grinder. Stir in salt.

2. Trim fat from ribs. Place ribs in a shallow roasting pan. Generously sprinkle rub mixture over both sides of ribs; rub in with your fingers. Cover pan with foil. Bake ribs for 2 to 2½ hours or until very tender. Drain off fat.

3. At least 1 hour before grilling, soak wood chips in enough water to cover. Drain wood chips.

4. For a charcoal grill, sprinkle wood chips over medium coals. Place ribs on the grill rack directly over the coals. Grill, covered, about 10 minutes or until ribs are browned, turning once and brushing occasionally with Mango Mojo. (For a gas grill, preheat grill. Reduce heat to medium. Add wood chips according to the manufacturer's directions. Place ribs on grill rack. Grill as above.) Drizzle ribs with remaining Mango Mojo.

5. Serve ribs with Black-Eyed Pea Salsa.

MANGO MOJO: In a food processor or blender, combine 2 medium mangoes, pitted, peeled, and chopped; 2 tablespoons honey; 2 tablespoons grated fresh ginger; 2 tablespoons Key lime juice or lime juice; and 2 tablespoons bourbon, if desired. Cover and process until smooth. Stir in 1 fresh jalapeño chile pepper, seeded and finely chopped,* and ¼ cup chopped green onions.

BLACK-EYED PEA SALSA: Place 4 slices cored fresh pineapple, 1 medium whole roma tomato, two ½-inch-thick slices sweet onion, and 1 fresh jalapeño chile pepper on the grill rack directly over medium coals. Grill, uncovered, for 5 to 10 minutes or until lightly charred and onion is tender, turning occasionally. Chop pineapple, tomato, and onion. Seed and finely chop jalapeño.* Place in a medium bowl. Add one 15-ounce can black-eyed peas, rinsed and drained; ½ teaspoon finely shredded lime peel; 1 tablespoon lime juice; 1 tablespoon chopped fresh cilantro; 1 teaspoon olive oil; 1 clove garlic, minced; ½ teaspoon ground cumin; and ¼ teaspoon salt. Gently stir to mix.

***TEST KITCHEN TIP:** Because chile peppers contain volatile oils that can burn your skin and eyes, avoid direct contact with chiles as much as possible. When working with chile peppers, wear plastic or rubber gloves. If your bare hands do touch the chile peppers, wash your hands and nails well with soap and warm water.

PER SERVING: 373 cal., 10 g total fat (3 g sat. fat), 115 mg chol., 532 mg sodium, 35 g carb., 5 g fiber, 36 g pro. Exchanges: 0.5 fruit, 1.5 starch, 4.5 lean meat, 0.5 fat. Carb choices: 2.

Grilled Bass with Lemon and Herbs
Striped bass is high in heart-healthy omega-3 fatty acids.
SERVINGS 4 (3 ounces cooked fish and 1 tablespoon herb mixture each)
CARB. PER SERVING 0 g

- 1 pound fresh or frozen striped bass fillets
- 2 teaspoons olive oil
- 2 tablespoons snipped fresh flat-leaf parsley
- 1 tablespoon snipped fresh basil and/or chives
- 2 teaspoons finely shredded lemon peel
- 1 teaspoon snipped fresh rosemary

1. Thaw fish, if frozen. Rinse fish; pat dry with paper towels. Cut fish into four serving-size pieces. Brush with oil; sprinkle with ¼ teaspoon *salt* and ⅛ teaspoon *black pepper*. Measure thickness of fish.

2. For a charcoal grill, place fish on a greased grill rack directly over medium coals. Grill, uncovered, for 4 to 6 minutes per ½-inch thickness of fish or until fish flakes easily when tested with fork; carefully turn once halfway through grilling. (For a gas grill, preheat grill. Reduce heat to medium. Place fish on a greased grill rack over heat. Cover and grill as above.)

▶ **QUICK TIP**
Fish tends to stick to grill racks—even clean ones. Reduce sticking by using a paper towel to apply vegetable oil to the cool grill rack. Then place the rack over the coals.

Grilled Bass with Lemon and Herbs

3. In a small bowl, combine parsley, basil, lemon peel, and rosemary. Sprinkle on fish.
PER SERVING: 131 cal., 5 g total fat (1 g sat. fat), 90 mg chol., 225 mg sodium, 0 g carb., 0 g fiber, 20 g pro. Exchanges: 3 lean meat. Carb choices: 0.

Herbed Fish and Vegetables with Lemon Mayo

A bit of green onion along with a touch of lemon peel and juice turn ordinary mayonnaise into an extraordinary topping for steamed fish.

SERVINGS 2 (1 piece fish with about ⅔ cup vegetables and 2 tablespoons Lemon Mayo each)

CARB. PER SERVING 13 g

- 2 6-ounce fresh or frozen skinless flounder, sole, cod, or perch fillets, ½ to ¾ inch thick
- 2 tablespoons assorted snipped fresh herbs (such as parsley, basil, oregano, and thyme)
- 1 cup matchstick-size pieces carrot
- 1 cup matchstick-size pieces zucchini and/or yellow summer squash
- ½ of a lemon, thinly sliced
- 1 recipe Lemon Mayo (right)

1. Thaw fish, if frozen. Rinse fish; pat dry with paper towels. Using a sharp knife, make shallow bias cuts in the fish fillets, spacing cuts ¾ inch apart. Sprinkle herbs over fillets, tucking into cuts.

Herbed Fish and Vegetables with Lemon Mayo

2. Place a steamer insert in a large saucepan or large deep skillet with a tight-fitting lid. Add water to the saucepan or skillet until just below the steamer insert. Bring water to boiling. Place carrot and squash in the steamer basket. Place fish on top of vegetables. Arrange lemon slices on top of fish. Cover and steam over medium heat for 6 to 8 minutes or until fish flakes easily when tested with a fork, adding more water as needed to maintain steam.

3. To serve, divide fish and vegetables between two serving plates. Serve with Lemon Mayo.

LEMON MAYO: In a small bowl, stir together 3 tablespoons light mayonnaise, 1 tablespoon thinly sliced green onion, ¼ teaspoon finely shredded lemon peel, and 1 teaspoon lemon juice.

PER SERVING: 270 cal., 10 g total fat (2 g sat. fat), 90 mg chol., 340 mg sodium, 13 g carb., 4 g fiber, 34 g pro. Exchanges: 1.5 vegetable, 4 lean meat, 1 fat. Carb choices: 1.

Fish Tacos

Keep the marinating time to 30 minutes; if the fish sits much longer, the acidic lime juice will "cook" it.

SERVINGS 4 (2 tacos each)

CARB. PER SERVING 30 g

- 1 pound fresh or frozen firm-flesh fish fillets (such as halibut or salmon), about 1 inch thick
- ¼ cup tequila, lime juice, or lemon juice
- 2 tablespoons lime juice or lemon juice
- 1 fresh jalapeño or serrano chile pepper, seeded and finely chopped (see tip, page 29)
- 2 cloves garlic, minced
- ¼ teaspoon ground cumin
- ¼ teaspoon salt
- 8 8-inch corn or flour tortillas
- 1½ cups shredded lettuce
- 1 cup chopped red and/or green sweet peppers (2 small)
- 1 medium red onion, halved and thinly sliced
- Snipped fresh cilantro (optional)

1. Thaw fish, if frozen. Rinse fish; pat dry with paper towels. Place fish in a resealable plastic bag set in a shallow dish. For marinade: In a small bowl, stir together tequila, lime juice, chile pepper, garlic, cumin, and salt. Pour marinade over fish in bag; seal bag and turn to coat fish. Marinate in the refrigerator for 30 minutes, turning fish occasionally.

QUICK TIP ❨

Tacos make great party fare. For appetizer-size tacos, use twenty-four 4-inch corn tortillas.

Fish Tacos

2. Meanwhile, preheat oven to 350°F. Stack tortillas and wrap tightly in foil. Bake tortillas about 10 minutes or until heated through.

3. Preheat broiler. Drain fish, discarding marinade. Pat fish dry with paper towels. Place fish on the greased unheated rack of a broiler pan. Broil 4 inches from heat for 5 minutes. Using a wide spatula, carefully turn fish. Broil for 3 to 7 minutes more or just until fish flakes easily when tested with a fork. Using a fork, break broiled fish into ½-inch chunks.

4. To assemble tacos, divide lettuce among warm tortillas, placing lettuce on one half of each tortilla. Top lettuce with fish, sweet peppers, and red onion. Fold tortillas in half over filling. If desired, serve with cilantro.

GRILLING DIRECTIONS: To grill the fish, place fish fillets in a well-greased wire grill basket. For a charcoal grill, place fish on the grill rack directly over medium coals. Grill, uncovered, for 8 to 12 minutes or just until fish flakes easily when tested with a fork, turning once. (For a gas grill, preheat grill. Reduce heat to medium. Place fish in grill basket over heat. Cover and grill as above.)

PER SERVING: 283 cal., 4 g total fat (1 g sat. fat), 36 mg chol., 162 mg sodium, 30 g carb., 5 g fiber, 27 g pro. Exchanges: 1 vegetable, 1.5 starch, 3 lean meat. Carb choices: 2.

Chili-Lime Catfish
with Corn Sauté

Chile-Lime Catfish with Corn Sauté

*Stirring the snipped fresh cilantro into the corn mixture just
before serving retains the herb's bright color and flavor.*

SERVINGS 4 (1 piece fish and ½ cup corn mixture each)
CARB. PER SERVING 25 g

- 4 4- to 5-ounce fresh or frozen skinless catfish, sole, or tilapia fillets
- 1 tablespoon lime juice
- 1 teaspoon ground ancho chile pepper or chili powder
- ¼ teaspoon salt
- 2 teaspoons canola oil
- 2⅔ cups loose-pack frozen gold and white whole kernel corn, thawed
- ¼ cup finely chopped red onion
- 2 teaspoons finely chopped seeded fresh jalapeño chile pepper (see tip, page 29)
- 2 cloves garlic, minced
- 1 tablespoon snipped fresh cilantro
- Lime wedges (optional)

1. Thaw fish, if frozen. Rinse fish; pat dry with paper towels. In a small bowl, stir together lime juice, ancho chile pepper, and salt. Brush mixture evenly over both sides of each fish fillet. Measure thickness of fish.

2. In a large nonstick skillet, heat 1 teaspoon of the oil over medium-high heat. Add fish fillets to hot oil; cook for 4 to 6 minutes per ½-inch thickness or until fish flakes easily when tested with a fork, turning once halfway through cooking. Remove from skillet. Cover to keep warm.

3. In the same skillet, cook corn, onion, jalapeño chile pepper, and garlic in the remaining 1 teaspoon oil about 2 minutes or until vegetables are heated through and just starting to soften, stirring occasionally. Remove from heat. Stir in cilantro.

4. To serve, divide corn mixture among four serving plates. Top with fish. If desired, serve with lime wedges.

PER SERVING: 278 cal., 12 g total fat (2 g sat. fat), 53 mg chol., 216 mg sodium, 25 g carb., 3 g fiber, 21 g pro. Exchanges: 1.5 starch, 2.5 lean meat, 1 fat. Carb choices: 1.5.

Thai Sole and Vegetables en Papillote

The fish and vegetables bake to perfection in parchment paper packets.

SERVINGS 4 (1 piece fish and about ½ cup vegetables each)

CARB. PER SERVING 10 g

- 4 4- to 5-ounce fresh or frozen skinless sole or cod fillets
  Parchment paper
- 8 ounces fresh thin green beans, trimmed
- 2 medium red sweet peppers, thinly sliced
- 1 small onion, cut into thin wedges
- ¼ to ½ teaspoon crushed red pepper
- 4 cloves garlic, thinly sliced
- 2 teaspoons canola oil
- 1½ teaspoons finely shredded lemon peel
- 2 tablespoons thinly sliced fresh basil (optional)

1. Preheat oven to 400°F. Thaw fish, if frozen. Rinse fish; pat dry with paper towels. Set aside.

2. Tear off four 20×12-inch pieces of parchment paper; fold each piece in half crosswise and crease. Unfold paper and lay flat. On half of each parchment piece, arrange beans, sweet peppers, and onion. Sprinkle each with some of the crushed red pepper and garlic. Top each with a piece of fish. Drizzle with oil. Sprinkle with lemon peel. To make packets, fold paper over fish and vegetables. Fold each of the open sides over ½ inch, then fold over again ½ inch.

3. Place packets on a large baking sheet. Bake about 15 minutes or until fish flakes easily when tested with a fork. (Carefully open the packets to test doneness.) If desired, sprinkle with basil just before serving.

PER SERVING: 157 cal., 4 g total fat (0 g sat. fat), 52 mg chol., 95 mg sodium, 10 g carb., 4 g fiber, 21 g pro. Exchanges: 1.5 vegetable, 3 lean meat. Carb choices: 1.5.

Salmon Alfredo

Plan so the rest of your meal is low in sodium because canned salmon is generally high in sodium.

SERVINGS 6 (1 cup noodle mixture and ⅓ cup salmon mixture each)

CARB. PER SERVING 23 g

- 3 cups dried wide noodles
- 3 cups broccoli florets
- 1½ cups fat-free milk
- 3 tablespoons all-purpose flour
- 1 tablespoon dried chives
- 2 cloves garlic, minced
- 1 14.75-ounce can salmon, drained, skin and bones removed, and broken into chunks
- ½ teaspoon finely shredded lemon peel
- 2 tablespoons coarsely shredded Parmesan cheese

1. Cook noodles according to package directions, adding broccoli for the last 3 minutes of cooking; drain and keep warm.

2. Meanwhile, in a medium saucepan, whisk together milk and flour; add chives and garlic. Cook and stir over medium heat until thickened and bubbly. Add salmon and lemon peel. Heat through.

3. Place noodle mixture on a serving platter; spoon salmon mixture on top. Sprinkle with Parmesan cheese and, if desired, *freshly ground black pepper.*

PER SERVING: 227 cal., 5 g total fat (1 g sat. fat), 76 mg chol., 351 mg sodium, 23 g carb., 2 g fiber, 23 g pro. Exchanges: 1 vegetable, 1 starch, 2.5 lean meat. Carb choices: 1.5.

QUICK SALMON ALFREDO: Use 1 teaspoon bottled minced garlic, purchased broccoli florets, and two 7.1-ounce pouches skinless, boneless pink salmon.

PER SERVING: 202 cal., 4 g total fat (2 g sat. fat), 42 mg chol., 404 mg sodium, 23 g carb., 2 g fiber, 19 g pro. Exchanges: 1 starch, 1 vegetable, 2 lean meat. Carb choices: 1.5.

Thai Sole and Vegetables en Papillote

Grilled Halibut Sarandeado

The Spanish word sarandeado *roughly means "barbecued."*
SERVINGS 4 (1 fish portion and 2 green onions each)
CARB. PER SERVING 9 g

- 4 6-ounce fresh or frozen halibut or grouper fillets
- ½ cup freshly squeezed lemon juice
- 1 medium fresh serrano chile pepper, seeded and chopped (see tip, page 35)
- 1 tablespoon Worcestershire sauce
- ¾ teaspoon black pepper
- ½ teaspoon salt
- 8 green onions, trimmed
- 2 teaspoons canola oil
- ¼ cup coarsely chopped cilantro
- 1 lemon, cut into wedges

1. Thaw fish, if frozen. Place fish fillets in a resealable plastic bag set in a shallow dish.
2. In a blender, combine lemon juice, chile, Worcestershire sauce, ½ teaspoon of the black pepper, and ¼ teaspoon of the salt. Cover and blend until smooth. Pour lemon mixture over fish. Seal bag and refrigerate for 30 minutes, turning once. (Do not marinate longer than 30 minutes.) Drain, reserving marinade. Brush green onions with canola oil.
3. Lightly grease an unheated grill rack. For a charcoal grill, place fish on the grill rack directly over medium coals. Grill, uncovered, for 4 to 6 minutes per ½-inch thickness or until fish flakes easily when tested with a fork, turning once and brushing with reserved marinade halfway through grilling. Discard remaining marinade. Add green onions to grill for the last 4 minutes of grilling, turning once halfway through grilling. (For a gas grill, preheat grill. Reduce heat to medium. Place fish on greased grill rack. Cover and grill as above.)
4. Sprinkle fish with cilantro. Season with the remaining ¼ teaspoon each salt and black pepper. Serve with lemon wedges and grilled green onions.
PER SERVING: 236 cal., 6 g total fat (1 g sat. fat), 54 mg chol., 433 mg sodium, 9 g carb., 2 g fiber, 37 g pro. Exchanges: 0.5 vegetable, 0.5 carb., 5 lean meat. Carb choices: 0.5.

Thai Tuna Kabobs

Thread the chunks of tuna on the skewers perpendicular to the grain of the fish. This will keep the chunks of fish from flaking apart and falling off the skewers as they cook.

SERVINGS 4 (2 kabobs each)
CARB. PER SERVING 8 g

- 1 pound fresh or frozen tuna steaks
- ¼ cup snipped fresh cilantro
- 1 to 2 Thai chile peppers, serrano peppers, or jalapeño peppers, seeded and finely chopped*
- 1 teaspoon finely shredded lemon peel or lime peel
- 3 tablespoons lemon juice or lime juice
- 3 tablespoons rice vinegar
- 1 teaspoon toasted sesame oil
- 1 teaspoon sesame seeds
- 1 medium red onion, peeled and cut into 8 wedges
- 2 medium zucchini, sliced or cut into 1-inch pieces
- Lime wedges (optional)

1. Thaw fish, if frozen. Rinse fish; pat dry with paper towels. Cut fish into 1-inch cubes; set aside. For marinade: In a small bowl, stir together 2 tablespoons of the cilantro, the peppers, lemon or lime peel, lemon or lime juice, rice vinegar, sesame oil, and sesame seeds; set aside.

2. On eight metal or wooden** skewers, alternately thread tuna, onion wedges, and zucchini. Arrange skewers on a platter or in a shallow pan. Remove ¼ cup of the marinade and brush over skewers. Cover and refrigerate for 2 to 4 hours. Cover and chill remaining marinade mixture.

3. For a charcoal grill, place skewers on the grill rack directly over medium coals. Grill, uncovered, for 10 to 12 minutes or until tuna flakes easily when tested with a fork but is still slightly pink inside, turning occasionally. (For a gas grill, preheat grill. Reduce heat to medium. Place skewers on grill rack. Cover and grill as above.)

4. Transfer kabobs to a serving platter; sprinkle with remaining cilantro and serve with remaining marinade as sauce. If desired, serve with lime wedges.

*TEST KITCHEN TIP: Because chile peppers contain volatile oils that can burn your skin and eyes, avoid direct contact with chiles as much as possible. When working with chile peppers, wear plastic or rubber gloves. If your bare hands do touch the chile peppers, wash your hands and nails well with soap and warm water.

**TEST KITCHEN TIP: If using wooden skewers, soak in water for 30 minutes before using.

PER SERVING: 215 cal., 7 g total fat (2 g sat. fat), 43 mg chol., 58 mg sodium, 8 g carb., 2 g fiber, 28 g pro. Exchanges: 1.5 vegetable, 3.5 lean meat, 0.5 fat. Carb choices: 0.5.

Tuna-Noodle Casserole

Panko, a variety of bread crumbs commonly used in Japanese cooking, is coarser than traditional bread crumbs. Look for it with the bread crumbs and coatings in the supermarket.

SERVINGS 6 (1 cup each)
CARB. PER SERVING 27 g

- 4 ounces dried medium noodles (2½ cups)
- 3 tablespoons panko (Japanese-style bread crumbs) or fine dry bread crumbs
- 1 tablespoon melted butter
- 10 ounces fresh green beans, trimmed and cut into 2-inch pieces, or one 10-ounce package frozen cut green beans
- 1 cup sliced fresh mushrooms
- ¾ cup chopped red or green sweet pepper
- ½ cup chopped onion
- ½ cup sliced celery
- ½ cup water
- 2 cloves garlic, minced
- 1 10.75-ounce can reduced-sodium and reduced-fat condensed cream of mushroom soup
- ½ cup fat-free milk
- ½ cup shredded reduced-fat American or process Swiss cheese (2 ounces)
- 2 4.5-ounce cans very low sodium chunk white tuna in spring water, drained and flaked

1. Preheat oven to 350°F. Cook noodles according to package directions; drain and set aside.

2. Meanwhile, toss panko with butter; set aside.

3. In a large saucepan, combine green beans, mushrooms, sweet pepper, onion, celery, the water, and garlic. Bring to boiling; reduce heat. Cover; simmer about 5 minutes or until vegetables are tender.

4. Stir soup and milk into vegetable mixture. Cook and stir until heated through. Remove from heat, then stir in cheese until it melts. Stir in noodles and tuna.

5. Spoon mixture into a 2-quart casserole. Sprinkle panko mixture around outside edge of casserole. Bake, uncovered, for 25 to 30 minutes or until tuna mixture is bubbly and panko is golden.

PER SERVING: 228 cal., 6 g total fat (2 g sat. fat), 49 mg chol., 403 mg sodium, 27 g carb., 3 g fiber, 18 g pro. Exchanges: 1 vegetable, 1.5 starch, 1.5 lean meat, 0.5 fat. Carb choices: 2.

▶ QUICK TIP
If fresh green beans aren't looking their best at the market, try fresh snow peas instead.

Dilled Shrimp with Beans and Carrots

Pasta with Asparagus and Shrimp

Dilled Shrimp with Beans and Carrots

Grab your sharpest paring knife for cutting the carrots into matchstick-size strips.

SERVINGS 4 (⅓ cup rice and 1 cup shrimp mixture each)

CARB. PER SERVING 27 g

1	pound fresh or frozen large shrimp in shells
1⅓	cups water
⅔	cup regular brown rice
1	tablespoon butter
3	medium carrots, cut into thin julienne strips
8	ounces fresh green beans, trimmed and cut into 1-inch pieces
¼	cup reduced-sodium chicken broth
1	teaspoon finely shredded lemon peel
½	teaspoon dried dillweed

1. Thaw shrimp, if frozen. Peel and devein shrimp, leaving tails intact if desired. Rinse shrimp; pat dry with paper towels. Set aside.

2. In a medium saucepan, bring the water and rice to boiling; reduce heat. Simmer, covered, about 40 minutes or until rice is tender and most of the liquid is absorbed.

3. Meanwhile, in a large skillet, melt butter over medium heat. Add carrots and green beans; cook and stir for 4 to 5 minutes or until vegetables are crisp-tender. Add broth, shrimp, lemon peel, and dillweed to bean mixture. Cook, uncovered, over medium heat for 3 to 4 minutes or until shrimp are opaque, stirring occasionally.

4. To serve, divide rice among four bowls. Divide shrimp mixture among bowls.

PER SERVING: 245 cal., 6 g total fat (2 g sat. fat), 173 mg chol., 284 mg sodium, 27 g carb., 4 g fiber, 22 g pro. Exchanges: 1.5 vegetable, 1.5 starch, 2 lean meat. Carb choices: 2.

QUICK DILLED SHRIMP WITH BEANS AND CARROTS: Use 12 ounces cooked, peeled shrimp in place of the shrimp in shells. Add with the broth, lemon peel, and dillweed and just heat through. Use one 8.8-ounce pouch cooked brown rice in place of the water and regular brown rice, and cook according to package directions. Use 1½ cups purchased julienned carrots in place of the 3 medium carrots.

PER SERVING: 298 cal., 6 g total fat (2 g sat. fat), 180 mg chol, 264 mg sodium, 33 g carb., 4 g fiber, 27 g pro. Exchanges: 1.5 starch, 1.5 vegetable, 2.5 lean meat. Carb choices: 2.

Pasta with Asparagus and Shrimp

Fat-free half-and-half makes this elegant pasta dish rich and creamy, yet ideal for diabetes meal plans.

SERVINGS 4 (1¼ cups each)

CARB. PER SERVING 38 g

12	ounces fresh or frozen medium shrimp in shells
6	ounces dried whole wheat bow tie pasta
12	ounces fresh asparagus, trimmed and cut into 1-inch pieces
1	tablespoon olive oil
4	cloves garlic, minced
2	teaspoons snipped fresh lemon thyme or thyme, or ½ teaspoon dried thyme, crushed
⅓	cup fat-free half-and-half

1. Thaw shrimp, if frozen. Peel and devein shrimp, leaving tails intact if desired. Rinse shrimp; pat dry with paper towels. Set aside.

2. In a large saucepan, cook pasta according to package directions, adding the asparagus for the last 2 minutes of cooking. Drain pasta mixture and return to pan.

3. Meanwhile, in a large skillet, heat oil over medium-high heat. Add garlic and dried thyme (if using). Cook and stir for 10 seconds. Add shrimp; cook for 2 to 3 minutes or until shrimp turn opaque, stirring frequently. Stir in half-and-half; reduce heat. Heat through. Remove from heat.

4. Add shrimp mixture and fresh thyme (if using) to the pasta mixture in pan. Toss to coat.

PER SERVING: 315 cal., 6 g total fat (1 g sat. fat), 130 mg chol., 157 mg sodium, 38 g carb., 4 g fiber, 25 g pro. Exchanges: 1 vegetable, 2 starch, 2.5 lean meat. Carb choices: 2.5.

Vegetable
Lasagna

Vegetable Lasagna

Sprinkle ½ cup shredded fresh spinach and ¼ teaspoon black pepper over the lasagna just before serving.

SERVINGS 12 (one 3¼×3-inch piece each)

CARB. PER SERVING 21 g

- 9 dried whole grain lasagna noodles
- 1 medium leek, chopped (about ½ cup)
- 3 medium zucchini, thinly sliced
- 2 cups sliced fresh mushrooms
- ¾ cup bottled roasted red peppers, drained and cut into bite-size strips
- ¼ cup chopped fresh basil
- 1 24-ounce carton fat-free cottage cheese (scant 3 cups)
- ½ cup refrigerated or frozen egg product, thawed, or 1 egg, lightly beaten
- 2 cloves garlic, minced
- 1 10-ounce package frozen chopped spinach, thawed and well drained
- 1 cup shredded low-fat mozzarella cheese

1. Preheat oven to 350° F. Cook lasagna noodles according to package directions; drain. Rinse with cold water; drain again. Lightly coat a 3-quart rectangular baking dish with *nonstick cooking spray*; set aside.
2. Lightly coat a large skillet with cooking spray. Heat skillet over medium heat. Add leek and cook about 4 minutes or until just tender, stirring occasionally. Stir in zucchini, mushrooms, and roasted red peppers. Cook and stir for 8 to 10 minutes or until vegetables are tender. Remove from heat and stir in basil.
3. Meanwhile, in a food processor or blender, combine cottage cheese, egg, and garlic. Cover and process or blend until smooth. Stir in spinach.
4. Layer 3 lasagna noodles in bottom of the prepared baking dish. Top with half of the zucchini mixture. Spread one-third of the cottage cheese mixture on top. Repeat, ending with a layer of noodles. Spread

remaining cottage cheese mixture on top. Sprinkle with mozzarella cheese. Spray a piece of foil with cooking spray and place over the cheese. Bake for 45 minutes; uncover and bake for 5 minutes more. Let stand for 10 minutes before serving.
PER SERVING: 156 cal., 2 g total fat (1 g sat. fat), 7 mg chol., 300 mg sodium, 21 g carb., 4 g fiber, 14 g pro. Exchanges: 1 vegetable, 1 starch, 1.5 lean meat. Carb choices: 1.5.

Baked Stuffed Shells

To ensure the filling is creamy rather than runny, use extra-firm, silken-style tofu and finely shredded Parmesan or Romano cheese.

SERVINGS 6 (2 shells each)

CARB. PER SERVING 32 g

- 1 teaspoon olive oil
- ½ cup chopped onion
- 2 cloves garlic, minced
- 1 14.5-ounce can no-salt-added diced tomatoes, undrained
- 1 8-ounce can no-salt-added tomato sauce
- 1 tablespoon snipped fresh basil or ½ teaspoon dried basil, crushed
- 2 teaspoons snipped fresh oregano or ½ teaspoon dried oregano, crushed
- ¼ teaspoon salt
- 12 dried jumbo macaroni shells
- 1 12.3-ounce package extra-firm, silken-style tofu (fresh bean curd)
- ¼ cup refrigerated or frozen egg product, thawed, or 1 egg, lightly beaten
- ½ cup finely shredded Parmesan or Romano cheese (2 ounces)
- ½ cup shredded reduced-fat mozzarella cheese (2 ounces)

1. Preheat oven to 350°F. For sauce: In a medium saucepan, heat oil over medium heat. Add onion and garlic; cook and stir about 3 minutes or until onion is tender. Carefully add undrained tomatoes, tomato sauce, dried basil and oregano (if using), and salt. Bring to boiling; reduce heat. Simmer, uncovered, about 15 minutes or until desired consistency. Remove from heat; stir in snipped fresh basil and oregano (if using). Set aside ¾ cup of the sauce; spoon the remaining sauce into a 2-quart rectangular baking dish. Set aside.

2. Meanwhile, cook pasta according to package directions; drain. Rinse with cold water; drain again.

3. For filling: Place tofu in a blender or food processor. Cover and blend or process until smooth. Add egg, Parmesan cheese, and ¼ teaspoon *black pepper;* cover and blend or process just until combined. Spoon about 3 tablespoons of the filling into each pasta shell. Arrange filled shells, filling sides up, on top of sauce in baking dish. Spoon the reserved ¾ cup sauce over top.

4. Bake, covered, about 35 minutes or until heated through. Uncover and sprinkle with mozzarella cheese. Bake, uncovered, about 2 minutes more or until cheese melts. Let stand for 10 minutes before serving. If desired, top with 2 tablespoons *shredded fresh basil.*

PER SERVING: 234 cal., 5 g total fat (2 g sat. fat), 10 mg chol., 357 mg sodium, 32 g carb., 3 g fiber, 14 g pro. Exchanges: 1 vegetable, 2 starch, 1 lean meat. Carb choices: 2.

Marinated Tofu with Edamame Stir-Fry

Cooking the tofu slices on a stovetop grill pan browns them nicely. If you don't have a grill pan, use a nonstick skillet.

SERVINGS 4 (1 slice tofu and about 1 cup vegetable mixture each)

CARB. PER SERVING 25 g

¼ cup rice vinegar

2 tablespoons reduced-sodium soy sauce

1 tablespoon toasted sesame oil

1 tablespoon honey

1 tablespoon finely chopped, peeled fresh ginger or 1 teaspoon ground ginger

2 cloves garlic, minced

1 16- to 18-ounce package firm or extra-firm tofu (fresh bean curd), drained and cut into 4 slices

3 cups sliced, stemmed shiitake mushrooms and/or button mushrooms

2 medium red, yellow, and/or orange sweet peppers, cut into bite-size strips

½ cup chopped red onion

4 cups coarsely shredded bok choy

1 cup frozen shelled sweet soybeans (edamame), thawed

½ teaspoon cornstarch

1 tablespoon sesame seeds, toasted

1. For marinade: In a 2-quart rectangular baking dish, combine vinegar, soy sauce, 1½ teaspoons of the sesame oil, the honey, ginger, and garlic. Add tofu slices, turning to coat. Marinate at room temperature for 30 minutes, turning tofu once halfway through marinating time.

2. Coat an unheated nonstick grill pan with *nonstick cooking spray.* Preheat over medium-high heat. Transfer tofu slices to grill pan, reserving marinade in baking dish. Cook tofu for 4 to 6 minutes or until heated through and starting to brown, turning once.

3. Meanwhile, in a large nonstick skillet, heat the remaining 1½ teaspoons sesame oil over medium-high heat. Add mushrooms, sweet peppers, and red onion. Cook and stir for 3 to 5 minutes or until crisp-tender. Add bok choy and soybeans. Cook and stir for 2 to 3 minutes more or until bok choy is wilted. Whisk cornstarch into the reserved marinade; add to vegetable mixture. Cook and stir until thickened and bubbly. Cook and stir for 1 minute more.

4. Divide vegetable mixture among four serving bowls. If desired, cut tofu slices in half. Place tofu on top of vegetable mixture. Sprinkle with sesame seeds and, if desired, ¼ teaspoon *crushed red pepper.*

PER SERVING: 293 cal., 12 g total fat (1 g sat. fat), 0 mg chol., 323 mg sodium, 25 g carb., 6 g fiber, 21 g pro. Exchanges: 2 vegetable, 1 starch, 2 lean meat, 1.5 fat. Carb choices: 1.5.

Marinated Tofu with Edamame Stir-Fry

fresh salad meals

Beautifully arranged on a platter or simply tossed in a bowl with an assortment of good-for-you-ingredients, a salad makes a complete meal. Enjoy one of these fresh-tastic creations loaded with leafy greens, hearty grains, lean meats, crunchy veggies, and more.

Mediterranean Chicken Salad

When you're grilling or broiling chicken breasts, cook some extra pieces to use in this salad. Or if you prefer, pick up some packaged cooked chicken breast strips or cubes at the supermarket.

SERVINGS 6 (about 1½ cups each)
CARB. PER SERVING 24 g

⅓ cup lemon juice
2 tablespoons snipped fresh mint
2 tablespoons snipped fresh basil
2 tablespoons olive oil
1 tablespoon honey
¼ teaspoon black pepper
5 cups shredded romaine lettuce
2 cups cut-up cooked chicken breast
2 roma tomatoes, cut into wedges
1 15-ounce can garbanzo beans (chickpeas), rinsed and drained
2 tablespoons pitted Kalamata olives, quartered
2 tablespoons crumbled reduced-fat feta cheese
12 whole Kalamata olives

1. For dressing: In a screw-top jar, combine lemon juice, mint, basil, oil, honey, and pepper. Cover and shake well.
2. Place lettuce on a large platter. Top with chicken, tomatoes, beans, the quartered olives, and cheese. Drizzle dressing over salad. Garnish individual servings with whole olives.

PER SERVING: 252 cal., 9 g total fat (1 g sat. fat), 41 mg chol., 422 mg sodium, 24 g carb., 5 g fiber, 19 g pro. Exchanges: 1 vegetable, 1 starch, 2 lean meat, 1 fat. Carb choices: 1.5.

Chicken Salad Lettuce Cups

Go ahead, indulge. Each serving includes three of these springy chicken-filled lettuce cups.

SERVINGS 4 (3 lettuce cups each)
CARB. PER SERVING 14 g

- ¼ cup light mayonnaise
- 2 tablespoons white balsamic vinegar or regular balsamic vinegar
- 1 large clove garlic, minced
- ⅛ teaspoon salt
- 3 cups coarsely chopped cooked chicken breast
- 1 large red-skin apple, cored and coarsely chopped
- 1 cup coarsely chopped, seeded cucumber
- 1 cup chopped Bibb or Boston lettuce or red leaf lettuce
- ½ cup chopped bottled roasted red sweet peppers
- ¼ cup thinly sliced green onions (2)
- 12 large leaves Bibb or Boston lettuce or red leaf lettuce
- 2 tablespoons pine nuts, toasted

1. In a large bowl, whisk together mayonnaise, vinegar, garlic, and salt. Add chicken, apple, cucumber, chopped lettuce, roasted sweet peppers, and green onions. Toss to coat.
2. To serve, divide lettuce leaves among serving plates. Spoon about ½ cup of the chicken mixture into each lettuce leaf. Sprinkle chicken mixture with pine nuts.
PER SERVING: 297 cal., 11 g total fat (2 g sat. fat), 95 mg chol., 257 mg sodium, 14 g carb., 2 g fiber, 35 g pro. Exchanges: 1.5 vegetable, 0.5 fruit, 4.5 lean meat, 1 fat. Carb choices: 1.

Chicken Salad Lettuce Cups

Mexican Chicken Salad Stacks

If you're in a hurry, simply toss the ingredients together and serve this seasoned-chicken medley in salad bowls.

SERVINGS 4 (1 small chicken breast half, 1 cup romaine mixture, ¼ avocado, ½ orange, and 1 tablespoon cheese each)
CARB. PER SERVING 16 g

- 4 small skinless, boneless chicken breast halves (1 to 1¼ pounds total)
- 1 teaspoon ancho chile powder or chili powder
- ½ teaspoon dried oregano, crushed
- ½ teaspoon dried thyme, crushed
- ⅛ teaspoon salt
- ⅛ teaspoon black pepper
- 2 tablespoons orange juice
- 1 tablespoon olive oil
- 1 tablespoon white wine vinegar
- 1 teaspoon honey
- 4 cups shredded romaine lettuce
- 1 small avocado, halved, seeded, peeled, and sliced
- 2 oranges, peeled and sectioned
- ¼ cup crumbled queso fresco or shredded Monterey Jack cheese (1 ounce)

1. Place each chicken breast half between two pieces of plastic wrap. Using the flat side of a meat mallet, pound chicken until about ½ inch thick. Remove plastic wrap.
2. Preheat broiler. In a small bowl, stir together chile powder, oregano, thyme, salt, and black pepper. Sprinkle spice mixture evenly over chicken pieces; rub in with your fingers.
3. Place chicken on the unheated rack of a broiler pan. Broil 4 to 5 inches from the heat for 6 to 8 minutes or until chicken is tender and no longer pink (170°F), turning once halfway through broiling. Slice chicken.
4. Meanwhile, in a medium bowl, whisk together the orange juice, oil, vinegar, and honey. Add lettuce; toss to coat.
5. To assemble, divide lettuce mixture among four dinner plates. Top with chicken, avocado slices, and orange sections. Sprinkle with cheese.
PER SERVING: 276 cal., 11 g total fat (2 g sat. fat), 68 mg chol., 153 mg sodium, 16 g carb., 6 g fiber, 30 g pro. Exchanges: 1 vegetable, 0.5 fruit, 4 lean meat, 1 fat. Carb choices: 1.

Mexican Chicken
Salad Stacks

Cran-Apple
Chicken Salad

Cran-Apple Chicken Salad

*Festive enough for a special occasion, yet easy enough
for a weeknight meal, this pretty platter
goes together in minutes.*

SERVINGS 4 (2 cups each)
CARB. PER SERVING 19 g

1 5- to 8-ounce package mixed salad greens
2 cups shredded cooked chicken breast*
1 medium Braeburn or Gala apple, cored and chopped
1 stalk celery, thinly bias-sliced (½ cup)
⅓ cup dried cranberries
1 medium shallot, minced (4 teaspoons)
2 tablespoons white wine vinegar
2 tablespoons canola oil
1 tablespoon frozen apple juice concentrate
1 teaspoon poppy seeds
½ teaspoon Dijon-style mustard
⅛ teaspoon salt
¼ cup shredded white cheddar cheese (1 ounce)

1. Place salad greens on a serving platter. Top with
chicken, apple, celery, and cranberries.
2. For dressing: In a screw-top jar, combine shallot,
vinegar, canola oil, apple juice concentrate, poppy
seeds, mustard, and salt. Cover and shake well.
3. Drizzle dressing over salad. Sprinkle salad
with cheese.

*TEST KITCHEN TIP: You will need about 8 ounces of
cooked skinless, boneless chicken breast for 2 cups
of shredded meat.

PER SERVING: 261 cal., 12 g total fat (3 g sat. fat), 56 mg chol.,
190 mg sodium, 19 g carb., 3 g fiber, 20 g pro. Exchanges:
1 vegetable, 1 fruit, 2.5 lean meat, 1.5 fat. Carb choices: 1.

Southwestern Chicken and Black Bean Salad

Deli-roasted chicken is a quick option if you don't have cooked chicken on hand.

SERVINGS 4 (2½ cups each)
CARB. PER SERVING 31 g

- 10 cups torn romaine lettuce leaves
- 1 15-ounce can no-salt-added black beans, rinsed and drained
- 1½ cups chopped cooked chicken or turkey breast
- 1½ cups red and/or yellow cherry tomatoes, halved
- ½ cup bottled light Caesar salad dressing
- 1½ teaspoons chili powder
- ½ teaspoon ground cumin
- ½ cup broken baked tortilla chips (about 1 ounce)
- 2 tablespoons snipped fresh cilantro or parsley
  Fresh cilantro sprigs (optional)

1. In a large salad bowl, combine romaine, black beans, chicken, and tomatoes.
2. For dressing: In a small bowl, whisk together salad dressing, chili powder, and cumin. Pour dressing over salad and toss gently to coat. Sprinkle with tortilla chips and snipped cilantro. If desired, garnish with cilantro sprigs.
PER SERVING: 293 cal., 7 g total fat (2 g sat. fat), 55 mg chol., 445 mg sodium, 31 g carb., 9 g fiber, 26 g pro. Exchanges: 2 vegetable, 1.5 starch, 2.5 lean meat, 0.5 fat. Carb choices: 2.

Chicken, Pear, and Parmesan Salad

Chicken, Pear, and Parmesan Salad

Enjoy a Bistro-style meal for around $2 per serving.

SERVINGS 4 (about 2½ cups each)
CARB. PER SERVING 26 g

- 2 tablespoons cider vinegar or white wine vinegar
- 2 tablespoons olive oil or canola oil
- 1 tablespoon honey
- 5 cups torn fresh spinach leaves
- 2 cups shredded or chopped cooked chicken breast
- 2 pears, cored and cut into cubes
- ½ of a small red onion, thinly sliced
- ¼ cup dried cranberries or raisins
- 1 ounce Parmesan cheese, shaved

1. For dressing: In a small screw-top jar, combine vinegar, oil, honey, ¼ teaspoon *salt*, and ¼ teaspoon *black pepper*. Cover and shake well.
2. In a large salad bowl, combine spinach, chicken, pears, onion, and cranberries. Drizzle dressing over salad and toss to coat evenly. Sprinkle with cheese.
PER SERVING: 275 cal., 8 g total fat (2 g sat. fat), 64 mg chol., 343 mg sodium, 26 g carb., 4 g fiber, 26 g pro. Exchanges: 1 vegetable, 1.5 fruit, 3.5 lean meat, 0.5 fat. Carb choices: 2.

Chopped Chef's Salad

Everything is chopped—prep can't get any easier!

SERVINGS 4 (2 cups each)
CARB. PER SERVING 8 g

- 8 cups chopped romaine and/or iceberg lettuce
- 6 ounces cooked turkey breast, chopped
- 1 medium cucumber, seeded and chopped
- 1 large tomato, chopped
- 2 hard-cooked eggs, chopped
- ⅓ cup shredded reduced-fat sharp cheddar cheese
- 1 recipe Herb Vinaigrette (below)

1. In a large salad bowl, combine lettuce, turkey, cucumber, tomato, eggs, and cheese. Pour dressing over salad and toss to combine.
HERB VINAIGRETTE: In a screw-top jar, combine 2 tablespoons white wine vinegar; 2 tablespoons olive oil; 1 tablespoon chopped fresh basil, thyme, and/or oregano or 1 teaspoon dried Italian seasoning; ½ teaspoon Dijon-style mustard; and ¼ teaspoon black pepper. Cover and shake well.
PER SERVING: 221 cal., 12 g total fat (3 g sat. fat), 147 mg chol., 148 mg sodium, 8 g carb., 3 g fiber, 21 g pro. Exchanges: 1.5 vegetable, 2.5 medium-fat meat. Carb choices: 0.5.

When you can, leave the skin on potatoes. It helps them retain nutrients, provides a good dose of fiber, and makes preparation fast and easy.

Warm Yukon Gold and
Sweet Potato Salad

Warm Yukon Gold and Sweet Potato Salad

Give the salad a gentle toss before serving. This will help mix in the spinach so all of it will become partially wilted.

SERVINGS 4 (2 cups spinach, ¾ cup potatoes, and ⅓ cup sausage mixture each)

CARB. PER SERVING 26 g

- 8 ounces Yukon gold potatoes, scrubbed and cut into ½-inch slices
- 8 ounces sweet potato, peeled and cut into ½-inch slices (1 medium)
- 7 ounces smoked turkey sausage, cut into ½-inch slices
- 1 small red onion, cut into thin wedges
- 1 stalk celery, thinly sliced (½ cup)
- 2 tablespoons olive oil
- 2 tablespoons cider vinegar
- 1 teaspoon Dusseldorf or spicy brown mustard
- 1 teaspoon snipped fresh sage or ½ teaspoon dried sage, crushed
- ¼ teaspoon black pepper
- ⅛ teaspoon celery seeds
- 1 5- to 6-ounce package fresh baby spinach

1. In a large saucepan, cook potatoes and sweet potatoes in enough boiling salted water to cover about 10 minutes or until tender; drain.

2. Meanwhile, in a large skillet, cook sausage, onion, and celery in hot olive oil over medium heat about 5 minutes or until onion is tender and sausage is browned. Stir in vinegar, mustard, sage, pepper, and celery seeds.

3. Place spinach in a serving bowl. Top with potatoes and sweet potato. Spoon sausage mixture over top.

PER SERVING: 253 cal., 12 g total fat (2 g sat. fat), 33 mg chol., 560 mg sodium, 26 g carb., 4 g fiber, 10 g pro. Exchanges: 1.5 vegetable, 1 starch, 0.5 medium-fat meat, 1.5 fat. Carb choices: 2.

Turkey Wild Rice Salad

If you purchase turkey from the deli, choose oven-roasted rather than smoked because it is lower in sodium.

SERVINGS 6 (1 cup each)

CARB. PER SERVING 32 g

- 1 6-ounce package long grain and wild rice mix
- 8 ounces cooked turkey breast, chopped
- 1 medium apple, cored and chopped
- 1 stalk celery, thinly sliced (½ cup)

Turkey Wild Rice Salad

- ¼ cup dried cherries
- ¼ cup chopped pecans, toasted
- 2 tablespoons cider vinegar
- 2 tablespoons canola oil
- ½ teaspoon snipped fresh thyme or ¼ teaspoon dried thyme, crushed
- ¼ teaspoon black pepper
- ⅛ teaspoon salt

1. Prepare long grain and wild rice mix according to package directions, omitting the seasoning packet. Discard the seasoning packet or reserve for another use. Spread rice mixture on a baking sheet to cool completely.

2. In a serving bowl, combine rice mixture, turkey, apple, celery, dried cherries, and pecans. For dressing: In a screw-top jar, combine vinegar, oil, thyme, pepper, and salt. Cover and shake well. Pour dressing over salad and toss to combine. Cover and chill until ready to serve or up to 24 hours.

PER SERVING: 252 cal., 8 g total fat (2 g sat. fat), 31 mg chol., 225 mg sodium, 32 g carb., 3 g fiber, 15 g pro. Exchanges: 2 starch, 1 lean meat, 1 fat. Carb choices: 2.

Beefy Pasta Salad

*Lean beef, fiber-rich multigrain pasta,
and summer-fresh corn, tomatoes, and basil make
this recipe a real winner for a diabetes-friendly meal.*

SERVINGS 4 (1⅓ cups each)

CARB. PER SERVING 28 g

 1 cup dried multigrain penne pasta (about 3½ ounces)
 2 ears of corn, husks and silks removed
12 ounces boneless beef sirloin steak, trimmed of fat and cut into thin bite-size strips, or 2 cups shredded cooked beef pot roast (10 ounces)*
 1 cup cherry tomatoes, halved
 ¼ cup shredded fresh basil
 2 tablespoons finely shredded Parmesan cheese
 3 tablespoons white wine vinegar
 1 tablespoon olive oil
 1 clove garlic, minced
 ¼ cup finely shredded Parmesan cheese

1. In a 4- to 6-quart Dutch oven, cook pasta according to package directions, adding corn for the last 3 minutes of cooking time. Using tongs, transfer corn to a large cutting board. Drain pasta. Rinse pasta in cold water and drain again; set aside. Cool corn until easy to handle.
2. Meanwhile, coat an unheated large nonstick skillet with *nonstick cooking spray*. Preheat skillet over medium-high heat. Add beef strips. Cook for 4 to 6 minutes or until slightly pink in the center, stirring occasionally. (If using shredded beef, cook until heated through.) Remove from heat and cool slightly.
3. On a cutting board, place an ear of corn pointed end down. While holding corn firmly at stem end to keep in place, use a sharp knife to cut corn from cob, leaving corn in planks; rotate cob as needed to cut corn from all sides. Repeat with the remaining ear of corn. In a large bowl, combine pasta, beef, tomatoes, basil, and the 2 tablespoons Parmesan cheese.
4. In a screw-top jar, combine vinegar, oil, garlic, ¼ teaspoon *salt*, and ⅛ teaspoon *black pepper*. Cover and shake well. Pour over pasta mixture; toss gently to coat. Gently fold in corn planks or place corn planks on top of individual servings. Serve immediately. Garnish with the ¼ cup Parmesan cheese.
*TEST KITCHEN TIP: If you have leftover beef pot roast, use it in this pasta salad. Simply shred the meat and use 2 cups of it in the salad.
PER SERVING: 313 cal., 10 g total fat (3 g sat. fat), 41 mg chol., 341 mg sodium, 28 g carb., 4 g fiber, 28 g pro. Exchanges: 0.5 vegetable, 1.5 starch, 3 lean meat, 1 fat. Carb choices: 2.

Warm Fajita Salad

*All the sizzling goodness of lime-and-cilantro-flavored
beef strips combined with cool, crisp greens
makes for a low-carb salad sensation.*

SERVINGS 4 (2 cups salad greens and ¾ cup beef-vegetable mixture plus tomatoes and tortilla strips each)

CARB. PER SERVING 19 g

12 ounces boneless beef top sirloin steak
 ¼ cup lime juice
 ¼ cup reduced-sodium chicken broth
 1 tablespoon snipped fresh cilantro
 2 to 3 teaspoons honey
1½ teaspoons cornstarch
 2 cloves garlic, minced
 ½ teaspoon ground cumin
 ¼ teaspoon salt
 ¼ teaspoon black pepper
   Nonstick cooking spray
 2 small green, red, and/or yellow sweet peppers, cut into thin strips
 2 small onions, cut into thin wedges
 1 tablespoon vegetable oil
 1 10-ounce package torn mixed salad greens
12 red and/or yellow cherry tomatoes, halved or quartered
 1 recipe Baked Tortilla Strips (below)

1. If desired, partially freeze meat for easier slicing. Trim fat from meat. Cut meat into thin bite-size strips. For sauce: In a small bowl, combine lime juice, broth, cilantro, honey, cornstarch, and garlic; set aside. Sprinkle meat strips with cumin, salt, and black pepper; toss to coat.
2. Coat a large skillet with cooking spray. Preheat over medium-high heat. Add sweet peppers and onions; cook and stir for 3 to 4 minutes or until crisp-tender. Remove from skillet. Pour oil into hot skillet. Add meat; cook and stir for 2 to 3 minutes or until meat is slightly pink in the center. Push meat from center of skillet.
3. Stir sauce; add to center of skillet. Cook and stir until thickened and bubbly. Return cooked vegetables to skillet. Stir all ingredients together to coat with sauce. Cook and stir until heated through.
4. To serve, divide salad greens and tomatoes among four dinner plates. Spoon meat mixture on top of greens mixture. Sprinkle with Baked Tortilla Strips.
BAKED TORTILLA STRIPS: Preheat oven to 400°F. Cut one 6-inch corn tortilla into ⅛- to ¼-inch strips; cut long strips in half crosswise. Place strips on an ungreased baking

Warm
Fajita Salad

sheet. Coat with cooking spray; sprinkle lightly with paprika and chili powder. Bake about 8 minutes or until strips are golden and crisp, stirring once.

PER SERVING: 223 cal., 8 g total fat (2 g sat. fat), 52 mg chol., 246 mg sodium, 19 g carb., 4 g fiber, 21 g pro. Exchanges: 2 vegetable, 1.5 starch, 2.5 lean meat, 0.5 fat. Carb choices: 1.

Polenta and Catfish Salad

Arugula, Pear, and Pork Salad

If you wish, omit the pork from the mix and serve the salad alongside grilled boneless pork loin chops.

SERVINGS 4 (1½ cups each)

CARB. PER SERVING 12 g

- 1 5- to 6-ounce package fresh baby arugula or baby spinach
- 1½ cups cooked pork loin, cut into 1-inch pieces
- 1 medium pear, cored and sliced
- 1 ounce blue cheese, crumbled
- ¼ cup sliced almonds, toasted
- 2 tablespoons olive oil
- 1 tablespoon lemon juice
- 1 tablespoon white wine vinegar
- 2 teaspoons honey
- 1 clove garlic, minced
- ¼ teaspoon cracked black pepper
- ⅛ teaspoon salt

1. Arrange arugula on a serving platter. Top with pork, pear, blue cheese, and almonds.

2. For dressing: In a screw-top jar, combine olive oil, lemon juice, vinegar, honey, garlic, pepper, and salt. Cover and shake well. Drizzle dressing over salad.

PER SERVING: 261 cal., 14 g total fat (3 g sat. fat), 59 mg chol., 224 mg sodium, 12 g carb., 2 g fiber, 22 g pro. Exchanges: 1 vegetable, 0.5 carb., 2.5 lean meat, 2 fat. Carb choices: 1.

Polenta and Catfish Salad

To kick up the heat, pass a bottle of hot pepper sauce.

SERVINGS 4 (2½ cups salad and 2 teaspoons dressing each)

CARB. PER SERVING 18 g

- 12 ounces fresh or frozen catfish fillets
- ½ of a 16-ounce tube refrigerated cooked polenta, sliced ½ inch thick and cut into sticks
- Nonstick cooking spray
- 1 tablespoon vegetable oil
- 2 teaspoons salt-free Cajun seasoning
- 8 cups chopped romaine or iceberg lettuce
- 1 large tomato, chopped
- 1 medium green sweet pepper, cut into bite-size strips
- 2 tablespoons light mayonnaise or salad dressing
- 1 tablespoon cider vinegar
- 1 teaspoon Creole mustard or spicy brown mustard

1. Thaw fish, if frozen. Cut catfish into bite-size strips; set aside. Preheat oven to 400°F. Place polenta on a lightly greased baking sheet. Lightly coat polenta with cooking spray. Bake for 15 to 20 minutes or until golden brown on the edges.

2. In a large nonstick skillet, cook catfish in hot oil over medium heat for 4 to 6 minutes or until lightly browned and fish flakes when tested with a fork. Sprinkle with 1 teaspoon of the Cajun seasoning.

3. Arrange lettuce on a serving platter. Top with polenta, catfish, tomato, and sweet pepper.

4. For dressing: In a small bowl, whisk together mayonnaise, vinegar, mustard, and remaining 1 teaspoon Cajun seasoning. Serve dressing with salad.

PER SERVING: 249 cal., 12 g total fat (2 g sat. fat), 42 mg chol., 341 mg sodium, 18 g carb., 4 g fiber, 16 g pro. Exchanges: 1 vegetable, 1 starch, 1.5 lean meat, 2 fat. Carb choices: 1.

Wilted Spinach and Trout Salad

Measure the thickness of the fish before you begin broiling.

SERVINGS 4 (1½ cups each)

CARB. PER SERVING 8 g

- 12 ounces fresh or frozen trout fillets
- ⅛ to ¼ teaspoon cayenne pepper
- 1 5- to 6-ounce package baby spinach
- 1 8-ounce package fresh button mushrooms, quartered
- 1 medium leek, sliced
- 3 cloves garlic, thinly sliced
- 2 tablespoons olive oil
- 1 large roma tomato, chopped
- 2 tablespoons red wine vinegar

1. Thaw fish, if frozen. Preheat broiler. Sprinkle trout with ¼ teaspoon *salt* and the cayenne pepper. Arrange trout fillets, skin sides down, on a greased unheated rack of a broiler pan. Broil 4 inches from the heat for 4 to 6 minutes per ½-inch thickness of fish or until fish flakes when tested with a fork. Keep warm.

2. Arrange spinach on a serving platter; set aside. In a large skillet, cook mushrooms, leek, and garlic in hot oil over medium heat about 4 minutes or until tender. Add tomato and cook 1 minute more or until softened. Add vinegar and heat through. Add mixture to spinach; toss to coat and lightly wilt. Top with trout.

PER SERVING: 222 cal., 12 g total fat (2 g sat. fat), 50 mg chol., 212 mg sodium, 8 g carb., 2 g fiber, 21 g pro. Exchanges: 2 vegetable, 2.5 lean meat, 1.5 fat. Carb choices: 0.5.

Grilled Salmon Salad Niçoise

This captivating combo gives salad niçoise a twist by substituting grilled salmon for the classic tuna.

SERVINGS 6 (about 1 ounce cooked salmon, $2/3$ of an egg, 1 cup greens, about $3/4$ cup vegetables, and about $1\frac{1}{2}$ tablespoons vinaigrette each)

CARB. PER SERVING 12 g

- 2 4- to 5-ounce fresh or frozen skinless salmon fillets
- 8 tiny new potatoes
- 8 ounces fresh green beans, trimmed
- ¼ teaspoon lemon-pepper seasoning
  Nonstick cooking spray
- 6 cups torn mixed salad greens
- 8 grape tomatoes or cherry tomatoes, halved
- ½ cup snipped fresh chives
- 4 hard-cooked eggs, cut into wedges
- ¼ cup niçoise olives, pitted, and/or other pitted olives
- 1 recipe Lemon Vinaigrette (page 53)

1. Thaw fish, if frozen. Rinse salmon; pat dry with paper towels. Set aside. Peel a strip around the center of each potato. In a covered large saucepan, cook potatoes in enough lightly salted boiling water to cover for 10 minutes. Add green beans. Return to boiling; reduce heat. Cover and simmer about 5 minutes more or until potatoes and beans are tender. Drain. Rinse with cold water to cool quickly; drain again. Set aside.

2. Meanwhile, measure thickness of salmon fillets. Sprinkle salmon with lemon-pepper seasoning. Lightly coat both sides of salmon fillets with cooking spray.

3. For a charcoal grill, place salmon fillets on the grill rack directly over medium coals. Grill, uncovered, for 4 to 6 minutes per ½-inch thickness or until fish flakes easily when tested with a fork, turning once halfway through grilling if fish is over ¾ inch thick. (For a gas grill, preheat grill. Reduce heat to medium. Place salmon fillets on grill rack over heat. Cover and grill as above.) Cut salmon into serving-size pieces.

Grilled Salmon
Salad Niçoise

4. Line six plates with salad greens. Arrange salmon, potatoes, green beans, tomatoes, chives, eggs, and olives on greens. Drizzle with Lemon Vinaigrette.

LEMON VINAIGRETTE: In a screw-top jar, combine $\frac{1}{2}$ teaspoon finely shredded lemon peel; $\frac{1}{4}$ cup lemon juice; 2 tablespoons olive oil; 1 clove garlic, minced; $\frac{1}{8}$ teaspoon salt; and $\frac{1}{8}$ teaspoon black pepper. Cover and shake well.

PER SERVING: 242 cal., 16 g total fat (3 g sat. fat), 162 mg chol., 221 mg sodium, 12 g carb., 4 g fiber, 14 g pro. Exchanges: 1 vegetable, 0.5 starch, 1.5 medium-fat meat, 1.5 fat. Carb choices: 1.

Asian Sesame Noodles with Shrimp

Toast the sesame seeds in a dry, small skillet over medium heat until golden, shaking frequently.

SERVINGS 4 ($1\frac{1}{4}$ cups each)
CARB. PER SERVING 35 g

---

  8 ounces fresh or frozen shrimp, peeled and deveined
  6 ounces udon noodles
  1 cup snow peas, trimmed and halved diagonally
$\frac{2}{3}$ cup julienned carrots
$\frac{1}{2}$ cup thinly sliced bok choy
  2 tablespoons rice vinegar
  1 tablespoon canola oil
  2 teaspoons grated fresh ginger
  1 teaspoon reduced-sodium soy sauce
  1 teaspoon toasted sesame oil
  1 clove garlic, minced
$\frac{1}{2}$ teaspoon honey
$\frac{1}{4}$ teaspoon crushed red pepper
$\frac{1}{8}$ teaspoon salt
  1 teaspoon sesame seeds, toasted

1. Thaw shrimp, if frozen. Cook noodles according to package directions, adding shrimp and snow peas for the last 3 minutes of cooking time; drain. Rinse under cold running water to stop cooking; drain again.

2. In a salad bowl, combine noodle mixture, carrots, and bok choy. In a screw-top jar, combine rice vinegar, canola oil, ginger, soy sauce, sesame oil, garlic, honey, crushed red pepper, and salt. Pour over noodle mixture and toss to coat. Sprinkle with sesame seeds. Cover and chill until ready to serve or up to 2 hours.

PER SERVING: 285 cal., 7 g total fat (1 g sat. fat), 86 mg chol., 284 mg sodium, 35 g carb., 4 g fiber, 19 g pro. Exchanges: 0.5 vegetable, 2 starch, 1.5 lean meat, 0.5 fat. Carb choices: 2.

Asian Sesame Noodles with Shrimp

▶ QUICK TIP
If you like their looks, leave the tails on the shrimp when you remove the peels and veins.

Iceberg Wedges with Shrimp and Blue Cheese Dressing

Wedges of crisp lettuce dressed up with grilled shrimp, crisp bacon, colorful tomatoes, sliced red onion, and chunky blue cheese dressing—now that's a salad that satisfies!

SERVINGS 6 (2 lettuce wedges, about 6 shrimp, and 2 tablespoons dressing each)
CARB. PER SERVING 8 g

- 1½ pounds fresh or frozen large shrimp in shells
- 3 tablespoons lemon juice
- ¼ teaspoon black pepper
- ½ cup light mayonnaise or salad dressing
- ¼ to ½ teaspoon bottled hot pepper sauce
- 2 tablespoons crumbled blue cheese
- 3 to 4 tablespoons fat-free milk
- Nonstick cooking spray
- 1 large head iceberg lettuce, cut into 12 wedges
- 1 large tomato, chopped
- ⅓ cup thinly sliced, quartered red onion
- 2 slices turkey bacon, cooked and crumbled

1. Thaw shrimp, if frozen. Peel and devein shrimp, leaving tails intact if desired. Rinse shrimp; pat dry with paper towels. In a medium bowl, combine shrimp, 2 tablespoons of the lemon juice, and ⅛ teaspoon of the black pepper. Toss to coat. Set aside.

Iceberg Wedges with Shrimp and Blue Cheese Dressing

2. For dressing: In a small bowl, combine the remaining 1 tablespoon lemon juice, the remaining ⅛ teaspoon black pepper, the mayonnaise, and hot pepper sauce. Stir in blue cheese. Stir in enough of the milk to make desired consistency.

3. Coat an unheated grill pan with cooking spray. Preheat grill pan over medium-high heat. Thread shrimp onto six 10- to 12-inch-long skewers.* Place skewers on grill pan. Cook for 3 to 5 minutes or until shrimp are opaque, turning once halfway through cooking. (If necessary, cook shrimp skewers half at a time.)

4. Place 2 lettuce wedges on each of six serving plates. Top with shrimp, tomato, red onion, and bacon. Serve with dressing.

*TEST KITCHEN TIP:** If using wooden skewers, soak skewers in enough water to cover for at least 30 minutes before using.
PER SERVING: 190 cal., 10 g total fat (2 g sat. fat), 129 mg chol., 360 mg sodium, 8 g carb., 1 g fiber, 18 g pro. Exchanges: 1.5 vegetable, 2 lean meat, 1.5 fat. Carb choices: 0.5.

Scallop Salad with Basil Vinaigrette

Balsamic vinegar adds a touch of sweetness to the light basil dressing that partners deliciously with the scallops, greens, and mixed veggies. Pictured on page 56.

SERVINGS 4 (1½ cups salad greens, about ¾ cup tomato mixture, and 2 or 3 scallops each)
CARB. PER SERVING 21 g

- 1 pound fresh or frozen sea scallops
- ¼ cup snipped fresh basil
- 3 tablespoons balsamic vinegar
- 2 tablespoons lemon juice
- 2 tablespoons olive oil
- 2 teaspoons Dijon-style mustard
- ½ teaspoon black pepper
- Nonstick cooking spray
- 6 cups torn mixed salad greens
- 3 roma tomatoes, seeded and chopped
- 1 medium red sweet pepper, chopped (¾ cup)
- 1 cup fresh corn kernels or frozen whole kernel corn, thawed
- ½ of a medium English cucumber, chopped
- 2 tablespoons finely shredded Parmesan cheese

1. Thaw scallops, if frozen. Rinse scallops; pat dry with paper towels. For vinaigrette: In a screw-top jar, combine basil, vinegar, lemon juice, oil, mustard, and ¼ teaspoon of the black pepper. Cover and shake well. Set aside.

2. Sprinkle scallops with the remaining ¼ teaspoon black pepper. Coat an unheated large nonstick skillet with cooking spray. Preheat over medium-high heat. Add scallops. Cook for 2 to 4 minutes or until scallops are opaque, turning once halfway through cooking.

3. Meanwhile, divide salad greens among four serving plates. In a large bowl, combine tomatoes, sweet pepper, corn, and cucumber. Add half of the vinaigrette; toss to coat. Add to serving plates with greens. Add scallops to salads and brush with some of the remaining vinaigrette. Pass the remaining vinaigrette. Sprinkle with Parmesan cheese.

PER SERVING: 261 cal., 9 g total fat (2 g sat. fat), 39 mg chol., 282 mg sodium, 21 g carb., 4 g fiber, 23 g pro. Exchanges: 2 vegetable, 0.5 starch, 2.5 lean meat, 1 fat. Carb choices: 1.5.

Roasted Vegetable Tabbouleh

When you're tired of fresh green salads, try this mix of hearty bulgur and roasted vegetables. It's a great make-and-take for lunch.

SERVINGS 4 (1½ cups each)
CARB. PER SERVING 45 g

- ¾ cup bulgur
- 3 medium carrots, chopped (1½ cups)
- 1 small red onion, chopped (⅓ cup)
- Nonstick cooking spray
- 1 15- to 16-ounce can garbanzo beans (chickpeas), rinsed and drained
- ½ cup chopped fresh parsley
- ½ teaspoon finely shredded lemon peel
- 3 tablespoons lemon juice
- 2 tablespoons water
- 2 tablespoons olive oil
- 2 teaspoons snipped fresh thyme
- ¼ teaspoon black pepper
- ⅛ teaspoon salt
- 1 medium tomato, chopped

1. Preheat oven to 400°F. Cook bulgur according to package directions; cool. Spread carrots and red onion in a 15×10×1-inch baking pan. Lightly coat with cooking spay and stir to coat. Roast, uncovered, for 20 to

Roasted Vegetable
Tabbouleh

25 minutes or until tender and lightly browned.

2. In a large bowl, combine cooked bulgur, roasted vegetables, garbanzo beans, parsley, lemon peel, lemon juice, the water, olive oil, thyme, pepper, and salt. Toss to combine. Cover and chill for 4 to 24 hours. Stir in tomato before serving.

PER SERVING: 254 cal., 8 g total fat (1 g sat. fat), 0 mg chol., 492 mg sodium, 45 g carb., 11 g fiber, 10 g pro. Exchanges: 1 vegetable, 2.5 starch, 1 fat. Carb choices: 3.

Scallop Salad with Basil Vinaigrette
recipe on page 54

Asian Tofu Salad

Quinoa Salad
with Seared Tuna

Top It Wisely

A salad of leafy greens topped with a few fresh veggies and some lean protein can make a quick, nutritious lunch. Remember to be health-conscious with the toppings, too. Use these four hints for smart toppings.

1. **Skip the croutons.** If you have room for the carbs, opt for a couple of whole grain crackers instead.

2. **Go light on cheese.** Cheese adds fat and calories. When you're craving cheese, use just a tablespoon. And opt for a high-flavor cheese such as feta or Parmesan.

3. **Keep it on the side.** Choose any dressing you like and serve it on the side. Dip your fork in the container prior to each bite and you will get a taste of the dressing while consuming a fraction of the calories.

4. **Think outside the dressing bottle.** Make your own dressings with different herbs and seasonings.

Asian Tofu Salad

The slices of protein-rich tofu that top this salad are seasoned in a chili sauce-and-peanut butter marinade and sautéed in sesame oil for bold, rich flavor.

SERVINGS 6 (1¼ cups salad and 2 slices tofu each)
CARB. PER SERVING 18 g

¼ cup reduced-sodium soy sauce
¼ cup sweet chili sauce
1 tablespoon creamy peanut butter
1 clove garlic, minced
1 teaspoon grated fresh ginger
1 16- to 18-ounce package firm water-packed tofu (fresh bean curd)
1 teaspoon toasted sesame oil
4 cups shredded romaine lettuce
1½ cups chopped, peeled jicama
1 medium red sweet pepper, thinly sliced
1 cup coarsely shredded carrots
2 tablespoons unsalted dry-roasted peanuts
2 tablespoons snipped fresh cilantro

1. In a small bowl, whisk together soy sauce, chili sauce, peanut butter, garlic, and ginger. Pat tofu dry with paper towels. Cut tofu crosswise into 12 slices. Place tofu in a 2-quart rectangular baking dish. Drizzle with 3 tablespoons of the soy sauce mixture, turning to coat tofu. Let marinate at room temperature for 30 minutes, turning tofu occasionally. Set aside the remaining soy sauce mixture for dressing.

2. In a very large nonstick skillet, heat sesame oil over medium-high heat. Remove tofu slices from the marinade. Add remaining marinade to the skillet; add tofu slices. Cook for 5 to 6 minutes or until lightly browned, turning once halfway through cooking.

3. In a large bowl, combine lettuce, jicama, sweet pepper, and carrots. Divide among six serving plates. Top with tofu, peanuts, and cilantro. Serve with reserved dressing mixture.

PER SERVING: 179 cal., 7 g total fat (1 g sat. fat), 0 mg chol., 515 mg sodium, 18 g carb., 3 g fiber, 11 g pro. Exchanges: 1.5 vegetable, 0.5 carb., 1 medium-fat meat, 0.5 fat. Carb choices: 1.

Quinoa Salad with Seared Tuna

Quinoa, a tiny bean-shape grain, is protein-rich and lower in carbohydrate than many other grains. Look for it in the organic or grain section of your supermarket.

SERVINGS 6 (1 cup each)
CARB. PER SERVING 31 g

12 ounces fresh or frozen tuna steaks
1½ cups quinoa
3 cups water
¼ teaspoon salt
1 large tomato, chopped
1 cup seeded and chopped cucumber
½ cup crumbled reduced-fat feta cheese (2 ounces)
¼ cup chopped red onion
2 tablespoons olive oil
2 tablespoons lemon juice
1 teaspoon honey
½ teaspoon snipped fresh oregano or ¼ teaspoon dried oregano, crushed
¼ teaspoon black pepper
Nonstick cooking spray
⅛ teaspoon salt
⅛ teaspoon black pepper
Fresh oregano leaves

1. Thaw fish, if frozen. Rinse quinoa well in a fine-mesh sieve. Bring the water and ¼ teaspoon salt to boiling. Add quinoa; reduce heat. Simmer, covered, about 15 minutes or until most of the water is absorbed and quinoa is tender. Drain if necessary. Spread quinoa in a shallow baking pan to cool slightly.

2. On a serving platter, combine quinoa, tomato, cucumber, feta cheese, and red onion.

3. For dressing: In a screw-top jar, combine olive oil, lemon juice, honey, snipped oregano, and ¼ teaspoon pepper. Cover and shake well. Add dressing to quinoa mixture and toss to combine.

4. Lightly coat a grill pan or large skillet with cooking spray. Heat grill pan over medium-high heat. Sprinkle tuna steaks with ⅛ teaspoon salt and ⅛ teaspoon pepper. Cook tuna on grill pan for 4 to 6 minutes per ½-inch thickness of fish, turning once, or until browned on both sides, fish begins to flake when tested with a fork, and center is just pink. Thinly slice tuna steaks and serve on top of salad. Garnish with fresh oregano leaves.

PER SERVING: 316 cal., 11 g total fat (3 g sat. fat), 25 mg chol., 332 mg sodium, 31 g carb., 4 g fiber, 22 g pro. Exchanges: 0.5 vegetable, 2 carb., 2 lean meat, 1 fat. Carb choices: 2.

comforting
soups and stews

Ah, lift the lid and nothing says comfort quite like a hearty pot of soup. Loaded with fiber-rich vegetables, protein-packed meats, and more nourishing ingredients, each pot is pumped with flavor as well as good nutrition. Tomatoey, brothy, or even creamy, these versions are diabetes-friendly.

Mediterranean Meatball Soup

Baking the meatballs is a fuss-free way to cook them without adding fat.

SERVINGS 6 (1½ cups each)
CARB. PER SERVING 31 g

¾ cup soft whole wheat bread crumbs
¼ cup refrigerated or frozen egg product, thawed, or 1 egg, lightly beaten
4 cloves garlic, minced
2 teaspoons snipped fresh rosemary or ½ teaspoon dried rosemary, crushed
¼ teaspoon black pepper
1 pound lean ground beef
1 tablespoon olive oil
3 medium carrots, peeled and coarsely chopped
2 medium yellow and/or red sweet peppers, cut into bite-size strips
½ cup chopped onion (1 medium)
2 cups lower-sodium beef broth
1 15-ounce can Great Northern beans, rinsed and drained
½ cup quick-cooking barley
4 cups packaged fresh baby spinach leaves

1. Preheat oven to 350°F. In a large bowl, combine bread crumbs, egg, half of the garlic, half of the rosemary, and the black pepper. Add ground beef; mix well. Shape meat mixture into 1½-inch meatballs. Place meatballs in a foil-lined 15×10×1-inch baking pan. Bake for 15 minutes or until done in centers (160°F). Set aside.
2. In a Dutch oven, heat oil over medium heat. Add carrots, sweet peppers, onion, and the remaining garlic; cook for 5 minutes, stirring occasionally. Add beef broth, 2 cups *water*, beans, barley, and the remaining rosemary. Bring to boiling; reduce heat. Simmer, covered, for 15 minutes or until barley is tender.
3. Add meatballs to barley mixture; heat through. Stir in spinach just before serving.
PER SERVING: 301 cal., 10 g total fat (3 g sat. fat), 49 mg chol., 400 mg sodium, 31 g carb., 7 g fiber, 25 g pro. Exchanges: 1.5 vegetable, 1.5 starch, 2.5 lean meat, 0.5 fat. Carb choices: 2.

Adobo Black Bean Chili

This thick, flavorful chili is packed with nutrients and takes just 30 minutes to prepare!

SERVINGS 4 (1½ cups each)

CARB. PER SERVING 35 g

- 12 ounces lean ground beef
- ½ cup chopped onion (1 medium)
- ¾ cup chopped green sweet pepper (1 medium)
- 2 cloves garlic, minced
- 1 15-ounce can no-salt-added black beans, rinsed and drained, or 1¾ cups cooked black beans
- 1 14.5-ounce can no-salt-added diced tomatoes, undrained
- 1 8-ounce can no-salt-added tomato sauce
- ½ cup frozen whole kernel corn
- 1 tablespoon canned chipotle chile peppers in adobo sauce, finely chopped
- 2 teaspoons chili powder
- 1 teaspoon dried oregano, crushed
- 1 teaspoon ground cumin
- ¼ teaspoon black pepper
- ¼ cup light sour cream
- 2 tablespoons shredded reduced-fat cheddar cheese

1. In a 4-quart Dutch oven, cook ground beef, onion, sweet pepper, and garlic until meat is brown and onion is tender; drain fat. Stir in beans, diced tomatoes, tomato sauce, corn, chile peppers, chili powder, oregano, cumin, and black pepper. Bring to boiling; reduce heat. Simmer, covered, for 20 minutes, stirring occasionally.

2. Top each serving with sour cream and cheddar cheese.

PER SERVING: 317 cal., 7 g total fat (3 g sat. fat), 59 mg chol., 184 mg sodium, 35 g carb., 10 g fiber, 28 g pro. Exchanges: 1.5 vegetable, 2 starch, 2.5 lean meat, 0.5 fat. Carb choices: 2.

Beefy Italian Vegetable Soup

Wow, a generous serving with just over 200 calories!

SERVINGS 4 (2 cups each)

CARB. PER SERVING 17 g

- 12 ounces boneless beef sirloin steak, trimmed of fat and cut into bite-size pieces
- 1 teaspoon vegetable oil
- 8 ounces fresh button mushrooms, quartered
- ½ cup chopped onion (1 medium)
- 3 cloves garlic, minced
- 1 tablespoon balsamic vinegar
- 2 14-ounce cans lower-sodium beef broth
- 1 14.5-ounce can no-salt-added diced tomatoes, undrained
- ¼ cup dry red wine (optional)
- ½ teaspoon dried Italian seasoning, crushed
- ¼ teaspoon fennel seeds, crushed
- 3 cups escarole or kale, chopped
- 1 cup fresh green beans, trimmed and bias-sliced into bite-size pieces
- ¾ cup chopped yellow sweet pepper (1 medium)

1. In a Dutch oven, brown beef in hot oil over medium-high heat. Remove meat with a slotted spoon.

2. Add mushrooms, onion, and garlic to Dutch oven. Cook and stir about 6 minutes or until vegetables are tender and mushrooms are browned. Add vinegar; stir to remove browned bits from the bottom of the pan.

3. Add broth, tomatoes, wine (if desired), Italian seasoning, fennel seeds, and ¼ teaspoon *black pepper*. Bring to boiling. Add beef, escarole, green beans, and sweet pepper; reduce heat. Simmer, covered, for 15 minutes or until vegetables and beef are tender.

PER SERVING: 209 cal., 5 g total fat (1 g sat. fat), 36 mg chol., 469 mg sodium, 17 g carb., 5 g fiber, 25 g pro. Exchanges: 1.5 vegetable, 0.5 starch, 3 lean meat. Carb choices: 1.

Adobo Black Bean Chili

Southwestern Steak and Potato Soup

You can't beat a slow cooker for cooking soup. Big pieces of meat and vegetables in a sassy broth are sure to please.

SERVINGS 14 (1 cup each)
CARB. PER SERVING 12 g

2 pounds boneless beef sirloin steak, cut ¾ inch thick
3 medium potatoes, cut into ¾-inch pieces (3 cups)
1 16-ounce package frozen cut green beans
1 medium onion, sliced and separated into rings
2 teaspoons dried basil, crushed
4 cloves garlic, minced
2 16-ounce jars thick and chunky salsa
2 14-ounce cans lower-sodium beef broth

1. Trim fat from beef. Cut beef into ¾-inch pieces. Set aside.

2. In a 6-quart slow cooker, combine potatoes, green beans, and onion. Add beef. Sprinkle with basil and garlic. Pour salsa and broth over beef and vegetable mixture in cooker.

3. Cover and cook on low-heat setting for 8 to 10 hours or on high-heat setting for 4 to 5 hours. Stir before serving.

PER SERVING: 142 cal., 3 g total fat (1 g sat. fat), 27 mg chol., 532 mg sodium, 12 g carb., 3 g fiber, 17 g pro. Exchanges: 1 starch, 2 lean meat. Carb choices: 1.

Chicken-Squash
Noodle Soup
recipe on page 64

Pork and Hominy
Soup

German Potato-
Sausage Soup
recipe on page 64

Sodium Savers

Soups tend to be loaded with sodium.
Keep the sodium level in check by
trying some of these helpful tips
when making your favorite bowls.

1. **When time allows,** make
   broth or stock from scratch.
2. **If you must use canned
   broth,** choose one that is
   reduced in sodium.
3. **Substitute no-salt-added
   canned tomato products**
   for the regular variety.
4. **Start with dry beans** and
   cook your own following the
   package directions.
5. **If you use canned beans,**
   be sure to give them a good
   rinse and drain.
6. **Go for fresh or frozen
   vegetables** instead of the
   canned varieties.
7. **Try salt-free seasonings**
   such as herbs and spices.
8. **Use minimal salt when
   making a pot of soup.** Pass
   the salt so it can be added
   only as needed.

Pork and Hominy Soup

The flavor of the soup will depend on the chile powder you use. For a milder flavor, choose pasilla or ancho chile, but for a spicy, smoky flavor, choose chipotle chile powder.

SERVINGS 4 (2 cups each)
CARB. PER SERVING 29 g

- 12 ounces pork tenderloin, trimmed of fat and cut into bite-size pieces
- 1 medium fresh poblano or Anaheim chile pepper, seeded and chopped*
- 1 large onion, cut into thin wedges
- 3 cloves garlic, minced
- 2 teaspoons vegetable oil
- 1 15.5-ounce can golden or white hominy, rinsed and drained
- 1 14.5-ounce can no-salt-added diced tomatoes, undrained
- 1 14-ounce can reduced-sodium chicken broth
- 1¾ cups water
- 1 tablespoon lime juice
- 2 teaspoons snipped fresh oregano or 1 teaspoon dried oregano, crushed
- 1 teaspoon ground cumin
- 1 teaspoon ground pasilla, ancho, or chipotle chile pepper powder
- ¼ teaspoon black pepper
- ¼ cup sliced radishes, shredded cabbage, and/or sliced green onions

1. In a Dutch oven, cook pork, poblano, onion, and garlic in hot oil over medium heat about 5 minutes or until tender. Stir in hominy, tomatoes, broth, the water, lime juice, oregano, cumin, pasilla pepper powder, and black pepper. Bring to boiling; reduce heat. Simmer, covered, for 15 minutes.

2. Top each serving with radishes, cabbage, and/or green onions.

*TEST KITCHEN TIP: Because chile peppers contain volatile oils that can burn your skin and eyes, avoid direct contact with chiles as much as possible. When working with chile peppers, wear plastic or rubber gloves. If your bare hands do touch the chile peppers, wash your hands and nails well with soap and warm water.

PER SERVING: 258 cal., 6 g total fat (1 g sat. fat), 55 mg chol., 569 mg sodium, 29 g carb., 6 g fiber, 23 g pro. Exchanges: 1 vegetable, 1.5 starch, 2.5 lean meat. Carb choices: 2.

Chunky Beer-Pork Chili

Lean pork tenderloin cooks up tender in just 5 minutes. Give credit to smoky chipotle chile peppers for the simmer-all-day flavor.

SERVINGS 4 (1 cup each)
CARB. PER SERVING 29 g

- 12 ounces pork tenderloin, trimmed of fat and cut into ¾-inch pieces
- 2 teaspoons chili powder
- 2 teaspoons ground cumin
- 1 tablespoon canola oil
- ½ cup chopped onion (1 medium)
- 4 cloves garlic, minced
- 1 medium yellow or red sweet pepper, cut into ½-inch pieces
- 1 cup beer or lower-sodium beef broth
- ¼ cup bottled picante sauce or salsa
- 2 to 3 teaspoons finely chopped canned chipotle chile pepper in adobo sauce*
- 1 15- to 16-ounce can small red beans or pinto beans, rinsed and drained
- ½ cup light sour cream
- 2 tablespoons snipped fresh cilantro

1. Place pork in a medium bowl. Add chili powder and cumin; toss gently to coat. Set aside.

2. In large saucepan, heat oil over medium heat. Add onion and garlic; cook and stir for 3 minutes. Add pork. Cook and stir until pork is browned.

3. Stir in sweet pepper, beer, picante sauce, and chipotle chile pepper. Bring to boiling; reduce heat. Simmer, covered, about 5 minutes or until pork is tender. Stir in beans; heat through.

4. Top each serving with sour cream. Garnish with cilantro.

*TEST KITCHEN TIP: Because chile peppers contain volatile oils that can burn your skin and eyes, avoid direct contact with chiles as much as possible. When working with chile peppers, wear plastic or rubber gloves. If your bare hands do touch the chile peppers, wash your hands and nails well with soap and warm water.

PER SERVING: 313 cal., 9 g total fat (2 g sat. fat), 64 mg chol., 510 mg sodium, 29 g carb., 7 g fiber, 27 g pro. Exchanges: 0.5 vegetable, 2 starch, 3 lean meat, 0.5 fat. Carb choices: 2.

German Potato-Sausage Soup

Three German favorites—sausage, caraway seeds, and beer—star in this easy-to-fix soup. Pictured on page 62.

SERVINGS 6 (1⅓ cups each)
CARB. PER SERVING 16 g

- 12 ounces bulk turkey sausage
- 8 ounces fresh button mushrooms, sliced
- ½ cup chopped onion (1 medium)
- ½ cup chopped celery (1 stalk)
- 1 teaspoon caraway seeds, crushed
- ¼ teaspoon black pepper
- 1¾ cups lower-sodium beef broth
- ½ cup light beer, nonalcoholic beer, or lower-sodium beef broth
- 2 medium potatoes, cubed
- 1 cup small broccoli florets
- 2 cups shredded cabbage
- 1½ cups fat-free milk

1. In a Dutch oven, cook sausage, mushrooms, onion, and celery over medium heat until sausage is browned, stirring to break up sausage as it cooks. Drain off fat.
2. Add caraway seeds and pepper to sausage mixture in Dutch oven. Add broth and beer; bring to boiling. Add potatoes. Simmer, covered, for 10 minutes. Add broccoli. Cover and simmer about 5 minutes more or until potatoes and broccoli are tender.
3. Stir cabbage and milk into sausage-broccoli mixture. Cook for 2 to 3 minutes or just until cabbage is tender and soup is heated through.

PER SERVING: 179 cal., 5 g total fat (1 g sat. fat), 44 mg chol., 522 mg sodium, 16 g carb., 3 g fiber, 17 g pro. Exchanges: 1 vegetable, 1 starch, 2 lean meat. Carb choices: 1.

Chicken-Squash Noodle Soup

Ceramic mugs make great serving bowls for this colorful take on all-time-favorite chicken and noodle soup. Pictured on page 62.

SERVINGS 6 (1½ cups each)
CARB. PER SERVING 20 g

- 1 pound skinless, boneless chicken breast halves, cut into 1-inch pieces
- ½ teaspoon poultry seasoning
- 1 tablespoon canola oil
- ½ cup chopped onion (1 medium)
- ½ cup chopped celery (1 stalk)
- ½ cup chopped carrot (1 medium)
- 2 cloves garlic, minced
- 3 14-ounce cans reduced-sodium chicken broth
- 1½ cups dried medium noodles
- 1 medium zucchini or yellow summer squash, quartered lengthwise and cut into 1-inch-thick pieces
- 1¾ cups fat-free milk
- ¼ cup all-purpose flour
- ¼ cup snipped fresh parsley

1. In a large bowl, combine chicken pieces and poultry seasoning; toss to coat. In a Dutch oven, heat oil over medium heat. Add chicken pieces; cook for 3 to 5 minutes or until chicken pieces are browned, stirring to brown all sides. Using a slotted spoon, transfer chicken to bowl and set aside.
2. In the same Dutch oven, cook onion, celery, carrot, and garlic over medium heat about 5 minutes or just until tender, stirring occasionally. Add chicken broth; bring to boiling. Add chicken, noodles, and zucchini. Return to boiling; reduce heat. Simmer, covered, for 5 minutes.
3. In a medium bowl, whisk milk and flour together until combined; stir into chicken mixture. Cook and stir until bubbly. Cook and stir for 1 minute more.
4. Sprinkle with parsley just before serving.

PER SERVING: 215 cal., 4 g total fat (1 g sat. fat), 53 mg chol., 560 mg sodium, 20 g carb., 2 g fiber, 25 g pro. Exchanges: 0.5 vegetable, 1 starch, 3 lean meat. Carb choices: 1.

Moroccan-Spiced Chicken Lentil Stew

A blend of garlic, cumin, coriander, black pepper, and cinnamon perfectly seasons this hearty stew.

SERVINGS 8 (1⅓ cups each)
CARB. PER SERVING 26 g

- 2 pounds skinless, boneless chicken thighs, trimmed of fat and cut into 2- to 3-inch chunks
- 2 cloves garlic, minced
- ½ teaspoon ground cumin
- ½ teaspoon ground coriander
- ¼ teaspoon black pepper
- ¼ teaspoon ground cinnamon
- Nonstick cooking spray
- 1¼ cups dry brown lentils, rinsed and drained
- 1 medium onion, cut into thin wedges
- 2 14-ounce cans reduced-sodium chicken broth

Moroccan-Spiced
Chicken Lentil Stew

1 cup water
1 large yellow summer squash, quartered lengthwise and cut into 1-inch-thick pieces
½ cup snipped dried apricots or golden raisins
2 tablespoons sliced green onion (optional)

1. In a large bowl, combine chicken, garlic, cumin, coriander, pepper, and cinnamon; toss to coat. Coat an unheated very large nonstick skillet with cooking spray. Preheat over medium heat. Add chicken to hot skillet; cook until browned, turning to brown all sides.

2. Transfer chicken to a 4- to 5-quart slow cooker. Add lentils and onion to cooker. Pour broth and the water over all in cooker.

3. Cover and cook on low-heat setting for 7 to 8 hours or on high-heat setting for 3½ to 4 hours. If using low-heat setting, turn to high-heat setting. Add squash and apricots to cooker. Cover and cook for 15 minutes more or just until squash is tender.

4. If desired, sprinkle each serving with sliced green onion.

PER SERVING: 274 cal., 5 g total fat (1 g sat. fat), 94 mg chol., 318 mg sodium, 26 g carb., 10 g fiber, 32 g pro. Exchanges: 0.5 fruit, 1 starch, 4 lean meat. Carb choices: 2.

Thai Chicken Soup

Thai Chicken Soup

Depending on the brand, Thai seasoning's ingredients may vary. Look for it along with other spice blends in your supermarket.

SERVINGS 5 (1⅓ cups each)
CARB. PER SERVING 10 g

- ½ cup chopped onion (1 medium)
- 1 tablespoon grated fresh ginger
- 3 cloves garlic, minced
- 2 14-ounce cans reduced-sodium chicken broth
- 1 14-ounce can light unsweetened coconut milk
- 1 tablespoon lime juice
- 2 teaspoons Thai seasoning
- 2 medium carrots, thinly bias-sliced
- ½ of a fresh jalapeño chile pepper, julienned or finely chopped (see tip, page 63)
- 1½ cups shredded cooked chicken breast or turkey breast
- 1 cup fresh shiitake, straw, and/or button mushrooms, sliced
- ⅔ cup fresh snow peas, trimmed and halved diagonally
- 1 tablespoon chopped fresh basil

1. Lightly coat a Dutch oven with *nonstick cooking spray.* Heat over medium heat. Add onion, ginger, and garlic to Dutch oven. Cook and stir for 2 to 3 minutes or until tender. Stir in broth, coconut milk, lime juice, and Thai seasoning. Bring to boiling; reduce heat. Add carrots and jalapeño. Simmer, covered, for 5 minutes. Add chicken, mushrooms, snow peas, and basil. Cook about 3 minutes more or until heated through.
PER SERVING: 159 cal., 6 g total fat (3 g sat. fat), 36 mg chol., 566 mg sodium, 10 g carb., 2 g fiber, 16 g pro. Exchanges: 0.5 vegetable, 0.5 carb., 2 lean meat, 0.5 fat. Carb choices: 0.5.

Curried Chicken-Noodle Soup

Sweet potatoes vary in size. You'll need about 1½ cups chopped for this colorful soup.

SERVINGS 6 (1⅓ cups each)
CARB. PER SERVING 25 g

- 2 14-ounce cans reduced-sodium chicken broth
- 1 to 3 teaspoons green or red Thai curry paste
- 10 ounces skinless, boneless chicken breast halves
- 1 5-ounce package dried Japanese curly wheat-flour noodles or angel hair pasta, broken
- 1 medium sweet potato, peeled and chopped
- 1 medium tomato, chopped
- 1 cup light unsweetened coconut milk
- ½ cup lightly packed fresh cilantro leaves

1. In a Dutch oven, combine broth, 1¾ cups *water,* and the curry paste. Cover and bring to boiling.
2. Meanwhile, slice chicken crosswise into ¼-inch strips; sprinkle lightly with *salt* and set aside. Add noodles, sweet potato, and tomato to broth mixture. Return to boiling; reduce heat. Simmer, covered, for 4 minutes, stirring once to break up noodles. Add chicken; simmer for 2 to 3 minutes more or until chicken is tender and no longer pink. Stir in coconut milk. Remove soup from heat and sprinkle with cilantro.
PER SERVING: 197 cal., 3 g total fat (2 g sat. fat), 27 mg chol., 409 mg sodium, 25 g carb., 2 g fiber, 16 g pro. Exchanges: 1.5 starch, 1.5 lean meat. Carb choices: 1.5.

Chicken Fajita Chili

Let your slow cooker rescue you on a busy day.

SERVINGS 6 (1½ cups each)
CARB. PER SERVING 22 g

- 2 pounds skinless, boneless chicken breast halves, cut into 1-inch pieces
- 1 tablespoon chili powder
- 1 teaspoon fajita seasoning
- ½ teaspoon ground cumin
- 2 cloves garlic, minced
- 2 14.5-ounce cans no-salt-added diced tomatoes, undrained
- 1 16-ounce package frozen pepper (yellow, green, and red) and onion stir-fry vegetables
- 1 15-ounce can cannellini beans (white kidney beans), rinsed and drained
- 3 tablespoons shredded reduced-fat cheddar cheese

1. In a bowl, combine chicken, chili powder, fajita seasoning, cumin, and garlic; toss to coat. Coat an unheated large skillet with *nonstick cooking spray.* Preheat skillet over medium-high heat. Cook chicken, half at a time, until browned, stirring occasionally.
2. Place chicken in a 3½- or 4-quart slow cooker. Add tomatoes, frozen vegetables, and beans. Cover and cook on low-heat setting for 4 to 5 hours or on high-heat setting for 2 to 2½ hours.
3. Top each serving with shredded cheese.
PER SERVING: 271 cal., 3 g total fat (1 g sat. fat), 90 mg chol., 320 mg sodium, 22 g carb., 7 g fiber, 42 g pro. Exchanges: 1.5 vegetable, 1 starch, 5 lean meat. Carb choices: 1.5.

Mexican Chicken Soup

Full of fresh vegetable flavor, this hearty soup is worthy of the made-from-scratch broth.

SERVINGS 6 (1½ cups each)
CARB. PER SERVING 14 g

2 to 2½ pounds chicken breast halves, skin removed
6 cups water
2 cups coarsely chopped onions (2 large)
2 cups coarsely chopped celery (4 stalks)
1 cup coarsely chopped tomato (1 large)
½ cup snipped fresh cilantro
1 teaspoon salt
1 teaspoon ground cumin
¼ to ½ teaspoon cayenne pepper
¼ to ½ teaspoon black pepper
1½ cups chopped carrots (3 medium)
1 or 2 fresh poblano chile peppers
1 medium avocado, peeled, seeded, and sliced
3 tablespoons fresh cilantro sprigs

1. In a Dutch oven, combine chicken breast halves, the water, 1 cup of the onions, 1 cup of the celery, the tomato, the snipped cilantro, salt, cumin, cayenne pepper, and black pepper. Bring to boiling; reduce heat. Simmer, covered, for 40 to 50 minutes or until chicken is tender. Remove chicken pieces and set aside to cool slightly. Strain the broth mixture, reserving broth and discarding the vegetables.

2. Return the broth to the Dutch oven. Add the remaining 1 cup onion, the remaining 1 cup celery, and the carrots. Bring to boiling; reduce heat. Simmer, covered, about 20 minutes or until vegetables are tender.

3. Meanwhile, preheat oven to 425°F. Line a baking sheet with foil; set aside. Cut chile peppers in half lengthwise and remove seeds, stems, and veins.* Place pepper halves, cut sides down, on prepared baking sheet. Bake for 20 to 25 minutes or until skins are blistered and dark. Wrap peppers in the foil; let stand about 15 minutes or until cool enough to handle. Using a sharp knife, loosen the edges of the skins from the pepper halves; gently and slowly pull off the skins in strips. Discard skins. Chop peppers.

4. Remove chicken from bones; discard bones. Chop the chicken. Stir chicken and poblano peppers into broth mixture. Heat through.

5. Add avocado slices and cilantro sprigs to each serving.

*TEST KITCHEN TIP: Because chile peppers contain volatile oils that can burn your skin and eyes, avoid direct contact with chiles as much as possible. When working with chile peppers, wear plastic or rubber gloves. If your bare hands do touch the chile peppers, wash your hands and nails well with soap and warm water.

PER SERVING: 203 cal., 5 g total fat (1 g sat. fat), 57 mg chol., 518 mg sodium, 14 g carb., 5 g fiber, 25 g pro. Exchanges: 1 vegetable, 0.5 starch, 3 lean meat. Carb choices: 1.

Turkey and Rice Soup

Round out this tasty bowl with a salad of fresh spinach, apple, and a drizzle of poppy seed dressing.

SERVINGS 6 (1½ cups each)
CARB. PER SERVING 16 g

2 14-ounce cans reduced-sodium chicken broth
1½ cups water
1 teaspoon snipped fresh rosemary or ¼ teaspoon dried rosemary, crushed
¼ teaspoon black pepper
½ cup thinly sliced carrot (1 medium)
½ cup thinly sliced celery (1 stalk)
⅓ cup thinly sliced onion (1 small)
1 cup instant brown rice
1 cup frozen cut green beans
2 cups chopped cooked turkey breast or chicken breast
1 14.5-ounce can no-added-salt diced tomatoes, undrained
Fresh rosemary sprigs (optional)

1. In a large saucepan or Dutch oven, combine broth, the water, snipped or dried rosemary, and pepper. Add carrot, celery, and onion. Bring to boiling.

2. Stir in uncooked rice and frozen green beans. Return to boiling; reduce heat. Simmer, covered, for 10 to 12 minutes or until vegetables are tender.

3. Stir in turkey and tomatoes; heat through. If desired, garnish each serving with rosemary sprigs.

PER SERVING: 143 cal., 1 g total fat (0 g sat. fat), 39 mg chol., 384 mg sodium, 16 g carb., 3 g fiber, 18 g pro. Exchanges: 1 vegetable, 0.5 starch, 2 lean meat. Carb choices: 1.

Mexican
Chicken Soup

▶ QUICK TIP

Firm-ripe avocados are best for slicing. Select one that yields to gentle pressure when you lightly squeeze it.

QUICK TIP ◖

When purchasing a wine to use for cooking, select a bottle that is reasonably priced and has the same flavor qualities that you enjoy for drinking.

Fish and Vegetable Soup

Chop the potatoes into equal-size pieces so they cook evenly.

SERVINGS 4 (2 cups each)

CARB. PER SERVING 23 g

- 12 ounces fresh or frozen cod, haddock, or pike fillets
- 8 ounces round red potatoes, chopped
- 2 medium carrots, sliced (1 cup)
- 1 small bulb fennel, chopped
- 1 medium shallot, sliced
- 2 cloves garlic, minced
- 2 teaspoons olive oil
- 2 14-ounce cans reduced-sodium chicken broth
- 1 14.5-ounce can no-salt-added diced tomatoes, undrained
- ½ cup dry white wine or water
- ½ teaspoon snipped fresh thyme or ¼ teaspoon dried thyme, crushed
- ¼ teaspoon crushed red pepper

1. Thaw fish, if frozen. Rinse fish; pat dry with paper towels. Cut fish into bite-size pieces; set aside.

2. In a Dutch oven, cook potatoes, carrots, fennel, shallot, and garlic in hot oil over medium-high heat for 6 to 8 minutes or until just tender, stirring occasionally. Add broth, tomatoes, wine, thyme, and crushed red pepper. Bring to boiling; reduce heat. Simmer, covered, for 20 minutes. Stir in fish. Simmer, uncovered, about 3 minutes more or until fish flakes when tested with a fork.

PER SERVING: 217 cal., 3 g total fat (0 g sat. fat), 37 mg chol., 605 mg sodium, 23 g carb., 5 g fiber, 21 g pro. Exchanges: 1.5 vegetable, 1 starch, 2 lean meat. Carb choices: 1.5.

Caribbean Fish Stew

Ginger, jerk seasoning, lime, and garlic turn simple white fish into a tropical delight.

SERVINGS 6 (1⅔ cups each)
CARB. PER SERVING 33 g

- 2 pounds sweet potatoes, peeled and coarsely chopped
- 1¼ cups chopped red sweet pepper (1 large)
- ½ cup chopped onion (1 medium)
- 1 tablespoon grated fresh ginger
- ½ teaspoon finely shredded lime peel
- 1 tablespoon lime juice
- 1 teaspoon Jamaican jerk seasoning
- 2 cloves garlic, minced
- 2 14-ounce cans reduced-sodium chicken broth
- 1 14.5-ounce can no-salt-added diced tomatoes, undrained
- 1 pound fresh or frozen firm white fish
- 2 tablespoons snipped fresh cilantro

1. In a 4- to 5-quart slow cooker, combine sweet potatoes, sweet pepper, onion, ginger, lime peel, lime juice, jerk seasoning, and garlic. Pour broth and tomatoes over vegetables.
2. Cover and cook on low-heat setting for 6 to 8 hours or on high-heat setting for 3 to 4 hours.
3. Thaw fish, if frozen. Rinse fish; pat dry with paper towels. Cut fish into 1-inch pieces. If using low-heat setting, turn to high-heat setting. Stir in fish. Cover and cook about 15 minutes more or until fish flakes easily when tested with a fork.
4. Sprinkle each serving with cilantro.
PER SERVING: 231 cal., 2 g total fat (0 g sat. fat), 24 mg chol., 522 mg sodium, 33 g carb., 6 g fiber, 21 g pro. Exchanges: 1 vegetable, 2 starch, 2 lean meat. Carb choices: 2.

Seafood-Corn Chowder

The addition of halibut, scallops, and clams turns ordinary corn chowder into an extraordinary meal-in-a-bowl.

SERVINGS 6 (1⅓ cups each)
CARB. PER SERVING 15 g

- 8 ounces fresh or frozen skinless halibut fillets
- 4 fresh or frozen sea scallops (about 8 ounces total)
- 1 tablespoon canola oil
- ½ cup chopped onion (1 medium)
- ¾ cup chopped green sweet pepper (1 medium)
- 2 cloves garlic, minced
- 4 medium tomatoes, cored and coarsely chopped
- 2 cups lower-sodium vegetable broth
- 1 cup water
- 1 cup fresh or frozen whole kernel corn
- 1 teaspoon ground cumin
- ¼ teaspoon black pepper
- 1 10-ounce can or two 3.53-ounce packages whole baby clams, drained
- ¼ cup snipped fresh cilantro

1. Thaw halibut and scallops, if frozen. Rinse seafood; pat dry with paper towels. Cut halibut into 1-inch pieces and cut large scallops into halves or quarters; set aside.
2. In a large saucepan, heat oil over medium heat. Add onion, sweet pepper, and garlic; cook about 5 minutes or until tender, stirring occasionally. Stir in tomatoes, broth, the water, corn, cumin, and black pepper. Bring to boiling; reduce heat. Cover and simmer for 10 minutes.
3. Add halibut and scallops to tomato mixture. Return to boiling; reduce heat. Simmer, uncovered, for 2 to 3 minutes more or until halibut flakes easily when tested with a fork and scallops are opaque.
4. Stir in clams and cilantro just before serving. If desired, sprinkle with *cracked black pepper*.
PER SERVING: 205 cal., 5 g total fat (0 g sat. fat), 50 mg chol., 319 mg sodium, 15 g carb., 2 g fiber, 26 g pro. Exchanges: 1 vegetable, 0.5 starch, 3 lean meat. Carb choices: 1.

Seafood-Corn Chowder

Asian Shrimp and
Vegetable Soup

and mushrooms; cook for 5 minutes, stirring occasionally. Add ginger and garlic; cook and stir for 1 minute more.

3. Add chicken broth, the water, soybeans, soy sauce, and, if desired, crushed red pepper to mushroom mixture. Bring to boiling; reduce heat. Simmer, covered, about 5 minutes or just until carrots are tender.

4. Add shrimp and pea pods and/or bok choy. Return to boiling; reduce heat. Simmer, uncovered, for 2 to 3 minutes or until shrimp are opaque. Stir in green onion tops just before serving. If desired, garnish with slivered green onion.

PER SERVING: 136 cal., 4 g total fat (0 g sat. fat), 65 mg chol., 489 mg sodium, 10 g carb., 3 g fiber, 16 g pro. Exchanges: 1 vegetable, 2 lean meat, 0.5 fat. Carb choices: 0.5.

Asian Shrimp and Vegetable Soup

To give this full-of-flavor soup a hint of heat, add the crushed red pepper.

SERVINGS 6 (1⅓ cups each)
CARB. PER SERVING 10 g

12 ounces fresh or frozen large shrimp in shells
4 green onions
2 teaspoons canola oil
1 cup thinly sliced carrots (2 medium)
8 ounces fresh shiitake or oyster mushrooms, stemmed and coarsely chopped
1 tablespoon grated fresh ginger or 1 teaspoon ground ginger
2 cloves garlic, minced
2 14-ounce cans reduced-sodium chicken broth
2 cups water
1 cup frozen shelled sweet soybeans (edamame)
1 tablespoon reduced-sodium soy sauce
¼ teaspoon crushed red pepper (optional)
1 cup trimmed sugar snap peas and/or coarsely shredded bok choy
2 tablespoons slivered green onion (optional)

1. Thaw shrimp, if frozen. Peel and devein shrimp. Rinse shrimp; pat dry with paper towels. Set aside. Diagonally slice the whole green onions into 1-inch-long pieces, keeping white parts separate from green tops. Set green tops aside.

2. In a large nonstick saucepan, heat oil over medium heat. Add white parts of the green onions, the carrots,

Shrimp Gazpacho

The color of this chilly favorite varies depending on the ripeness and the variety of the tomatoes.

SERVINGS 4 (1½ cups each)
CARB. PER SERVING 17 g

2½ pounds Brandywine heirloom tomatoes or desired tomatoes, chopped
1½ cups seeded and chopped cucumber (1 medium)
¾ cup chopped green or red sweet pepper (1 medium)
¾ cup low-sodium vegetable juice or tomato juice
½ cup clam juice
¼ cup chopped onion
3 tablespoons red wine vinegar or dry sherry
2 tablespoons snipped fresh cilantro
2 tablespoons olive oil
1 clove garlic, minced
¼ teaspoon ground cumin
1 8-ounce package frozen peeled, cooked shrimp, thawed
Lemon juice (optional)
Fresh cilantro leaves

1. In a large bowl, combine tomatoes, cucumber, sweet pepper, vegetable juice, clam juice, onion, vinegar, snipped cilantro, oil, garlic, and cumin. Cover and chill for 4 to 24 hours. Stir in shrimp before serving.

2. If desired, add lemon juice to taste. Garnish with cilantro leaves.

PER SERVING: 192 cal., 8 g total fat (1 g sat. fat), 111 mg chol., 372 mg sodium, 17 g carb., 5 g fiber, 17 g pro. Exchanges: 1.5 vegetable, 0.5 starch, 1.5 lean meat, 1 fat. Carb choices: 1.

Three-Bean Chili

Chocolate adds depth and richness to spicy chili for a flavor that's satisfying and unexpected.

SERVINGS 6 (1 cup each)
CARB. PER SERVING 44 g

- 1 15-ounce can no-salt-added red kidney beans, rinsed and drained
- 1 15-ounce can small white beans, rinsed and drained
- 1 15-ounce can no-salt-added black beans, rinsed and drained
- 1 14.5-ounce can diced tomatoes and green chiles, undrained
- 1 cup beer or reduced-sodium chicken broth
- 3 tablespoons chocolate-flavor syrup
- 1 tablespoon chili powder
- 2 teaspoons Cajun seasoning
- 3 tablespoons light sour cream
- 1½ tablespoons shredded reduced-fat cheddar cheese

1. In a 3½- or 4-quart slow cooker, combine kidney beans, white beans, black beans, undrained tomatoes, beer or broth, chocolate syrup, chili powder, and Cajun seasoning.

2. Cover and cook on low-heat setting for 6 to 8 hours or on high-heat setting for 3 to 4 hours. Top each serving with sour cream and cheddar cheese.

PER SERVING: 242 cal., 2 g total fat (1 g sat. fat), 4 mg chol., 576 mg sodium, 44 g carb., 14 g fiber, 15 g pro. Exchanges: 0.5 vegetable, 3 starch, 0.5 lean meat. Carb choices: 3.

Roasted Cauliflower Soup

Green onion is an accessible stand-in for the chives.

SERVINGS 4 (1½ cups each)
CARB. PER SERVING 20 g

- 1 large head cauliflower, cut into florets
- 1 small sweet onion, cut into wedges
- 4 cloves garlic, peeled
- Nonstick cooking spray
- 1 14-ounce can vegetable broth
- 1 cup low-fat milk
- ½ teaspoon ground coriander
- 2 tablespoons chopped fresh chives

1. Preheat oven to 400°F. In a 15×10×1-inch baking pan, spread cauliflower, onion, and garlic. Lightly coat with cooking spray; toss. Roast, uncovered, for 30 minutes or until tender and lightly browned, stirring once.

2. Transfer vegetables to a Dutch oven. Add broth, 1¾ cups *water,* the milk, coriander, ¼ teaspoon *black pepper,* and ⅛ teaspoon *salt.* Bring to boiling; reduce heat. Simmer, covered, for 15 to 20 minutes or until cauliflower is very tender. Cool slightly.

3. Transfer mixture, in batches, to a blender or food processor. Cover and blend until smooth. Return to Dutch oven. Heat through. Sprinkle with chives.

PER SERVING: 103 cal., 1 g total fat (0 g sat. fat), 3 mg chol., 554 mg sodium, 20 g carb., 5 g fiber, 7 g pro. Exchanges: 0.5 milk, 2 vegetable. Carb choices: 1.

Three-Bean Chili

Roasted Root Vegetable Soup

In the fall, when vitamin-rich root vegetables are in abundance, stir together a batch of this creamy soup.

SERVINGS 4 (1¼ cups each)
CARB. PER SERVING 31 g

- 2 medium carrots, peeled and cut into 1-inch-thick pieces
- 1 medium sweet potato, peeled and cut into 1-inch cubes
- 1 medium parsnip, peeled and cut into 1-inch-thick pieces
- ½ of a medium red onion, cut into thin wedges
- 3 cloves garlic, thinly sliced
- 1 tablespoon olive oil
- 1 teaspoon dried thyme, crushed
- ⅛ teaspoon black pepper
- 3 cups fat-free milk
- 1 cup reduced-sodium chicken broth
- ¼ cup all-purpose flour

1. Preheat oven to 425°F. In a 13×9×2-inch baking pan, combine carrots, sweet potato, parsnip, red onion, and garlic. Drizzle with oil; sprinkle with ½ teaspoon of the thyme and the pepper. Toss to coat. Cover with foil.

2. Bake for 20 minutes. Remove foil; stir vegetables. Bake, uncovered, for 15 to 20 minutes more or until vegetables are tender.

3. Meanwhile, in a large saucepan, whisk together milk, broth, flour, and the remaining ½ teaspoon thyme until smooth. Cook and stir over medium heat until thickened and bubbly. Add roasted vegetables. Cook and stir about 1 minute more or until heated through.

PER SERVING: 191 cal., 4 g total fat (1 g sat. fat), 4 mg chol., 359 mg sodium, 31 g carb., 3 g fiber, 9 g pro. Exchanges: 2 starch, 0.5 fat. Carb choices: 2.

Tomato-Basil Soup

This naturally sweet soup begs to be part of your meal plan as a salad, snack, or dessert.

Tomato-Basil Soup

Serve this fresh-tasting soup as a first course for a dinner party or a side dish at a luncheon.

SERVINGS 4 (1 cup soup and ¼ cup croutons each)

CARB. PER SERVING 23 g

- ½ cup chopped onion (1 medium)
- 2 cloves garlic, minced
- 2 teaspoons olive oil
- 2 14.5-ounce cans no-salt-added diced tomatoes
- 1½ cups ⅓-less-sodium vegetable broth or reduced-sodium chicken broth
- ¾ cup bottled roasted red sweet peppers, drained and chopped
- 2 tablespoons snipped fresh basil or 2 teaspoons dried basil, crushed
- 2 teaspoons balsamic vinegar
- 1 recipe Toasted Cheese Croutons (below)

1. In medium nonstick saucepan, cook onion and garlic in hot oil about 5 minutes or until tender, stirring occasionally. Add undrained tomatoes, broth, roasted peppers, and dried basil (if using). Bring to boiling; reduce heat. Simmer, covered, for 10 minutes to blend flavors. Cool slightly.

2. Transfer half of the tomato mixture to a blender or food processor. Cover and blend or process until smooth; add to remaining tomato mixture in saucepan. Heat through. Stir in fresh basil (if using) and vinegar just before serving. Top each serving with a few Toasted Cheese Croutons.

TOASTED CHEESE CROUTONS: Preheat broiler. Place four ¾-inch-thick slices whole grain baguette-style bread on a baking sheet. Broil 4 to 5 inches from the heat for 1 to 2 minutes or until lightly toasted. Turn bread slices over; sprinkle tops with ¼ cup shredded reduced-fat Italian cheese blend. Broil about 1 minute more or until cheese melts. Cool bread slices slightly. Cut into bite-size pieces.

PER SERVING: 146 cal., 4 g total fat (1 g sat. fat), 4 mg chol., 406 mg sodium, 23 g carb., 5 g fiber, 5 g pro. Exchanges: 1 vegetable, 1 starch, 0.5 fat. Carb choices: 1.5.

Watermelon Soup with Fresh Mint

Watermelon Soup with Fresh Mint

As if you need a reason to relish watermelon, it nourishes your body with vitamins C and A and is also a good source of the antioxidant lycopene.

SERVINGS 4 (¾ cup each)

CARB. PER SERVING 18 g

- 4 cups cut-up seedless watermelon
- 2 tablespoons lemon juice
- 2 tablespoons lime juice
- 2 tablespoons snipped fresh mint
- 1 tablespoon honey
- ¼ teaspoon ground ginger
- ¼ cup plain fat-free Greek yogurt or plain yogurt

1. In a blender or food processor, combine watermelon, lemon juice, lime juice, 1 tablespoon of the mint, the honey, and ginger. Cover and blend or process until nearly smooth. Cover and chill for 2 to 4 hours.

2. Top each serving with a spoonful of yogurt; sprinkle with remaining mint.

PER SERVING: 75 cal., 0 g total fat, 0 mg chol., 8 mg sodium, 18 g carb., 1 g fiber, 2 g pro. Exchanges: 1 fruit. Carb choices: 1.

sensational sandwiches

From toasty bread with melty cheese and meat concoctions to layers of veggies and meat combos stuffed between bread or inside a wrap, sandwiches are great family-friendly fare. Quick to make and fun to eat, they are an easy way to cram lots of healthful goodness into one easy bundle.

Mediterranean Chicken Panini

Another time, use the subtly seasoned Dried Tomato-Pepper Spread to spiff up a cold turkey sandwich.

SERVINGS 4 (1 sandwich each)
CARB. PER SERVING 35 g

Olive oil nonstick cooking spray
1 recipe Dried Tomato-Pepper Spread (below)
2 small skinless, boneless chicken breast halves
4 miniature squares whole wheat bagel bread
1 small zucchini

1. Lightly coat an unheated panini sandwich maker, covered indoor electric grill, or large nonstick skillet with cooking spray. Preheat according to manufacturer's directions or over medium heat. Add chicken. If using panini maker or grill, close lid and grill for 6 to 7 minutes or until chicken is no longer pink (170°F). (If using skillet, cook chicken for 10 to 12 minutes or until chicken is no longer pink, turning once.) Cool chicken slightly; split each chicken piece in half horizontally and cut crosswise into 2-inch-wide slices.
2. Spread the Dried Tomato-Pepper Spread on cut sides of bagel bread squares. Place chicken on bottoms of the bread squares. Using a vegetable peeler, cut very thin lengthwise strips from the zucchini. Place zucchini strips on top of the chicken. Place bagel square tops on top of the zucchini, spread sides down. Press down lightly. Lightly coat the top and bottom of each sandwich with cooking spray.
3. Place sandwiches on panini maker or grill or in skillet, adding in batches if necessary. If using panini maker or grill, close lid and grill for 2 to 3 minutes or until bread is toasted. (If using skillet, place a heavy skillet on top of sandwiches. Cook for 1 to 2 minutes or until bottoms are toasted. Using hotpads, carefully remove top skillet. Turn sandwiches and top again with skillet. Cook for 1 to 2 minutes more or until bread is toasted.)
DRIED TOMATO-PEPPER SPREAD: In a small bowl, combine ¼ cup dried tomatoes (not oil pack) and 2 tablespoons boiling water. Cover and let stand for 5 minutes. Transfer undrained tomato mixture to a food processor. Add ¼ cup drained bottled roasted red sweet peppers; 1 tablespoon balsamic vinegar; ½ teaspoon snipped fresh oregano or ¼ teaspoon dried oregano, crushed; 1 clove garlic, minced; and dash black pepper. Cover and process until smooth.
PER SERVING: 238 cal., 2 g total fat (0 g sat. fat), 33 mg chol., 354 mg sodium, 35 g carb., 5 g fiber, 21 g pro. Exchanges: 1 vegetable, 2 starch, 1.5 lean meat. Carb choices: 2.

Chicken-Spinach Focaccia Sandwiches

A Microplane or cheese grater makes quick work of shredding the hard-cooked eggs.

SERVINGS 6 (1 wedge each)
CARB. PER SERVING 21 g

- 1 8- to 9-inch Italian flatbread (focaccia)
- ¼ cup light mayonnaise
- ¼ cup chopped bottled roasted red sweet peppers
- 1 teaspoon capers, drained (optional)
- 2 cups fresh baby spinach and/or arugula
- 2 cups shredded cooked chicken breast (10 ounces)
- 1 medium tomato, quartered and thinly sliced
- ¼ cup thinly sliced red onion, cooked if desired*
- 2 hard-cooked eggs, shredded

1. Halve focaccia horizontally. Wrap and save the top half for another use. Set the bottom half aside. In a small bowl, combine mayonnaise, roasted red peppers, and, if using, capers. Spread mayonnaise mixture over the cut side of the focaccia half.
2. Arrange spinach on top of the mayonnaise mixture. Top with chicken, tomato, red onion, and eggs. Cut into wedges.

*TEST KITCHEN TIP: To cook onion, coat an unheated medium skillet with nonstick cooking spray. Preheat skillet over medium heat. Add red onion. Cook for 5 to 10 minutes or until onion is tender and lightly browned.

CHICKEN-SPINACH CIABATTA SANDWICHES: Substitute 6 multigrain ciabatta rolls, split, for the focaccia. Spread mayonnaise mixture on cut sides of rolls. Fill rolls with spinach, chicken, tomato, red onion, and eggs.

PER SERVING: 241 cal., 8 g total fat (2 g sat. fat), 114 mg chol., 132 mg sodium, 21 g carb., 2 g fiber, 21 g pro. Exchanges: 0.5 vegetable, 1 starch, 2.5 lean meat, 1 fat. Carb choices: 1.5.

Chicken-Spinach
Focaccia Sandwiches

Grilled Chicken, Spinach, and Pear Pitas

Warm pita bread is a delicious way to corral a sophisticated combination of spinach, pear, chicken, and a goat cheese sauce.

SERVINGS 6 (1 pita half each)
CARB. PER SERVING 24 g

- 12 ounces skinless, boneless chicken breast halves
- 1 tablespoon balsamic vinegar
- 3 whole wheat pita bread rounds, halved crosswise
- ¼ cup light mayonnaise
- 1 ounce soft goat cheese (chèvre)
- 1 tablespoon fat-free milk
- 1 teaspoon balsamic vinegar
- 1 green onion, thinly sliced
- 1½ cups fresh spinach leaves
- 1 small pear or apple, cored and thinly sliced

1. Brush chicken on both sides with some of the 1 tablespoon balsamic vinegar; set aside. For a charcoal grill, place chicken on the grill rack directly over medium coals. Grill, uncovered, for 12 to 15 minutes or until chicken is no longer pink (170°F), turning once and brushing with the remainder of the 1 tablespoon vinegar halfway through grilling. (For a gas grill, preheat grill. Reduce heat to medium. Place chicken on the grill rack over heat. Cover and grill as above.) Cut each chicken breast half into ½-inch-thick slices.
2. Meanwhile, wrap pita bread rounds in foil. Place on the grill rack directly over medium coals. Grill about 8 minutes or until bread is warm, turning once halfway through grilling.
3. For sauce: In a small bowl, use a fork to stir together mayonnaise, goat cheese, milk, and the 1 teaspoon vinegar. Stir in green onion.
4. To assemble, arrange spinach, pear slices, and chicken in pita bread halves. Spoon about 1 tablespoon sauce into each pita.

BROILING DIRECTIONS: Preheat broiler. Brush chicken with vinegar as directed. Place chicken breast halves on the ungreased rack of a broiler pan. Broil chicken 4 to 5 inches from the heat for 12 to 15 minutes or until chicken is no longer pink (170°F), turning once and brushing with the remainder of the 1 tablespoon balsamic vinegar halfway through broiling. Heat pitas according to package directions. Continue as directed in Step 3.

PER SERVING: 216 cal., 6 g total fat (2 g sat. fat), 39 mg chol., 293 mg sodium, 24 g carb., 3 g fiber, 18 g pro. Exchanges: 1.5 starch, 2 lean meat. Carb choices: 1.5.

Grilled Chicken, Spinach, and Pear Pitas

Moo Shu
Chicken Wraps

Tropical Chicken
Salad Wraps

Chicken, Kraut,
and Apple Panini

Round It Out

With a simple side, a sandwich can be a complete meal. There's no cooking required with these easy, nutritious ideas.

1. **Add a handful** of celery sticks.

2. **Slice a few** crunchy radishes.

3. **Seed and cut up** a small sweet pepper.

4. **Cut a small** tomato into wedges.

5. **Try a little guacamole** and a couple of baked tortilla chips.

6. **Go for some** raw cauliflower or broccoli florets.

7. **Drizzle a little** low-carb salad dressing over some mixed greens.

8. **Dip a few** cucumber slices into plain yogurt.

9. **Nibble on** a few fresh button mushrooms.

10. **Grab a couple** of small strawberries.

Tropical Chicken Salad Wraps

Rolled in lettuce, this fruited chicken mixture is a sandwich. Served on a bed of greens, it's a main-dish salad.

SERVINGS 4 (2 wraps each)
CARB. PER SERVING 14 g

    2 cups shredded cooked chicken breast
    2 cups finely shredded napa cabbage
    1 8-ounce can crushed pineapple, drained
    ⅓ cup light mayonnaise
    2 tablespoons flaked coconut, toasted
    1 tablespoon lime juice
    1 tablespoon snipped fresh cilantro
    1 teaspoon Jamaican jerk seasoning
    8 leaves Bibb or Boston lettuce
    Lime wedges (optional)

1. In a large bowl, combine chicken, cabbage, drained pineapple, mayonnaise, coconut, lime juice, cilantro, and Jamaican jerk seasoning.

2. Divide chicken mixture among lettuce leaves. Fold in sides and roll up. Secure with toothpicks if needed. If desired, serve with lime wedges.

PER SERVING: 243 cal., 10 g total fat (3 g sat. fat), 66 mg chol., 301 mg sodium, 14 g carb., 1 g fiber, 23 g pro. Exchanges: 1 vegetable, 0.5 fruit, 3 lean meat, 1 fat. Carb choices: 1.

Chicken, Kraut, and Apple Panini

If you buy a can of sauerkraut, you will have some left. Serve it another time with grilled pork chops.

SERVINGS 4 (1 sandwich each)
CARB. PER SERVING 21 g

    1 cup canned sauerkraut
    8 slices very thin sliced firm-texture whole wheat bread
    Nonstick cooking spray
    12 ounces sliced, cooked chicken breast
    1 apple, cored and thinly sliced
    4 thin slices reduced-fat Swiss cheese (2 ounces total)

1. Place sauerkraut in a colander and rinse with cold water. Drain well, using a spoon to press out excess liquid. Set aside.

2. Lightly coat one side of each bread slice with cooking spray. Place four bread slices, coated sides down, on a work surface. Top with chicken, sauerkraut, apple slices, and cheese. Top with remaining four bread slices, coated sides up.

3. Coat an unheated grill pan or large skillet with cooking spray. Preheat over medium-low heat for 1 to 2 minutes. Add sandwiches, in batches if necessary. Place a heavy skillet on top of sandwiches. Cook over medium-low heat for 6 to 8 minutes or until bottoms are toasted. Using hot pads, carefully remove top skillet. Turn sandwiches and top again with skillet. Cook for 6 to 8 minutes more or until bottoms are toasted.

PER SERVING: 283 cal., 7 g total fat (3 g sat. fat), 79 mg chol., 457 mg sodium, 21 g carb., 4 g fiber, 34 g pro. Exchanges: 1.5 starch, 4 lean meat. Carb choices: 1.5.

Moo Shu Chicken Wraps

This tasty take on an Asian classic uses chicken rather than the traditional pork.

SERVINGS 4 (1 wrap each)
CARB. PER SERVING 25 g

    12 ounces skinless, boneless chicken breast halves
    4 7- to 8-inch whole grain tortillas
    2 teaspoons canola oil or olive oil
    2 cups small broccoli florets
    ½ cup chopped onion (1 medium)
    ½ teaspoon ground ginger
    ¼ teaspoon black pepper
    3 tablespoons bottled hoisin sauce

1. Preheat oven to 350°F. Cut chicken into thin bite-size strips; set aside. Stack tortillas and wrap in foil; bake about 10 minutes or until heated through and softened.

2. Meanwhile, in a large nonstick skillet, heat 1 teaspoon of the oil over medium-high heat. Add broccoli, onion, ginger, and pepper. Cook and stir about 4 minutes or just until vegetables are tender; remove vegetable mixture from skillet. Add chicken and the remaining 1 teaspoon oil. Cook for 3 to 5 minutes or until chicken is no longer pink, stirring occasionally. Add vegetable mixture and hoisin sauce to chicken mixture. Heat through.

3. To assemble, use a slotted spoon to spoon chicken mixture onto tortillas, placing about ¾ cup of the mixture on one half of each tortilla. Roll up tortillas; cut in half to serve. If desired, serve skillet juices as a dipping sauce.

PER SERVING: 294 cal., 7 g total fat (2 g sat. fat), 50 mg chol., 574 mg sodium, 25 g carb., 12 g fiber, 30 g pro. Exchanges: 0.5 vegetable, 1.5 starch, 3.5 lean meat. Carb choices: 1.5.

Chicken "Brats"
with Apple Slaw

Chicken "Brats" with Apple Slaw

If you have extra crunchy slaw, serve it on the side.
SERVINGS 5 (1 sausage with bun and ⅓ cup slaw each)
CARB. PER SERVING 38 g

- 1 tablespoon spicy brown mustard
- 1 tablespoon maple syrup
- 1 cup finely shredded napa cabbage
- 1 small Granny Smith apple, cored and cut into thin strips or coarsely shredded
- ¼ cup thin wedges of red onion
- 1 tablespoon cider vinegar
- 1 tablespoon olive oil
- 1 12-ounce package cooked chicken-apple sausages (5)
- 5 whole wheat hot dog buns

1. In a small bowl, combine mustard and maple syrup; set aside.
2. In a medium bowl, combine cabbage, apple, and red onion. In a small bowl, whisk the vinegar, olive oil, and 1 teaspoon of the mustard mixture to blend. Drizzle over cabbage mixture and toss to coat.
3. Preheat a grill pan or griddle over medium heat. Add sausages and cook for 15 to 18 minutes or until heated through, turning occasionally.
4. Serve sausages on buns. Top with remaining mustard mixture and apple slaw.
PER SERVING: 321 cal., 11 g total fat (3 g sat. fat), 49 mg chol., 661 mg sodium, 38 g carb., 2 g fiber, 16 g pro. Exchanges: 2.5 starch, 1 medium-fat meat, 1 fat. Carb choices: 2.5.

Cajun Turkey Sandwiches

The tasty Cajun mayo spread will dress up any sandwich combo.
SERVINGS 4 (1 sandwich each)
CARB. PER SERVING 18 g

- ¼ cup light mayonnaise or salad dressing
- 1 teaspoon purchased salt-free Cajun seasoning or Homemade Salt-Free Cajun Seasoning
- 1 clove garlic, minced
- 8 very thin slices firm-texture whole wheat bread, toasted if desired
- 1 cup fresh spinach leaves

Cajun Turkey Sandwiches

- 8 ounces packaged lower-sodium sliced cooked turkey breast
- 4 tomato slices
- 1 small green sweet pepper or fresh poblano chile pepper,* seeded and sliced

1. In a small bowl, combine mayonnaise, Cajun seasoning, and garlic. Spread on one side of each of the bread slices.
2. To assemble, place four of the bread slices, spread sides up, on serving plates. Layer with spinach, turkey, tomato slices, and pepper slices. Top with remaining bread slices, spread sides down. Cut in half to serve.
HOMEMADE SALT-FREE CAJUN SEASONING: In a small bowl, stir together ¼ teaspoon white pepper, ¼ teaspoon garlic powder, ¼ teaspoon onion powder, ¼ teaspoon paprika, ¼ teaspoon black pepper, and ⅛ to ¼ teaspoon cayenne pepper.
***TEST KITCHEN TIP:** Because chile peppers contain volatile oils that can burn your skin and eyes, avoid direct contact with chiles as much as possible. When working with chile peppers, wear plastic or rubber gloves. If your bare hands do touch the chile peppers, wash your hands and nails well with soap and warm water.
PER SERVING: 194 cal., 7 g total fat (1 g sat. fat), 35 mg chol., 602 mg sodium, 18 g carb., 3 g fiber, 15 g pro. Exchanges: 0.5 vegetable, 1 starch, 1.5 lean meat, 1 fat. Carb choices: 1.

Turkey Swiss Panini

Flavors of Thanksgiving ring true in this toasty favorite. And it's a perfect way to use up some of the leftover bird.

SERVINGS 4 (1 sandwich each)
CARB. PER SERVING 30 g

Nonstick cooking spray
8 slices oatmeal bread
1 recipe Cranberry Mustard (below)
6 ounces sliced cooked turkey breast
1½ cups fresh baby arugula
4 thin slices Swiss cheese (2 ounces total)

1. Lightly coat an unheated panini sandwich maker or grill pan with cooking spray. Preheat panini maker according to manufacturer's directions or grill pan over medium heat.
2. Spread four of the bread slices with Cranberry Mustard. Top with turkey, arugula, Swiss cheese, and remaining bread slices.
3. Place sandwiches on panini maker or grill pan, in batches if necessary. If using panini maker, close lid and grill for 3 to 4 minutes or until golden brown. (If using grill pan, place a heavy skillet on top of sandwiches. Cook for 1 to 2 minutes or until bottoms are toasted. Using hotpads, carefully remove top skillet. Turn sandwiches and top again with skillet. Cook for 1 to 2 minutes more or until bread is toasted.)
CRANBERRY MUSTARD: In a small bowl, combine 1 tablespoon stone-ground mustard; 1 tablespoon light mayonnaise; 2 tablespoons chopped fresh cranberries; 1 teaspoon honey; 1 teaspoon snipped fresh sage or ½ teaspoon dried sage, crushed; and ¼ teaspoon cracked black pepper.
PER SERVING: 282 cal., 8 g total fat (3 g sat. fat), 50 mg chol., 495 mg sodium, 30 g carb., 2 g fiber, 21 g pro. Exchanges: 2 starch, 2 lean meat, 0.5 fat. Carb choices: 2.

Mexican Turnovers

Before baking the turnovers, use a sharp knife to cut a few slits in the top of each to allow steam to escape.

SERVINGS 6 (1 turnover each)
CARB. PER SERVING 41 g

Nonstick cooking spray
1 16-ounce loaf frozen honey-wheat bread dough, thawed
12 ounces ground turkey breast
1 small green sweet pepper, chopped
1 small onion, chopped
1 14.5-ounce can no-salt-added diced tomatoes
2 teaspoons snipped fresh oregano
⅓ cup shredded reduced-fat cheddar cheese
Fat-free milk

1. Preheat oven to 400°F. Lightly coat a baking sheet with cooking spray; set aside. Divide dough into six equal portions. Cover and let stand for 10 minutes.
2. Lightly coat a large nonstick skillet with cooking spray. Cook turkey, sweet pepper, and onion over medium heat for 5 minutes or until turkey is no longer pink. Add tomatoes and bring to boiling; reduce heat. Simmer, uncovered, about 8 minutes or until thickened.
3. On a lightly floured surface, roll each portion of dough to a 6- to 7-inch circle. Using a slotted spoon, spoon turkey mixture onto dough and sprinkle with cheese. Fold dough over and crimp edges with fingers to seal. Cut slits in top of each turnover. Place turnovers on prepared baking sheet. Brush tops with milk.
4. Bake for 15 to 20 minutes or until golden brown.
PER SERVING: 296 cal., 5 g total fat (1 g sat. fat), 31 mg chol., 531 mg sodium, 41 g carb., 5 g fiber, 25 g pro. Exchanges: 1 vegetable, 2.5 starch, 2 lean meat. Carb choices: 3.

Turkey Meatball Grinders

Put extra hot dog buns to use by making bread crumbs. Place in a food processor and pulse with several on/off turns to create crumbs.

SERVINGS 4 (1 sandwich each)
CARB. PER SERVING 43 g

Nonstick cooking spray
1 14.5-ounce can no-salt-added diced tomatoes
2 tablespoons no-salt-added tomato paste
1 tablespoon balsamic vinegar
2 cloves garlic, halved
1 teaspoon Italian seasoning, crushed
¼ teaspoon crushed red pepper
¼ teaspoon salt
1 egg, lightly beaten
⅔ cup soft whole grain or whole wheat bread crumbs
12 ounces ground turkey breast
1 medium red sweet pepper, cut into thin strips
1 small sweet onion, cut into thin wedges
2 teaspoons olive oil
4 whole grain or whole wheat hot dog buns, toasted
4 thin slices mozzarella cheese (1 ounce total)

Turkey Meatball Grinders

1. Preheat oven to 400°F. Coat a 15×10×1-inch baking pan with cooking spray; set aside. In a blender or food processor, combine undrained tomatoes, tomato paste, vinegar, garlic, Italian seasoning, crushed red pepper, and salt. Cover and blend or process until smooth.

2. In a large bowl, combine the egg, ¼ cup of the sauce, and bread crumbs. Add turkey and mix until combined. Form mixture into twelve 2-inch meatballs. Place meatballs in prepared baking pan. Bake about 15 minutes or until no longer pink (165°F).

3. Meanwhile, in a large skillet, cook sweet pepper and onion in hot oil over medium heat about 8 minutes or until very tender, stirring occasionally. Stir in remaining sauce. Heat through. Add meatballs and stir gently to coat with sauce.

4. Increase oven temperature to broil. Broil split buns 4 to 5 inches from the heat for 1 minute. Line buns with cheese slices. Broil about 1 minute more or until cheese is melted and bread is toasted.

5. Place three meatballs in each bun. Top with sauce.

PER SERVING: 364 cal., 8 g total fat (2 g sat. fat), 98 mg chol., 600 mg sodium, 43 g carb., 8 g fiber, 31 g pro. Exchanges: 1 vegetable, 2.5 starch, 3 lean meat. Carb choices: 3.

QUICK TIP
Turn your favorite sandwich into a toasty treat with the help of a panini sandwich maker or grill pan.

Roast Beef Panini

Roast Beef Panini

If you use deli-style roast beef, make sure it is low-sodium.
SERVINGS 4 (1 sandwich each)
CARB. PER SERVING 32 g

Nonstick cooking spray
8 slices marble rye, rye, or pumpernickel bread
1 recipe Horseradish Spread (below)
8 ounces leftover cooked roast beef, sliced
1 cup baby arugula or watercress
2 slices Havarti cheese, halved (about 1½ ounces total)
¼ cup thinly sliced red onion

1. Lightly coat an unheated panini sandwich maker or grill pan with cooking spray. Preheat panini maker according to manufacturer's directions or grill pan over medium heat.
2. Meanwhile, spread Horseradish Spread on one side of the bread slices. On half of the slices, place roast beef, arugula, cheese, and red onion. Top with remaining bread slices, spread sides down.
3. Place sandwiches on panini maker or grill pan, in batches if necessary. If using panini maker, close lid and grill for 2 to 3 minutes or until bread is toasted. (If using grill pan, place a heavy skillet on top of sandwiches. Cook for 1 to 2 minutes or until bottoms are toasted. Using hotpads, carefully remove top skillet. Turn sandwiches and top again with skillet. Cook for 1 to 2 minutes more or until bread is toasted.)
HORSERADISH SPREAD: In a small bowl, combine 2 tablespoons light mayonnaise, 1 tablespoon prepared horseradish, 1 teaspoon Dijon-style mustard, and ⅛ teaspoon caraway seeds.
PER SERVING: 333 cal., 11 g total fat (4 g sat. fat), 60 mg chol., 615 mg sodium, 32 g carb., 4 g fiber, 24 g pro. Exchanges: 2 starch, 2.5 lean meat, 1 fat. Carb choices: 2.

Pepper-Steak Quesadillas

Add a twist of zesty, fresh flavor by serving with lime wedges.
SERVINGS 4 (1 quesadilla each)
CARB. PER SERVING 20 g

8 ounces beef sirloin steak, trimmed of fat and cut into bite-size strips
1 teaspoon finely shredded lime peel
2 cloves garlic, minced
¼ teaspoon ground cumin

Pepper-Steak Quesadillas

4 7- to 8-inch whole wheat tortillas
Nonstick cooking spray
1 medium red sweet pepper, cut into thin bite-size strips
¼ cup thinly sliced green onions
½ cup chopped, peeled jicama
½ cup shredded reduced-fat Monterey Jack cheese (2 ounces)

1. In a medium bowl, combine steak, lime peel, garlic, and cumin. Cover and chill for 30 minutes to 4 hours.
2. Preheat oven to 300°F. Lightly coat one side of each tortilla with cooking spray. Place tortillas, coated sides down, on a clean work surface. Set aside. Coat an unheated extra-large nonstick skillet with cooking spray. Preheat skillet over medium heat. Add steak strips, sweet pepper, and green onions to hot skillet. Cook for 3 to 5 minutes or until steak is browned and pepper is crisp-tender, stirring occasionally. Remove from heat. Stir in jicama.
3. Divide steak mixture among tortillas, placing mixture on half of each tortilla. Sprinkle with cheese. Fold tortillas over filling; press down lightly.
4. Coat a clean, unheated extra-large nonstick skillet with cooking spray. Preheat skillet over medium-high heat; reduce heat to medium. Cook quesadillas, half at a time, in hot skillet about 3 minutes or until tortillas are browned, turning once halfway through cooking. Place quesadillas on a baking sheet; keep warm in the oven. Cut each quesadilla into three wedges.
PER SERVING: 267 cal., 9 g total fat (4 g sat. fat), 34 mg chol., 475 mg sodium, 20 g carb., 11 g fiber, 25 g pro. Exchanges: 0.5 vegetable, 1 starch, 3 lean meat, 1 fat. Carb choices: 1.

Asian Burgers

meats; mix well. Shape into six ½-inch-thick patties.
2. For a charcoal grill, place patties, pineapple, and red onion on the grill rack directly over medium coals. Grill pineapple and onion, uncovered, for 4 to 6 minutes or until lightly browned, turning once. Grill patties for 10 to 13 minutes or until no longer pink (160°F), turning once halfway through grilling. (For a gas grill, preheat grill. Reduce heat to medium. Place patties, pineapple, and onion on grill rack over heat. Cover and grill as above.)
3. Place pineapple on bun bottoms. Top with patties, onion, pea pods, and bun tops.
PER SERVING: 351 cal., 11 g total fat (4 g sat. fat), 72 mg chol., 416 mg sodium, 34 g carb., 3 g fiber, 28 g pro. Exchanges: 0.5 fruit, 1.5 starch, 3.5 lean meat, 1 fat. Carb choices: 2.

Grilled Cuban Pork Sandwiches
To cut the fat a bit, choose a reduced-fat cheese.
SERVINGS 4 (1 sandwich each)
CARB. PER SERVING 23 g

---

4 whole grain white flat sandwich rolls
1 recipe Spicy Mustard Spread (below)
8 ounces roasted pork loin, thinly sliced
4 thin slices Fontina or provolone cheese (1 ounce total)
8 dill pickle slices
¼ cup thinly sliced red onion

1. Lightly coat an unheated panini sandwich maker or grill pan with *nonstick cooking spray*. Preheat sandwich maker or grill pan over medium heat.
2. Meanwhile, spread cut sides of rolls with Spicy Mustard Spread. On roll bottoms, divide pork, cheese, pickles, and red onion. Add roll tops.
3. Place sandwiches on panini maker or grill pan, in batches if necessary. If using panini maker, close lid and grill for 3 to 4 minutes or until bread is toasted. (If using grill pan, place a heavy skillet on top of sandwiches. Cook for 2 to 3 minutes or until bottoms are toasted. Using hotpads, carefully remove top skillet. Turn sandwiches and top again with skillet. Cook for 2 to 3 minutes more or until bread is toasted.)
SPICY MUSTARD SPREAD: Combine 2 tablespoons yellow mustard; 2 teaspoons lime juice; ¼ teaspoon dried oregano, crushed; ¼ teaspoon ground cumin; and ⅛ teaspoon cayenne pepper.
PER SERVING: 261 cal., 10 g total fat (3 g sat. fat), 54 mg chol., 555 mg sodium, 23 g carb., 5 g fiber, 24 g pro. Exchanges: 1.5 starch, 3 lean meat, 0.5 fat. Carb choices: 1.5.

Asian Burgers
Hoisin sauce, five-spice powder, and crushed red pepper add tantalizing Asian notes to these beef-and-pork burgers.
SERVINGS 6 (1 burger each)
CARB. PER SERVING 34 g

---

3 tablespoons bottled hoisin sauce
1 tablespoon finely chopped onion
1 teaspoon five-spice powder
¼ teaspoon crushed red pepper
1 pound lean ground beef
8 ounces lean ground pork
6 ½-inch-thick slices peeled and cored fresh pineapple
6 ½-inch-thick slices red onion
6 whole wheat hamburger buns, split and toasted
½ cup fresh snow pea pods, strings and tips removed and halved lengthwise

1. In a large bowl, combine hoisin sauce, finely chopped onion, five-spice powder, and crushed red pepper. Add

> ▶ **QUICK TIP**
> ## If you choose, use a serrated knife to first cut the bread into six portions and then assemble each sandwich individually.

Banh Mi Vietnamese Sandwiches

Banh Mi Vietnamese Sandwiches
A crisp vegetable combo helps tame the fiery heat of the jalapeño. If you like heat, leave the seeds in the jalapeño.
SERVINGS 6 (1 portion each)
CARB. PER SERVING 26 g

- 12 ounces pork tenderloin
- 2 tablespoons Asian sweet chili sauce
- 1 tablespoon reduced-sodium soy sauce
- 1 small cucumber, seeded and cut into thin strips
- 1 small red sweet pepper, cut into thin strips
- 1 medium carrot, shredded
- ¼ cup sliced green onions
- ¼ cup bottled low-fat sesame ginger salad dressing
- 1 tablespoon lime juice
- 1 10-ounce loaf whole grain baguette-style French bread, split horizontally
- ¼ cup fresh cilantro leaves
- 1 fresh jalapeño chile pepper, seeded and thinly sliced*

1. Trim fat from meat. Cut meat crosswise into ½-inch slices. Press each piece with the palm of your hand to make an even thickness. In a small bowl, combine chili sauce and soy sauce. Brush sauce mixture onto pork. In a greased grill pan or extra-large skillet, cook meat over medium-high heat for 4 to 6 minutes or until slightly pink in center and juices run clear, turning once.

2. In a large bowl, combine cucumber, sweet pepper, carrot, green onions, salad dressing, and lime juice.

3. Place meat slices on the bottom half of the baguette. Top with vegetable mixture, cilantro, jalapeño slices, and top half of baguette. Cut into portions to serve.

***TEST KITCHEN TIP:** Because chile peppers contain volatile oils that can burn your skin and eyes, avoid direct contact with chiles as much as possible. When working with chile peppers, wear plastic or rubber gloves. If your bare hands do touch the chile peppers, wash your hands and nails well with soap and warm water.

PER SERVING: 220 cal., 4 g total fat (0 g sat. fat), 37 mg chol., 481 mg sodium, 26 g carb., 6 g fiber, 19 g pro. Exchanges: 0.5 vegetable, 1.5 starch, 2 lean meat. Carb choices: 2.

Sensational Sandwiches **89**

Catfish Po'Boys

Freshly made broccoli and pepper slaw works double duty—it's a crunchy condiment on the sandwich and a colorful, zesty side dish.

SERVINGS 4 (1 sandwich and ½ cup slaw each)
CARB. PER SERVING 47 g

- 4 fresh or frozen catfish fillets (12 ounces total)
- 1 teaspoon salt-free Cajun seasoning
- ⅛ teaspoon salt
- 2 teaspoons vegetable oil
- 2 tablespoons fat-free mayonnaise
- 1 tablespoon cider vinegar
- ¼ teaspoon bottled hot pepper sauce
- 3 cups packaged shredded broccoli (broccoli slaw mix)
- 1 medium red sweet pepper, cut into thin bite-size strips
- ¼ cup thinly sliced red onion
- 4 whole grain rolls, split and toasted

1. Thaw fish, if frozen. Rinse fish; pat dry with paper towels. Sprinkle fish with Cajun seasoning and salt. In a large skillet, heat oil over medium-high heat. Cook fish in hot oil for 4 to 6 minutes per ½-inch thickness of fish or until golden and fish flakes when tested with a fork.
2. In a bowl, combine mayonnaise, vinegar, and pepper sauce. Add broccoli, sweet pepper, and onion; toss to coat.

3. Place a fish fillet on the bottom half of each roll. Top each with ¼ cup slaw mixture and a roll top. Serve with remaining slaw.
PER SERVING: 372 cal., 11 g total fat (2 g sat. fat), 41 mg chol., 600 mg sodium, 47 g carb., 4 g fiber, 21 g pro. Exchanges: 1 vegetable, 3 starch, 1.5 lean meat, 1 fat. Carb choices: 3.

Tilapia Tacos with Charred Tomatillos and Sweet Onions

Use a fork and gently twist to break the cooked fish into bite-size chunks.

SERVINGS 4 (2 tacos each)
CARB. PER SERVING 32 g

- 1 pound fresh or frozen tilapia fillets
- 8 6- to 7-inch low-carb whole wheat flour tortillas
- 3 tomatillos, husks removed and halved
- 3 roma tomatoes, halved
- ½ of a medium sweet onion, sliced ½ inch thick
- 1 fresh jalapeño chile pepper, halved and seeded (see tip, page 89)
- 1 teaspoon ground coriander
- ½ teaspoon honey
- 2 cups finely shredded cabbage

1. Thaw fish, if frozen. Rinse fish; pat dry with paper towels. Preheat broiler. Wrap tortillas in foil; place on bottom rack of oven. Lightly coat the unheated rack of a broiler pan with *nonstick cooking spray*. Place tomatillos, tomatoes, sweet onion slices, and jalapeño halves on broiler rack. Broil 4 to 5 inches from the heat for 8 to 12 minutes, turning vegetables occasionally, or until tender and lightly charred, removing vegetables from rack as they are done. Remove broiler pan from oven.
2. Place fish on the broiler rack. Sprinkle with ½ teaspoon of the coriander, ¼ teaspoon *black pepper*, and ⅛ teaspoon *salt*. Broil fish for 4 to 6 minutes per ½-inch thickness of fish or until fish flakes easily when tested with a fork, turning once.
3. Coarsely chop tomatillos and tomatoes; transfer to a medium bowl. Add honey and gently mash. Chop onion and finely chop jalapeño; stir into tomatillo mixture along with the remaining ½ teaspoon coriander.
4. Break fish into bite-size chunks. Divide fish among tortillas. Top with tomatillo mixture and cabbage.
PER SERVING: 255 cal., 6 g total fat (1 g sat. fat), 57 mg chol., 505 mg sodium, 32 g carb., 19 g fiber, 34 g pro. Exchanges: 1.5 vegetable, 1.5 starch, 3.5 lean meat. Carb choices: 2.

Catfish Po'Boys

Pan Bagnat

Pan Bagnat

*If your baguette is thick and bready, hollow out some of the
interior of the loaf to make room for the yummy layers
(and cut the carb count!).*

SERVINGS 4 (1 portion each)
CARB. PER SERVING 35 g

- 1 10-ounce loaf whole grain baguette-style French bread,
  split lengthwise and toasted
- 1 tablespoon extra virgin olive oil
- 2 4.5-ounce pouches herb and garlic or lemon pepper
  marinated chunk light tuna
- 1 small green sweet pepper, cut into thin bite-size strips
- 1 medium tomato, thinly sliced
- 2 hard-cooked eggs, sliced
- ¼ cup thinly sliced red onion

1. Drizzle cut sides of baguette with olive oil. On the
bottom half of baguette, place tuna, sweet pepper,
tomato, eggs, and onion. Top with top half of baguette.
Cut crosswise into four portions.

PER SERVING: 360 cal., 12 g total fat (2 g sat. fat), 134 mg chol.,
610 mg sodium, 35 g carb., 10 g fiber, 28 g pro. Exchanges:
0.5 vegetable, 2 starch, 3 lean meat, 1 fat. Carb choices: 2.

Open-Face Egg Sandwiches

Roasted Tofu and Veggie Pockets

Grilled Vegetable Sandwiches

Nutritious Options

Make your favorite sandwiches as healthful as you can by trying some of these carb-, fat-, and sodium-cutting pointers.

1. **Opt for whole wheat** or whole grain bread.

2. **Go with one slice of bread** and serve it open-face.

3. **Use iceberg lettuce leaves as a wrap** instead of the traditional tortilla.

4. **For panini, spray the sandwich maker or grill pan** with nonstick cooking spray rather than slathering the bread with butter.

5. **Choose deli-style meats** that are low in sodium.

6. **Load on crunchy vegetables and leafy greens.** It's a good way to work in servings of healthful veggies.

7. **If cheese is a must,** purchase the reduced-fat variety.

8. **Go light** on any mayonnaise or sandwich spread.

Roasted Tofu and Veggie Pockets

A splash of balsamic vinaigrette enhances the tantalizing roasted flavor of this colorful tofu, zucchini, onion, and sweet pepper combination.

SERVINGS 6 (1 pita half each)
CARB. PER SERVING 23 g

½ of a 16- to 18-ounce package extra-firm water-packed tofu (fresh bean curd)
1 small zucchini, thinly sliced (6 ounces)
1 medium onion, halved and thinly sliced
1 red sweet pepper, cut into thin strips
1 tablespoon olive oil
¼ teaspoon salt
¼ teaspoon black pepper
3 large whole wheat pita bread rounds, halved
2 tablespoons bottled light balsamic vinaigrette
⅓ cup shredded mozzarella-flavor soy cheese

1. Preheat oven to 450°F. Drain tofu; pat tofu with paper towels until well dried. Using a sharp knife, cut tofu into ¼-inch-thick slices, then cut into ½-inch-wide strips. In a large bowl, combine tofu, zucchini, onion, and sweet pepper. Add oil, salt, and black pepper; toss to coat.
2. Lightly coat a 15×10×1-inch baking pan with *nonstick cooking spray*. Spread tofu mixture evenly in prepared pan. Roast, uncovered, for 10 to 12 minutes or until vegetables are tender, gently stirring once.
3. Open pita halves to create pockets. Divide roasted tofu and vegetables among pita pockets; drizzle with vinaigrette. Top with shredded soy cheese. Place the filled pitas, filled sides up, in a 2-quart square baking dish. Bake for 1 to 2 minutes or until cheese melts.
PER SERVING: 189 cal., 7 g total fat (1 g sat. fat), 0 mg chol., 433 mg sodium, 23 g carb., 4 g fiber, 9 g pro. Exchanges: 1 vegetable, 1 starch, 0.5 medium-fat meat, 1 fat. Carb choices: 1.5.

Grilled Vegetable Sandwiches

This crostini-style sandwich is a great way to work vitamin-loaded veggies into your meal plan.

SERVINGS 8 (1 open-face sandwich each)
CARB. PER SERVING 19 g

1 medium zucchini, sliced lengthwise
1 medium summer squash, sliced lengthwise
1 small red onion, cut into ½-inch slices
2 medium roma tomatoes, halved

Nonstick cooking spray
8 slices whole grain crusty country-style bread
1 cup shredded part-skim mozzarella cheese (4 ounces)
½ cup fresh basil leaves

1. Lightly coat zucchini, summer squash, onion, and tomatoes with cooking spray. Sprinkle with ¼ teaspoon *salt* and ¼ teaspoon *black pepper*.
2. For a charcoal grill, place zucchini, squash, and onion slices on the grill rack directly over medium coals. Grill, uncovered, for 6 to 8 minutes or until tender, turning once. Grill tomatoes about 3 minutes or until heated through and lightly charred, turning once. Grill bread slices for 1 minute; turn. Top with cheese and grill for 1 minute more. (For a gas grill, preheat grill. Reduce heat to medium. Place vegetables and bread on grill rack over heat. Cover and grill as directed.)
3. Cut up vegetables as desired. Top bread slices with vegetables and basil leaves.
PER SERVING: 141 cal., 4 g total fat (1 g sat. fat), 9 mg chol., 275 mg sodium, 19 g carb., 5 g fiber, 9 g pro. Exchanges: 1 vegetable, 1 starch, 0.5 medium-fat meat. Carb choices: 1.

Open-Face Egg Sandwiches

The soybean-avocado mixture is reminiscent of guacamole.

SERVINGS 4 (1 open-face sandwich each)
CARB. PER SERVING 16 g

1 cup frozen shelled sweet soybeans (edamame), thawed
1 small avocado, halved, seeded, and peeled
2 tablespoons lemon juice
2 cloves garlic, minced
½ cup chopped red sweet pepper
4 very thin slices firm-texture whole wheat bread, toasted
4 hard-cooked eggs, thinly sliced
Freshly ground black pepper

1. In a medium bowl, combine soybeans, avocado, lemon juice, garlic, and ¼ teaspoon *salt*; use a fork or potato masher to mash ingredients together until avocado is smooth and soybeans are coarsely mashed. Stir in sweet pepper.
2. Spread soybean mixture on of top bread slices. Arrange egg slices on top of soybean mixture. Sprinkle with black pepper.
PER SERVING: 221 cal., 12 g total fat (3 g sat. fat), 212 mg chol., 292 mg sodium, 16 g carb., 5 g fiber, 13 g pro. Exchanges: 1 starch, 1.5 medium-fat meat, 1 fat. Carb choices: 1.

A health-conscious menu consists of nutrient-rich ingredients from the meat and beans, grains, vegetables, and fruits groups. Create a well-rounded meal by first selecting a meat or other protein. Then based on your fat and carb guidelines, choose one of these vibrant, tasty sides.

Marinated Vegetable Salad

Use garden-fresh produce to make this summertime-favorite veggie quartet.

SERVINGS 6 (²/₃ cup each)
CARB. PER SERVING 5 g

- 2 medium red and/or yellow tomatoes or 4 roma tomatoes, cut into wedges
- ¾ cup chopped green sweet pepper (1 medium)
- 1 cup thinly sliced zucchini or yellow summer squash (1 small)
- ½ of a small red onion, thinly sliced
- 2 tablespoons snipped fresh parsley
- 2 tablespoons olive oil
- 2 tablespoons balsamic vinegar or wine vinegar
- 2 tablespoons water
- 1 tablespoon snipped fresh thyme or basil or 1 teaspoon dried thyme or basil, crushed
- 1 clove garlic, minced
- 2 tablespoons pine nuts, toasted (optional)

1. In a medium bowl, combine tomatoes, sweet pepper, zucchini, red onion, and parsley; set aside.

2. For dressing: In a screw-top jar, combine oil, vinegar, the water, thyme, and garlic. Cover and shake well. Pour over vegetable mixture. Toss gently to coat.

3. Let salad stand at room temperature for 30 to 60 minutes, stirring occasionally. If desired, garnish with pine nuts. Serve with a slotted spoon.

MAKE-AHEAD DIRECTIONS: Prepare as directed through Step 2. Cover and refrigerate for 4 to 24 hours, stirring once or twice. Let stand at room temperature about 30 minutes before serving. If desired, garnish with pine nuts. Serve with a slotted spoon.

PER SERVING: 65 cal., 5 g total fat (1 g sat. fat), 0 mg chol., 7 mg sodium, 5 g carb., 1 g fiber, 1 g pro. Exchanges: 1 vegetable, 1 fat. Carb choices: 0.

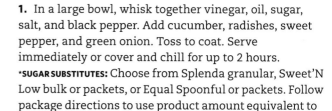

Add more food to your plate by taking advantage of nonstarchy veggies such as cucumbers and sweet peppers that are low in calories and high in nutrients.

Cucumber Radish Slaw

Seasoned with a light vinaigrette, this easy salad is a fresh-tasting partner for grilled steaks or chops.

SERVINGS 4 (¾ cup each)
CARB. PER SERVING 5 g

- 2 tablespoons cider vinegar
- 1 teaspoon olive oil
- ½ teaspoon sugar*
- ⅛ teaspoon salt
- ⅛ teaspoon black pepper
- 2 cups thinly sliced English cucumber
- 1 cup radishes, trimmed and thinly sliced
- ½ cup thinly sliced red sweet pepper strips
- 2 tablespoons finely chopped green onion (1)

1. In a large bowl, whisk together vinegar, oil, sugar, salt, and black pepper. Add cucumber, radishes, sweet pepper, and green onion. Toss to coat. Serve immediately or cover and chill for up to 2 hours.

***SUGAR SUBSTITUTES:** Choose from Splenda granular, Sweet'N Low bulk or packets, or Equal Spoonful or packets. Follow package directions to use product amount equivalent to ½ teaspoon sugar.

PER SERVING: 32 cal., 1 g total fat (0 g sat. fat), 0 mg chol., 87 mg sodium, 5 g carb., 1 g fiber, 1 g pro. Exchanges: 1 vegetable. Carb choices: 0.
PER SERVING WITH SUBSTITUTE: Same as above.

Gingered Lemon Broccoli Salad

With soy yogurt in the ginger-accented dressing and roasted soy nuts on top of the salad, you get a double dose of soy in this flavorful dish.

SERVINGS 8 (½ cup each)
CARB. PER SERVING 8 g

- 3 tablespoons light mayonnaise or salad dressing
- 2 tablespoons plain soy yogurt
- ¼ teaspoon finely shredded lemon peel
- 2 teaspoons lemon juice
- ¼ teaspoon grated fresh ginger
- 4 cups small broccoli and/or cauliflower florets
- ⅓ cup finely chopped red onion
- ¼ cup dried cranberries
- 3 tablespoons roasted soy nuts

1. In a large bowl, stir together mayonnaise, soy yogurt, lemon peel, lemon juice, and ginger. Add broccoli, red onion, and cranberries. Toss to coat. Cover and chill for 1 to 24 hours. Just before serving, sprinkle with soy nuts.

PER SERVING: 59 cal., 3 g total fat (0 g sat. fat), 2 mg chol., 54 mg sodium, 8 g carb., 2 g fiber, 2 g pro. Exchanges: 0.5 vegetable, 0.5 fat. Carb choices: 0.5.

Cucumber
Radish Slaw

Gingered Lemon Broccoli Salad

Greek Garden Pasta Salad

Dressing with fat-free yogurt and just a little light mayonnaise keeps the fat in check.

SERVINGS 12 (½ cup each)
CARB. PER SERVING 15 g

- 6 ounces dried whole grain or multigrain bow tie or rotini pasta (2⅔ cups)
- 1 6-ounce carton plain fat-free yogurt or plain fat-free Greek yogurt (⅔ cup)
- ⅓ cup light mayonnaise or salad dressing
- 2 tablespoons fat-free milk
- 2 tablespoons snipped fresh dillweed or 1½ teaspoons dried dillweed
- 2 tablespoons snipped fresh Italian (flat-leaf) parsley
- 1 teaspoon finely shredded lemon peel
- 1 tablespoon lemon juice
- ½ teaspoon freshly ground black pepper
- 1½ cups chopped English cucumber
- 1½ cups halved grape tomatoes
- ¾ cup chopped green sweet pepper (1 medium)
- ⅓ cup sliced green onions
- ⅓ cup quartered pitted Kalamata olives

1. Cook pasta according to package directions. Drain well. Rinse with cold water and drain again. Set aside.
2. In a large bowl, stir together yogurt, mayonnaise, milk, dillweed, parsley, lemon peel, lemon juice, and black pepper. Add pasta, cucumber, tomatoes, sweet pepper, and green onions. Toss gently to coat. Cover and chill in the refrigerator for 3 to 6 hours. To serve, fold in Kalamata olives.

PER SERVING: 98 cal., 3 g total fat (0 g sat. fat), 3 mg chol., 100 mg sodium, 15 g carb., 2 g fiber, 3 g pro. Exchanges: 1 starch, 0.5 fat. Carb choices: 1.

Curried Wild Rice Salad

Sprinkling a few chopped peanuts over the salad just before serving adds a delightful crunch.

SERVINGS 10 (½ cup each)
CARB. PER SERVING 25 g

- ⅔ cup wild rice, rinsed and drained
- ⅔ cup brown rice
- 1 cup frozen peas, thawed
- ¾ cup chopped red or yellow sweet pepper (1 medium)
- ¼ cup dried currants or raisins
- 2 tablespoons thinly sliced green onion (1)
- 3 tablespoons canola oil
- 3 tablespoons orange juice
- 1 tablespoon honey
- 1 teaspoon curry powder
- ¼ cup chopped peanuts (optional)

1. In a medium saucepan, combine 3 cups *water,* the uncooked wild rice, and uncooked brown rice. Bring to boiling; reduce heat. Simmer, covered, about 40 minutes or until rice is tender; drain if necessary.
2. Transfer cooked rice to a large bowl; let cool to room temperature. Add peas, sweet pepper, currants, and green onion to rice mixture.
3. In a screw-top jar, combine oil, orange juice, honey, curry powder, and ¼ teaspoon *salt.* Cover; shake well.
4. Pour orange juice mixture over rice mixture in bowl. Toss gently to combine. Cover and chill in the refrigerator for 4 to 24 hours.
5. Let salad stand at room temperature for 30 minutes before serving. If desired, sprinkle with chopped peanuts.
PER SERVING: 155 cal., 5 g total fat (0 g sat. fat), 0 mg chol., 80 mg sodium, 25 g carb., 2 g fiber, 4 g pro. Exchanges: 1.5 starch, 1 fat. Carb choices: 1.5.

New Potato-Cabbage Salad

Shave a few minutes off the prep time by substituting 4 cups purchased shredded cabbage with carrot (coleslaw mix) for the shredded cabbage and carrots.

SERVINGS 8 (¾ cup per each)
CARB. PER SERVING 11 g

- 12 ounces round red or small Yukon gold potatoes, cut into ½-inch-thick wedges
- 3 tablespoons light mayonnaise
- 2 tablespoons German-style mustard
- 3 tablespoons cider vinegar
- 3 cups shredded green cabbage
- 1 cup shredded carrots
- ½ cup thinly sliced celery (1 stalk)
- ½ cup thinly sliced green onions (4)
- 2 slices turkey bacon, cooked and chopped

1. In a covered large saucepan, cook potato wedges in enough boiling water to cover for 10 to 12 minutes or until tender. Drain well; set aside to cool.
2. Meanwhile, in a large bowl, whisk together mayonnaise and mustard. Gradually add vinegar, whisking until smooth. Add cooled potatoes, cabbage, carrots, celery, and green onions. Toss to coat. Cover and chill in the refrigerator for 2 to 24 hours. Toss before serving. Sprinkle with bacon.
PER SERVING: 82 cal., 3 g total fat (1 g sat. fat), 5 mg chol., 220 mg sodium, 11 g carb., 2 g fiber, 2 g pro. Exchanges: 0.5 vegetable, 0.5 starch, 0.5 fat. Carb choices: 1.

Caribbean Couscous Salad

Look for whole wheat couscous in the grains section of a large supermarket or at a health food store.

SERVINGS 10 (⅔ cup each)
CARB. PER SERVING 29 g

- 1 cup whole wheat couscous
- 1 15-ounce can black beans, rinsed and drained
- 2 cups coarsely shredded fresh spinach
- 1 medium mango, peeled, pitted, and chopped
- ¾ cup coarsely chopped red sweet pepper (1 medium)
- ¼ cup thinly sliced green onions (2)
- 1 recipe Ginger-Lime Vinaigrette (below)

1. In a medium saucepan, bring 1¼ cups *water* to boiling. Remove from heat. Stir in couscous; cover and let stand for 5 minutes. Fluff with a fork. Let stand at room temperature about 10 minutes or until cool.
2. In a bowl, stir together beans, spinach, mango, sweet pepper, and green onions. Add couscous and Ginger-Lime Vinaigrette. Toss to coat. Serve immediately or cover and chill in the refrigerator for up to 24 hours.
GINGER-LIME VINAIGRETTE: In a small bowl, whisk together ¼ cup snipped fresh cilantro, 3 tablespoons lime juice, 2 tablespoons canola oil, 1½ teaspoons grated fresh ginger or ½ teaspoon ground ginger, ⅛ teaspoon salt, and ⅛ teaspoon cayenne pepper.
PER SERVING: 156 cal., 3 g total fat (0 g sat. fat), 0 mg chol., 142 mg sodium, 29 g carb., 6 g fiber, 6 g pro. Exchanges: 2 starch. Carb choices: 2.

Potluck Sides

Side dishes make perfect potluck fare. Use these tips to select good-for-you foods and to avoid overeating.

1. **Take a 9-inch plate** with you so you won't try to load a larger one that may be provided.

2. **Spoon dishes** onto your plate, allowing space between each. No piling.

3. **Walk past** vegetable dishes that ooze with sauce or cheese. Instead spoon up crisp-cooked, vibrant veggies that are simply seasoned.

4. **Pass on** salads drenched in mayonnaise-base dressings. Seek those lightly dressed with a vinaigrette or yogurt dressing.

5. **Take small helpings** of high-carb favorites such as potato salad, pasta salad, and scalloped potatoes.

6. **Keep portions** on target by using an appropriate-size measuring cup to scoop up servings.

New Potato-Cabbage Salad

Caribbean Couscous Salad

To prevent the tomatoes and artichoke hearts from watering out too much, be sure to let them stand on a double thickness of paper towels before topping the focaccia.

from top to bottom:
Tomato-Artichoke
Focaccia, Green Apple
Slaw, Fiesta Corn Salad

Tomato-Artichoke Focaccia

This pizzalike bread will stand out at any picnic-style gathering or informal party.

SERVINGS 16 (1 piece each)

CARB. PER SERVING 26 g

3½ to 4 cups all-purpose flour
1 package active dry yeast
1 teaspoon salt
1¼ cups warm water (120°F to 130°F)
2 tablespoons olive oil
¼ cup cornmeal
  Nonstick cooking spray
1¼ pounds roma tomatoes and/or green or yellow tomatoes, thinly sliced
1 14-ounce can artichoke hearts, drained and quartered
1 tablespoon olive oil
1 tablespoon snipped fresh rosemary or 1 teaspoon dried rosemary, crushed
1 small red onion, very thinly sliced and separated into rings
4 cloves garlic, cut into thin slivers

1. In a large bowl, combine 1½ cups of the flour, the yeast, and salt. Add the warm water and the 2 tablespoons olive oil. Beat with an electric mixer on low to medium speed for 30 seconds, scraping side of bowl constantly. Beat on high speed for 3 minutes. Using a wooden spoon, stir in cornmeal and as much of the remaining flour as you can.

2. Turn out dough onto a lightly floured surface. Knead in enough of the remaining flour to make a moderately soft dough that is smooth and elastic (3 to 5 minutes total). Shape dough into a ball. Place dough in a lightly greased bowl, turning once to grease surface.

3. Cover and let dough rise in a warm place until double in size (45 to 60 minutes). Punch dough down; let rest for 10 minutes. Grease a 15×10×1-inch baking pan. Place dough in prepared baking pan. Gently pull and stretch dough in the baking pan into a 15×8-inch rectangle, being careful not to overwork dough.

4. Lightly coat dough with cooking spray. Cover loosely with plastic wrap; let dough rise in a warm place until nearly double in size (about 30 minutes).

5. Preheat oven to 450°F. Arrange tomato slices and artichoke quarters on a double thickness of paper towels. Let stand for 15 minutes. Change paper towels as necessary so all of the excess liquid is absorbed from tomatoes and artichokes. Using your fingers, press deep indentations in the dough 1½ to 2 inches apart. Brush dough with the 1 tablespoon olive oil. Sprinkle with rosemary. Arrange tomato slices, artichoke quarters, onion rings, and garlic slivers evenly on top of dough.

6. Bake about 25 minutes or until golden brown. Transfer to a wire rack to cool. Cut into pieces. Serve warm or at room temperature.

MAKE-AHEAD DIRECTIONS: Prepare dough as directed through Step 2. Cover and chill dough in the refrigerator for 16 to 24 hours. Punch dough down and continue as directed in Step 3, except increase the rising time in Step 4 to about 45 minutes.

PER SERVING: 148 cal., 3 g total fat (0 g sat. fat), 0 mg chol., 232 mg sodium, 26 g carb., 2 g fiber, 4 g pro. Exchanges: 2 starch. Carb choices: 2.

Green Apple Slaw

Tossing the apples with lemon juice prevents the slices from turning brown.

SERVINGS 12 (about ¾ cup each)

CARB. PER SERVING 10 g

- ½ cup light mayonnaise or salad dressing
- 2 teaspoons honey
- ½ teaspoon poppy seeds
- 4 Granny Smith apples, quartered and thinly sliced (4 cups)
- 1 tablespoon lemon juice
- 1½ cups coarsely chopped cabbage
- ¾ cup halved green seedless grapes
- ½ cup thinly sliced celery (1 stalk)

1. For dressing: In a small bowl, stir together mayonnaise, honey, and poppy seeds. Set aside.

2. In a large salad bowl, combine apples and lemon juice; toss to combine. Stir in cabbage, grapes, and celery. Pour dressing over apple mixture; toss gently to coat. Cover and chill in the refrigerator for 1 to 24 hours before serving.

PER SERVING: 67 cal., 3 g total fat (1 g sat. fat), 4 mg chol., 73 mg sodium, 10 g carb., 1 g fiber, 0 g pro. Exchanges: 0.5 fruit. Carb choices: 0.5.

Fiesta Corn Salad

Yellow corn, green soybeans, purplish red onion, and bright red tomatoes combine for a fiesta of color and flavor.

SERVINGS 12 (½ cup each)

CARB. PER SERVING 15 g

- 4 cups fresh or frozen whole kernel corn
- 1 cup frozen shelled sweet soybeans (edamame)
- ¼ cup chopped red onion
- ¼ cup snipped fresh cilantro
- 1 small fresh jalapeño chile pepper, seeded and finely chopped*
- 2 tablespoons olive oil
- ½ teaspoon finely shredded lime peel
- 2 tablespoons lime juice
- 1½ teaspoons cumin seeds, toasted**
- 2 cloves garlic, minced
- ¼ teaspoon chili powder
- 2 medium tomatoes, seeded and chopped
  Fresh cilantro (optional)

1. In a covered large saucepan, cook corn and soybeans in enough boiling water to cover for 2 minutes; drain. Rinse with cold water and drain again.

2. In a large bowl, stir together corn, soybeans, red onion, snipped cilantro, and chile pepper.

3. In a screw-top jar, combine olive oil, lime peel, lime juice, cumin seeds, garlic, and chili powder. Cover and shake well.

4. Pour lime mixture over corn mixture; toss gently to coat. Gently stir in tomatoes. If desired, garnish with additional cilantro. Serve immediately. (Or do not stir in tomatoes. Cover and chill in the refrigerator for up to 24 hours. Gently stir in tomatoes. Let stand for 30 minutes before serving.)

***TEST KITCHEN TIP:** Because chile peppers contain volatile oils that can burn your skin and eyes, avoid direct contact with chiles as much as possible. When working with chile peppers, wear plastic or rubber gloves. If your bare hands do touch the chile peppers, wash your hands and nails well with soap and warm water.

****TEST KITCHEN TIP:** To toast cumin seeds, place seeds in a dry small skillet. Heat over medium heat about 2 minutes or until fragrant, shaking skillet often.

PER SERVING: 96 cal., 4 g total fat (0 g sat. fat), 0 mg chol., 6 mg sodium, 15 g carb., 2 g fiber, 4 g pro. Exchanges: 1 starch, 0.5 fat. Carb choices: 1.

Farmer's Market
Salad Platter

Farmer's Market Salad Platter

A trip to a well-stocked farmer's market should yield the green beans and other vegetables you need.

SERVINGS 10 (about ½ cup arugula, ⅓ cup potatoes, ⅓ cup green beans, and ¼ cup tomatoes each)

CARB. PER SERVING 15 g

1¼ pounds tiny new potatoes, halved or quartered
12 ounces fresh green beans and/or yellow wax beans, trimmed
¼ cup white wine vinegar or champagne vinegar
3 tablespoons olive oil
1 medium shallot, finely chopped (2 tablespoons)
1 tablespoon capers, rinsed and drained
1 teaspoon Dijon-style mustard
¼ teaspoon freshly ground black pepper
5 cups fresh baby arugula or baby spinach
4 medium roma tomatoes, coarsely chopped

1. In a covered large saucepan, cook potatoes in enough boiling water to cover about 10 minutes or just until tender; drain. Rinse with cold water and drain again. If desired, cover and chill for up to 24 hours.

2. In a covered medium saucepan, cook beans in enough boiling water to cover about 10 minutes or just until crisp-tender; drain. Submerse beans in a bowl of ice water to cool quickly; drain again. If desired, cover and chill for up to 24 hours.

3. For dressing: In a screw-top jar, combine vinegar, olive oil, shallot, capers, mustard, and pepper. Cover and shake well. If desired, chill for up to 24 hours.

4. To serve, if dressing is chilled, let it stand at room temperature for 30 minutes. Arrange arugula on a platter. Arrange potatoes, beans, and tomatoes on top of arugula. Shake dressing well. Drizzle dressing over vegetables.

PER SERVING: 106 cal., 4 g total fat (1 g sat. fat), 0 mg chol., 49 mg sodium, 15 g carb., 3 g fiber, 3 g pro. Exchanges: 1 vegetable, 0.5 starch, 1 fat. Carb choices: 1.

Caesar-Style Salad with Crispy Parmesan Rounds

This flavorful salad is simple enough for a weeknight meal yet special enough for a dinner party.

SERVINGS 4 (1 cup salad, about 3 tablespoons croutons, and 1 Parmesan round each)

CARB. PER SERVING 7 g

½ cup finely shredded Parmesan cheese (2 ounces)
⅛ teaspoon freshly ground black pepper
¾ cup 1-inch cubes whole grain baguette-style bread
  Olive oil nonstick cooking spray
2 tablespoons light mayonnaise or salad dressing
1 tablespoon lemon juice
½ of a clove garlic, minced
⅛ teaspoon freshly ground black pepper
4 cups torn romaine lettuce
  Freshly ground black pepper (optional)

1. Preheat oven to 300°F. Line a large baking sheet with parchment paper or foil. Draw four 4-inch circles on the paper or foil, spacing circles at least 1 inch apart. In a small bowl, combine cheese and ⅛ teaspoon pepper. Divide mixture among circles, spreading evenly to edges of circles.

2. Bake for 10 to 15 minutes or until cheese is melted and just beginning to brown on the edges. Cool on baking sheet. Carefully remove cheese rounds from parchment paper or foil.

3. Meanwhile, for croutons: Place bread cubes in a small skillet. Lightly coat with cooking spray. Turn cubes; lightly coat again with cooking spray. Cook over medium-high heat for 3 to 5 minutes or until bread is lightly toasted, tossing cubes occasionally.

4. For dressing: In a small bowl, whisk together mayonnaise, lemon juice, garlic, and ⅛ teaspoon pepper until well mixed. Divide romaine among salad plates. Drizzle with dressing; top with croutons and Parmesan rounds. If desired, sprinkle with additional pepper.

PER SERVING: 96 cal., 6 g total fat (2 g sat. fat), 10 mg chol., 256 mg sodium, 7 g carb., 2 g fiber, 5 g pro. Exchanges: 1 vegetable, 0.5 lean meat, 1 fat. Carb choices: 0.5.

Stuffed Baby Watermelon

Watermelon tastes its best in this lime- and honey-tossed medley of melon, peaches, and grapes.

SERVINGS 6 (1⅓ cups each)

CARB. PER SERVING 19 g

1 teaspoon finely shredded lime peel
2 tablespoons lime juice
1 tablespoon honey
1 8-inch baby watermelon (about 5 pounds) or 7 cups watermelon balls or cut-up watermelon
½ of a medium white peach, white nectarine, yellow peach, or yellow nectarine, pitted and coarsely chopped (¾ cup)
½ cup seedless red grapes, halved
  Lime peel strips (optional)

1. In a large bowl, combine the 1 teaspoon lime peel, the lime juice, and honey; set aside.

2. If using baby watermelon, cut it in half crosswise; using a melon baller, scoop out flesh. Add watermelon balls or pieces to lime juice mixture. Add chopped peach and grapes; toss to coat. If desired, spoon fruit mixture back into watermelon halves and garnish with lime peel strips.

PER SERVING: 75 cal., 0 g total fat, 0 mg chol., 2 mg sodium, 19 g carb., 1 g fiber, 1 g pro. Exchanges: 1 fruit. Carb choices: 1.

Stuffed Baby Watermelon

Layered Vegetable Bake

Perk up a family meal by replacing ordinary spuds with this colorful roasted combo of Yukon gold potatoes, carrots, beets, and zucchini.

SERVINGS 8 (1 wedge each)
CARB. PER SERVING 14 g

- 1 pound Yukon gold potatoes
- 2 medium carrots, peeled and halved crosswise
  Butter-flavor nonstick cooking spray
- 4 packaged refrigerated cooked whole baby beets, very thinly sliced*
- 1 medium zucchini, very thinly sliced* (1¼ cups)
- 2 teaspoons olive oil
- ¼ teaspoon salt
- ¼ teaspoon ground black pepper

1. Scrub potatoes; remove eyes and/or sprouts. In a covered large saucepan, cook potatoes in enough boiling water to cover about 25 minutes or until tender, adding the carrot pieces for the last 4 minutes of cooking time. Drain; cool until easy to handle. Very thinly slice potatoes and carrots, keeping the carrots separate from the potatoes.*

2. Preheat oven to 400°F. Line a 9×1½-inch round baking pan with heavy foil. Generously coat foil with cooking spray. Layer half of the beet slices, half of the carrot slices, half of the zucchini slices, and half of the potato slices in pan. Drizzle with olive oil and sprinkle with half of the salt and half of the pepper. Layer remaining vegetable slices on top. Sprinkle with the remaining salt and pepper. Cover with foil; press down lightly with hands.

3. Bake for 30 to 35 minutes or until vegetables are tender. Let stand for 5 minutes. Remove top piece of foil. Invert vegetables onto a serving plate; peel off foil. Cut into eight wedges to serve.

*TEST KITCHEN TIP: Using a mandoline will allow you to cut the vegetables into very thin slices.

PER SERVING: 72 cal., 1 g total fat (0 g sat. fat), 0 mg chol., 95 mg sodium, 14 g carb., 2 g fiber, 2 g pro. Exchanges: 1 vegetable, 0.5 starch. Carb choices: 1.

Roasted Radishes with Chive Vinaigrette

Roasting brings out a bit of sweetness in zippy radishes.
Serve hot or at room temperature.

SERVINGS 6 (½ cup each)

CARB. PER SERVING 4 g

1½ pounds radishes, trimmed, scrubbed, and halved
   Olive oil nonstick cooking spray
2 tablespoons white wine vinegar
2 tablespoons olive oil
1 tablespoon chopped fresh chives
½ teaspoon Dijon-style mustard
¼ teaspoon black pepper
⅛ teaspoon salt

1. Preheat oven to 425°F. Place the radishes on a 15×10×1-inch baking pan. Lightly coat with cooking spray. Roast, uncovered, for 30 to 35 minutes or until tender and lightly browned, stirring once.
2. For vinaigrette: In a screw-top jar, combine vinegar, oil, chives, mustard, pepper, and salt. Drizzle over radishes and toss to coat.
PER SERVING: 60 cal., 5 g total fat (1 g sat. fat), 0 mg chol., 103 mg sodium, 4 g carb., 2 g fiber, 1 g pro. Exchanges: 1 vegetable, 1 fat. Carb choices: 0.

Grilled Sweet Potato Wedges

Grilling browns the sweet potatoes without all the calories and fat of frying. The lively coating of oregano, garlic powder, and cinnamon is the perfect partner for the subtly sweet taters.

SERVINGS 4 (½ cup each)

CARB. PER SERVING 17 g

1 medium sweet potato, scrubbed (12 ounces)
½ teaspoon dried oregano, crushed
¼ teaspoon garlic powder
⅛ teaspoon salt
⅛ teaspoon ground cinnamon
   Olive oil nonstick cooking spray
2 tablespoons snipped fresh cilantro

1. Cut sweet potato in half lengthwise. Cut each half in half crosswise. Cut each quarter lengthwise into 1-inch-thick wedges. In a covered medium saucepan, cook sweet potato wedges in enough boiling water to cover for 8 to 10 minutes or just until tender; drain well. Pat dry with paper towels.
2. In a small bowl, combine oregano, garlic powder, salt, and cinnamon. Coat sweet potato wedges with cooking spray. Sprinkle evenly with oregano mixture.
3. For a charcoal grill, place potato wedges on the grill rack directly over medium coals. Grill, uncovered, for 3 to 5 minutes or until potato wedges are lightly browned, turning once halfway through grilling. (For a gas grill, preheat grill. Reduce heat to medium. Place potato wedges on grill rack over heat. Cover and grill as above.)
4. To serve, sprinkle potato pieces with cilantro.
PER SERVING: 75 cal., 0 g total fat, 0 mg chol., 118 mg sodium, 17 g carb., 3 g fiber, 1 g pro. Exchanges: 1 starch. Carb choices: 1.

Grilled Sweet
Potato Wedges

Spring Risotto

*To achieve the creamy texture characteristic of risotto,
be sure to add the liquid a little at a time as directed.*

SERVINGS 6 (²/₃ cup each)

CARB. PER SERVING 25 g

- 1 tablespoon olive oil
- 1 medium fennel bulb, trimmed and chopped, or 1 medium onion, chopped (½ cup)
- 2 cloves garlic, minced
- 1 cup uncooked arborio rice
- 1 14-ounce can vegetable broth
- 1¾ cups water
- 12 ounces fresh asparagus and/or green beans, trimmed and cut into 1-inch pieces
- 2 cups coarsely chopped fresh arugula or spinach
- ½ cup chopped radishes
- ¼ cup snipped fresh flat-leaf parsley
- ¼ cup snipped fresh mint or basil

1. In a large saucepan, heat oil over medium heat. Add fennel and garlic; cook about 5 minutes or until fennel is tender, stirring occasionally. Add the rice. Cook about 5 minutes or until rice is golden brown, stirring frequently. Remove from heat.

2. Meanwhile, in a medium saucepan, bring broth and the water to boiling. Add green beans, if using. Cover and cook for 5 minutes. Add asparagus, if using. Cover and cook for 2 to 3 minutes more or just until vegetables are tender. Using a slotted spoon, transfer vegetables to a bowl, reserving broth mixture in saucepan. Set vegetables aside. Reduce heat; cover and keep broth mixture simmering.

3. Carefully stir 1 cup of the broth mixture into the rice mixture. Cook, stirring frequently, over medium heat until liquid is absorbed. Stir another 1 cup of the broth mixture into the rice mixture. Continue to cook, stirring frequently, until liquid is absorbed. Add another 1 cup of the broth mixture, ½ cup at a time, stirring frequently until the broth is absorbed. (This should take 18 to 20 minutes total.)

4. Stir in the remaining broth mixture. Cook and stir until rice is slightly firm (al dente) and creamy. Stir in cooked asparagus and/or beans, the arugula, radishes, parsley, and mint. Serve immediately.

PER SERVING: 129 cal., 2 g total fat (0 g sat. fat), 0 mg chol., 290 mg sodium, 25 g carb., 3 g fiber, 4 g pro. Exchanges: 1 vegetable, 1 starch, 0.5 fat. Carb choices: 1.5.

Spring Risotto

Green Beans with Cilantro

When shopping for green beans, select ones that are bright green and fresh-looking with no bruises, bulges, or brown spots.

SERVINGS 4 (¾ cup each)
CARB. PER SERVING 7 g

- 12 ounces fresh green beans, trimmed
- 2 cloves garlic, minced
- 2 teaspoons olive oil
- ¼ teaspoon salt
- ¼ teaspoon black pepper
- 2 tablespoons snipped fresh cilantro

1. Place a steamer basket in a large saucepan with a tight-fitting lid. Add water to just below the basket. Bring water to boiling over medium-high heat. Place beans in steamer basket. Cover; steam for 8 to 10 minutes or until beans are crisp-tender.
2. In a large nonstick skillet, cook garlic in hot oil over medium heat for 15 seconds, stirring constantly. Add beans, salt, and pepper. Cook for 3 minutes, tossing occasionally. Sprinkle with cilantro.

PER SERVING: 50 cal., 2 g total fat (0 g sat. fat), 0 mg chol., 152 mg sodium, 7 g carb., 3 g fiber, 2 g pro. Exchanges: 1.5 vegetable, 0.5 fat. Carb choices: 0.5.

Heartland Baked Beans

Starting with dry beans and slow baking are the keys to old-fashioned baked beans.

SERVINGS 12 (½ cup each)
CARB. PER SERVING 29 g or 27 g

- 1 pound dry navy beans or Great Northern beans (2⅓ cups)
- 3 ounces turkey bacon, chopped
- ¾ cup chopped onion (1 large)
- ½ cup chopped celery (1 stalk)
- 2 cloves garlic, minced
- 1 teaspoon grated fresh ginger or ½ teaspoon ground ginger
- 3 tablespoons packed brown sugar*
- ½ cup ketchup
- 2 tablespoons cider vinegar
- 1 teaspoon dry mustard
- ¼ teaspoon black pepper

Heartland
Baked Beans

1. Rinse and drain beans. In a 4- to 5-quart oven-going Dutch oven, combine beans and 8 cups *water*. Bring to boiling; reduce heat. Simmer, uncovered, for 2 minutes. Remove from heat. Cover and let stand for 1 hour. (Or place beans and 8 cups water in Dutch oven. Cover and let soak overnight.) Drain and rinse beans.
2. Return beans to Dutch oven. Stir in 8 cups fresh *water*. Bring to boiling; reduce heat. Cover and simmer for 1 to 1¼ hours or until beans are tender, stirring occasionally. Drain beans, reserving liquid.
3. Preheat oven to 300°F. In the same Dutch oven, combine turkey bacon, onion, celery, garlic, and ginger; cook over medium heat until onion is tender, stirring occasionally. Add brown sugar; cook and stir until sugar is dissolved. Stir in ketchup, vinegar, dry mustard, and pepper. Stir in drained beans and 1 cup of the reserved bean liquid. If desired, transfer mixture to a bean pot.
4. Bake, covered, about 2¼ hours or until desired consistency, stirring occasionally. If necessary, stir in additional reserved bean liquid.

*SUGAR SUBSTITUTES: Choose from Sweet'N Low Brown or Sugar Twin Granulated Brown. Follow package directions to use product amount equivalent to 3 tablespoons brown sugar.

PER SERVING: 170 cal., 2 g total fat (0 g sat. fat), 6 mg chol., 204 mg sodium, 29 g carb., 10 g fiber, 10 g pro. Exchanges: 2 starch, 0.5 lean meat. Carb choices: 2.

PER SERVING WITH SUBSTITUTE: Same as above, except 162 cal., 27 g carb.

eye-opening
breakfasts

Eating a nutritious breakfast each day is a great way to rev up your body's metabolic rate, and it's helpful in controlling your blood glucose. Whether you grab a high-fiber muffin on the way out or sit down to a protein-loaded egg bake, begin your day with a wholesome morning meal.

Herbed Turkey Strata

You can spoon out a single serving.
But for exact portions, cut the strata with a knife and
use a spatula to lift the pieces out.

SERVINGS 6 (¾ cup each)
CARB. PER SERVING 20 g

- 1 cup fresh asparagus cut into 1-inch pieces
- ¾ cup chopped red sweet pepper (1 medium)
- ⅓ cup thin wedges red onion
- 1 teaspoon canola oil
- 4 cups multigrain bread cubes (about 5½ slices)
- 2 cups shredded or cubed cooked turkey
- ½ cup low-fat cottage cheese
- 1 teaspoon snipped fresh sage or ½ teaspoon dried sage, crushed
- 1 teaspoon snipped fresh thyme or ½ teaspoon dried thyme, crushed
- 1 teaspoon snipped fresh rosemary or ½ teaspoon dried rosemary, crushed
- ¼ teaspoon salt
- 1¼ cups low-fat milk
- 1 cup refrigerated or frozen egg product, thawed, or 4 eggs, lightly beaten

1. In a large skillet, cook asparagus, sweet pepper, and onion in hot oil over medium heat about 4 minutes or until crisp-tender.

2. Grease a 2-quart square baking dish. Spread half of the bread cubes in the prepared dish. Top with turkey, asparagus mixture, cottage cheese, herbs, and salt. Top with remaining bread cubes.

3. In a medium bowl, whisk together milk and eggs. Pour evenly over the layers in the dish. Cover and chill for 2 to 24 hours.

4. Preheat oven to 325°F. Bake, uncovered, for 60 to 70 minutes or until the internal temperature registers 170°F on an instant-read thermometer. Let stand for 10 minutes before serving.

PER SERVING: 228 cal., 5 g total fat (1 g sat. fat), 39 mg chol., 394 mg sodium, 20 g carb., 5 g fiber, 26 g pro. Exchanges: 0.5 vegetable, 1 starch, 3 lean meat. Carb choices: 1.

Poached Eggs on Soft Polenta

*If you have an egg-poaching pan,
use it instead of the skillet.*

SERVINGS 4 (1 egg, ½ cup polenta mixture, and ½ cup tomato mixture each)

CARB. PER SERVING 23 g

- 1 **cup water**
- 1 **cup fat-free milk**
- ½ **cup cornmeal**
- ¼ **teaspoon salt**
- ¼ **cup finely shredded Asiago or Parmesan cheese (1 ounce)**
- ¼ **tablespoons fresh basil leaves or 1 teaspoon dried basil, crushed**
- 4 **eggs**
- 1 **small red onion, thinly sliced**
- 1 **teaspoon canola oil**
- 1 **pint grape or cherry tomatoes, halved**
- ¼ **teaspoon cracked black pepper**

1. In a small saucepan, bring the water to boiling. Meanwhile, in a medium bowl, combine milk, cornmeal, and salt. Slowly add cornmeal mixture to boiling water, stirring constantly. Cook and stir until mixture returns to boiling. Reduce heat to low. Cook for 10 to 15 minutes or until mixture is thick, stirring frequently. Stir in cheese and dried basil (if using). Place in a serving bowl; keep warm.

2. Lightly grease a large skillet. Half-fill skillet with water. Bring the water to boiling; reduce heat to simmering (bubbles should begin to break the surface of the water). Break one of the eggs into a measuring cup. Holding the lip of the cup as close to the water as possible, carefully slide egg into simmering water. Repeat with remaining eggs, allowing each egg an equal amount of space. Simmer eggs, uncovered, for 3 to 5 minutes or until the whites are completely set and yolks begin to thicken but are not hard. Remove eggs with a slotted spoon.

3. In a large skillet, cook onion in hot oil over medium heat about 5 minutes or until tender. Stir in tomatoes;

Poached Eggs
on Soft Polenta

cook and stir about 2 minutes more or until tomatoes begin to soften. Sprinkle with pepper.

4. Serve polenta topped with poached eggs and tomato mixture. Garnish with fresh basil leaves (if using).

PER SERVING: 218 cal., 9 g total fat (3 g sat. fat), 220 mg chol., 319 mg sodium, 23 g carb., 2 g fiber, 12 g pro. Exchanges: 0.5 vegetable, 1.5 starch, 1 medium-fat meat, 0.5 fat. Carb choices: 1.5.

Sweet Potato and Turkey Sausage Hash

Greek Frittata

Make sure your skillet is broilerproof before you begin—not all skillets can withstand the direct heat.

SERVINGS 4 (¼ of the frittata each)

CARB. PER SERVING 9 g

  2 cups refrigerated or frozen egg product, thawed, or 8 eggs, lightly beaten
  1 teaspoon snipped fresh oregano or ½ teaspoon dried oregano, crushed
  4 cups baby spinach
  ½ cup chopped onion (1 medium)
  2 cloves garlic, minced
  2 teaspoons canola oil
  1 tomato, chopped
  ¾ cup crumbled reduced-fat feta cheese (3 ounces)
  ¼ teaspoon black pepper

1. In a medium bowl, combine eggs and oregano; set aside.

2. In a large broilerproof skillet, cook spinach, onion, and garlic in hot oil over medium heat about 3 minutes or until onion is just tender. Add tomato; cook and stir for 1 minute more.

3. Pour the egg mixture over vegetables in the skillet. Cook over medium heat. As mixture sets, run a spatula around edge of skillet, lifting egg mixture so uncooked portion flows underneath. Continue cooking and lifting edge until mixture is almost set. Sprinkle with cheese and pepper.

4. Broil 4 to 5 inches from the heat for 1 to 2 minutes or until top is set.

PER SERVING: 157 cal., 5 g total fat (2 g sat. fat), 6 mg chol., 570 mg sodium, 9 g carb., 3 g fiber, 18 g pro. Exchanges: 1 vegetable, 2 lean meat, 0.5 fat. Carb choices: 0.5.

Sweet Potato and Turkey Sausage Hash

Roasting the potatoes allows you to cut the fat that is commonly used when pan-frying hash.

SERVINGS 4 (1 cup each)

CARB. PER SERVING 22 g

  2 medium russet potatoes, peeled (if desired) and diced
  1 medium sweet potato, peeled (if desired) and diced
     Nonstick cooking spray
  ½ of a 14-ounce ring smoked turkey sausage, halved lengthwise and sliced ½ inch thick
  ½ cup chopped green sweet pepper (1 small)
  ½ cup chopped onion (1 medium)
  1 tablespoon snipped fresh sage or 1 teaspoon dried sage, crushed
  ¼ teaspoon black pepper

1. Preheat oven to 400°F. Place russet and sweet potatoes on a 15×10×1-inch baking sheet. Lightly coat potatoes with cooking spray and toss to coat.

2. Bake about 20 minutes or until tender and lightly browned, turning once with a spatula.

3. Meanwhile, in a large nonstick skillet, cook sausage, sweet pepper, and onion for 8 to 10 minutes or until tender. Stir in sweet potato mixture, sage, and black pepper.

PER SERVING: 170 cal., 5 g total fat (1 g sat. fat), 33 mg chol., 493 mg sodium, 22 g carb., 3 g fiber, 10 g pro. Exchanges: 0.5 vegetable, 1.5 starch, 0.5 medium-fat meat. Carb choices: 1.5.

Mexican Breakfast Scramble (Migas)

A poblano is a milder form of chile than the jalapeño. Choose the pepper with the spice level you prefer.

SERVINGS 4 (1½ cups each)
CARB. PER SERVING 22 g

- 4 6-inch corn tortillas
- 2 3-ounce links cooked chicken sausage with seasoning, sliced
- 1 medium red sweet pepper, cut into bite-size strips
- 1 medium onion, halved and sliced
- 1 fresh poblano or jalapeño chile pepper, seeded and chopped*
- 2 cups refrigerated or frozen egg product, thawed, or 8 eggs, lightly beaten
- ⅛ teaspoon salt
- ¼ cup crumbled queso fresco or shredded reduced-fat Monterey jack cheese (1 ounce)

1. Preheat oven to 400°F. Place corn tortillas on a baking sheet. Bake for 6 to 8 minutes or until crisp. Break into coarse pieces; set aside.
2. In a large skillet, cook sausage, sweet pepper, onion, and chile pepper over medium heat for 6 minutes or until vegetables are tender and sausage is browned.
3. Add eggs, salt, queso fresco, and broken tortilla pieces. Cook, without stirring, until mixture begins to set on the bottom and around edge. With a spatula or large spoon, lift and fold the partially cooked egg mixture so the uncooked portion flows underneath. Continue cooking for 2 to 3 minutes or until egg mixture is cooked through but still glossy and moist. Immediately remove from heat.
***TEST KITCHEN TIP:** Because chile peppers contain volatile oils that can burn your skin and eyes, avoid direct contact with chiles as much as possible. When working with chile peppers, wear plastic or rubber gloves. If your bare hands do touch the chile peppers, wash your hands and nails well with soap and warm water.
PER SERVING: 227 cal., 5 g total fat (1 g sat. fat), 33 mg chol., 558 mg sodium, 22 g carb., 3 g fiber, 24 g pro. Exchanges: 0.5 vegetable, 1.5 starch, 2.5 lean meat. Carb choices: 1.5.

Green Eggs and Ham Breakfast Burritos

If you have regular salsa on hand, you can substitute it for the green variety.

SERVINGS 6 (1 burrito each)
CARB. PER SERVING 24 g

- 2 cups refrigerated or frozen egg product, thawed, or 8 eggs, lightly beaten
- 4 ounces cooked reduced-sodium ham, chopped
- ½ cup low-fat milk
- ¼ teaspoon black pepper
- 1 tablespoon canola oil
- 1 small zucchini, halved lengthwise and thinly sliced
- 1 tablespoon finely chopped, seeded jalapeño chile pepper*
- 6 8-inch low-carb whole wheat flour tortillas**
- 1 cup canned very low-sodium black beans, rinsed and drained
- 1 medium avocado, peeled, pitted, and sliced
- ½ cup shredded reduced-fat Monterey jack cheese (2 ounces)
- ½ cup bottled green salsa (salsa verde)

1. In a medium bowl, beat together eggs, ham, milk, and black pepper; set aside. In a large skillet, heat oil over medium heat. Add zucchini and cook about 5 minutes or until tender; remove with a slotted spoon and set aside. Add egg mixture to skillet. Cook over medium heat, without stirring, until mixture begins to set on the bottom and around edge. With a spatula or a large spoon, lift and fold the partially cooked egg mixture so the uncooked portion flows underneath. Continue cooking over medium heat for 2 to 3 minutes or until egg mixture is cooked through but still glossy and moist. Immediately remove from heat. Fold in zucchini and jalapeño.
2. On each of the tortillas, spoon some of the egg mixture, beans, avocado, cheese, and salsa verde. Fold in sides of tortillas. Roll up tightly. Serve warm.
***TEST KITCHEN TIP:** Because chile peppers contain volatile oils that can burn your skin and eyes, avoid direct contact with chiles as much as possible. When working with chile peppers, wear plastic or rubber gloves. If your bare hands do touch the chile peppers, wash your hands and nails well with soap and warm water.
****TEST KITCHEN TIP:** Stack tortillas and wrap in foil. Heat in a 350°F oven for 10 minutes.
PER SERVING: 270 cal., 10 g total fat (2 g sat. fat), 16 mg chol., 646 mg sodium, 24 g carb., 12 g fiber, 20 g pro. Exchanges: 0.5 vegetable, 1.5 starch, 2 lean meat, 1 fat. Carb choices: 1.5.

Green Eggs and Ham
Breakfast Burritos

Poblano Tofu Scramble

This Southwestern-style scramble is great for breakfast or a light supper. Don't skip the lime juice and tomatoes—they add a delightfully fresh note.

SERVINGS 4 (1 cup each)
CARB. PER SERVING 11 g

- 1 16- to 18-ounce package extra-firm water-packed tofu (fresh bean curd)
- 1 tablespoon olive oil
- 1 or 2 fresh poblano chile peppers, seeded and chopped* (½ to 1 cup total)
- ½ cup chopped onion (1 medium)
- 2 cloves garlic, minced
- 1 teaspoon chili powder
- ½ teaspoon ground cumin
- ½ teaspoon dried oregano, crushed
- ¼ teaspoon salt
- 1 tablespoon lime juice
- 2 roma tomatoes, seeded and chopped (about 1 cup)
  Fresh cilantro sprigs (optional)

1. Drain tofu; cut tofu in half and pat each half with paper towels until well dried. Crumble the tofu into a medium bowl. Set aside.

2. In a large nonstick skillet, heat olive oil over medium-high heat. Add poblano(s), onion, and garlic; cook and stir for 4 minutes. Add chili powder, cumin, oregano, and salt. Cook and stir for 30 seconds more.

3. Add crumbled tofu to poblano mixture. Reduce heat; cook for 5 minutes, gently stirring occasionally. Just before serving, drizzle with lime juice and fold in tomatoes. If desired, garnish with fresh cilantro.

***TEST KITCHEN TIP:** Because chile peppers contain volatile oils that can burn your skin and eyes, avoid direct contact with chiles as much as possible. When working with chile peppers, wear plastic or rubber gloves. If your bare hands do touch the chile peppers, wash your hands and nails well with soap and warm water.

PER SERVING: 182 cal., 10 g total fat (1 g sat. fat), 0 mg chol., 158 mg sodium, 11 g carb., 3 g fiber, 13 g pro. Exchanges: 0.5 vegetable, 0.5 starch, 1.5 medium-fat meat, 0.5 fat. Carb choices: 1.

Spiced Bran Muffins
with Dried Apricots

Italian Egg Sandwiches

*If you use bottled roasted red peppers, drain the peppers
on paper towels before cutting them into strips.*

SERVINGS 4 (1 sandwich each)

CARB. PER SERVING 29 g

Nonstick cooking spray

1 cup refrigerated or frozen egg product, thawed, or
4 eggs, lightly beaten

¼ teaspoon Italian seasoning, crushed

⅛ teaspoon salt

4 whole grain English muffins, split and toasted

2 tablespoons bottled reduced-fat or regular basil pesto

4 ounces cooked chicken breast, shredded

¼ cup roasted red sweet pepper, cut into bite-size strips

1. Lightly coat a large nonstick skillet with cooking
spray. In a small bowl, combine eggs, Italian seasoning,
and salt. Heat skillet over medium heat; pour in egg
mixture. Cook, without stirring, until mixture begins to
set on the bottom and around edge. With a spatula or a
large spoon, lift and fold the partially cooked egg
mixture so the uncooked portion flows underneath.
Continue cooking for 2 to 3 minutes or until egg
mixture is cooked through but still glossy and moist.
Immediately remove from heat.

2. Spread cut sides of English muffins with pesto. Top
bottom halves of muffins with egg mixture, chicken,
roasted red pepper, and muffin tops. Serve warm.

PER SERVING: 243 cal., 5 g total fat (1 g sat. fat), 26 mg chol.,
588 mg sodium, 29 g carb., 5 g fiber, 22 g pro. Exchanges:
2 starch, 2.5 lean meat. Carb choices: 2.

Spiced Bran Muffins with Dried Apricots

*You can swap dried cranberries, dried cherries,
or raisins for the dried apricots.*

SERVINGS 24 (1 muffin each)

CARB. PER SERVING 27 g

1 cup boiling water

3 cups whole bran cereal (not flakes)

2½ cups white whole wheat flour

½ cup packed brown sugar*

2 teaspoons baking powder

1 teaspoon ground cinnamon

1 teaspoon ground ginger

¼ teaspoon ground cloves

½ teaspoon baking soda

½ teaspoon salt

2 cups buttermilk

1 large very ripe banana, mashed (¾ cup)

½ cup refrigerated or frozen egg product, thawed, or
2 eggs, lightly beaten

¼ cup canola oil

½ cup snipped dried apricots

1. Preheat oven to 400°F. Grease twenty-four 2½-inch
muffin cups or line with paper bake cups. Spray paper
cups, if using, with *nonstick cooking spray*; set aside. In a
medium bowl, pour boiling water over cereal. Stir to
moisten cereal; set aside.

2. In another medium bowl, combine flour, brown
sugar, baking powder, cinnamon, ginger, cloves, baking
soda, and salt. In a large bowl, combine buttermilk,
banana, eggs, and oil. Stir cereal and flour mixtures into
buttermilk mixture just until moistened. Stir in apricots.

3. Spoon batter into prepared muffin cups, filling each
three-fourths full. Bake about 20 minutes or until a
wooden toothpick inserted in centers comes out clean.
Cool in muffin cups on a wire rack for 5 minutes.
Remove from muffin cups; serve warm.

*SUGAR SUBSTITUTES: We do not recommend sugar
substitutes for this recipe.

PER SERVING: 130 cal., 3 g total fat (0 g sat. fat), 1 mg chol.,
215 mg sodium, 27 g carb., 6 g fiber, 4 g pro. Exchanges:
1.5 starch, 0.5 carb., 0.5 fat. Carb choices: 2.

Chocolate and Ginger Spiked Scones

For tender, flaky layers, gently knead the dough just until nearly smooth.

SERVINGS 10 (1 wedge each)
CARB. PER SERVING 29 g or 26 g

    2   cups all-purpose flour
    ¼   cup sugar*
    1½ teaspoons baking powder
    ½   teaspoon ground ginger
    ⅛   teaspoon salt
    ¼   cup cold butter, cut up
    ¼   cup chopped bittersweet or semisweet chocolate
    2   tablespoons chopped crystallized ginger
    2   egg whites, lightly beaten
    ⅓   cup fat-free milk
        Nonstick cooking spray
        Fat-free milk

1. Preheat oven to 400°F. In a medium bowl, stir together flour, sugar, baking powder, ground ginger, and salt. Using a pastry blender, cut in butter until mixture resembles coarse crumbs. Stir in chocolate and crystallized ginger. Make a well in the center of the flour mixture.

2. In a small bowl, stir together egg whites and the ⅓ cup milk. Add milk mixture all at once to flour mixture. Stir just until moistened. Turn dough out onto a lightly floured surface. Knead dough by folding and gently pressing it for 10 to 12 strokes until nearly smooth.

3. Divide dough in half. Roll or pat each dough half into a 5-inch circle. Cut each circle into five wedges. Lightly coat a baking sheet with cooking spray; place wedges on baking sheet. Brush with additional milk. Bake about 15 minutes or until bottoms are browned. Serve warm.

*SUGAR SUBSTITUTES: Choose from Splenda Sugar Blend for Baking or Sun Crystals Granulated Blend. Follow package directions to use product amount equivalent to ¼ cup sugar.

PER SERVING: 187 cal., 6 g total fat (4 g sat. fat), 13 mg chol., 133 mg sodium, 29 g carb., 1 g fiber, 4 g pro. Exchanges: 1 starch, 1 carb., 1 fat. Carb choices: 2.

PER SERVING WITH SUBSTITUTE: Same as above, except 180 cal., 26 g carb.

Pear Hazelnut Coffee Cake

Use a sharp paring knife to cut a green- or red-skin pear into thin slices.

SERVINGS 10 (1 wedge each)
CARB. PER SERVING 32 g or 27 g

        Nonstick cooking spray
    1   medium pear
    ½   cup sugar*
    ¼   cup canola oil
    ¾   cup fat-free milk
    ⅓   cup refrigerated or frozen egg product, thawed, or 2 egg whites, lightly beaten
    ½   teaspoon vanilla
    ⅔   cup all-purpose flour
    ½   cup whole wheat flour
    2   teaspoons baking powder
    1   teaspoon finely shredded lemon peel
    ½   teaspoon ground nutmeg
    1¼ cups quick-cooking rolled oats
    2   tablespoons chopped hazelnuts or sliced almonds

1. Preheat oven to 375°F. Lightly coat a 9×1½-inch round baking pan with cooking spray; set aside. Core and slice the pear; set aside.

2. In a large bowl, stir together sugar and oil. Add milk, egg, and vanilla. Beat with an electric mixer on medium speed for 1 minute.

3. In a small bowl, combine all-purpose flour, whole wheat flour, baking powder, lemon peel, and nutmeg. Add to beaten mixture; beat until combined. Stir in oats. Spoon into prepared pan. Arrange sliced pears over batter. Sprinkle with hazelnuts.

4. Bake for 35 to 40 minutes or until a toothpick inserted near the center of the cake portion comes out clean. Cool in pan on a wire rack for 30 minutes. Cut into wedges. Serve warm.

*SUGAR SUBSTITUTES: Choose from Splenda Sugar Blend for Baking or Sun Crystals Granulated Blend. Follow package directions to use product amount equivalent to ½ cup sugar.

PER SERVING: 207 cal., 7 g total fat (1 g sat. fat), 0 mg chol., 97 mg sodium, 32 g carb., 3 g fiber, 5 g pro. Exchanges: 1 starch, 1 carb., 1.5 fat. Carb choices: 2.

PER SERVING WITH SUBSTITUTE: Same as above, except 192 cal., 27 g carb.

Pear Hazelnut
Coffee Cake

Herbed Crepes with Grilled Stone Fruits

Pick the season's best fruit selection to showcase in these tender crepes.

SERVINGS 7 (3 crepes each)
CARB. PER SERVING 32 g

½ cup refrigerated or frozen egg product, thawed, or 2 eggs, lightly beaten
1½ cups low-fat milk
½ cup all-purpose flour
½ cup whole wheat flour
1 tablespoon canola oil
1 tablespoon snipped fresh basil
½ teaspoon snipped fresh thyme
⅛ teaspoon salt
Nonstick cooking spray
6 cups sliced, pitted stone fruits, such as peaches, nectarines, apricots, and/or plums
⅔ cup plain low-fat Greek yogurt
1 tablespoon honey

1. In a blender or food processor, combine eggs, milk, flours, oil, basil, thyme, and salt. Cover and blend or process until smooth.
2. Lightly coat an 8-inch skillet with cooking spray; heat over medium heat. Spoon in 2 tablespoons batter; lift and tilt skillet to spread batter. Brown on one side for 30 to 60 seconds. Turn and cook for 10 to 15 seconds on the other side. (Or cook on a crepe maker according to manufacturer's directions.) Invert the crepe onto a sheet of waxed paper. Repeat with remaining batter, coating skillet occasionally with cooking spray.
3. Lightly coat a grill pan with cooking spray. Heat grill pan over medium heat. Grill sliced stone fruit, in two or three batches, for 3 to 4 minutes until warmed through and lightly browned, turning to brown and heat evenly.
4. In a small bowl, combine Greek yogurt and honey. Spread each crepe with 1 teaspoon of the yogurt mixture, top with ⅓ cup fruit, and roll up. Repeat with remaining crepes, yogurt mixture, and fruit.

MAKE-AHEAD DIRECTIONS: Crepes can be made up to 24 hours ahead of time and refrigerated, stacked between sheets of waxed paper, until ready to use, or frozen for up to 4 months in a freezer container. Thaw at room temperature 1 hour before using.

PER SERVING: 187 cal., 4 g total fat (1 g sat. fat), 4 mg chol., 106 mg sodium, 32 g carb., 3 g fiber, 9 g pro. Exchanges: 1 fruit, 0.5 starch, 0.5 carb., 1 lean meat, 0.5 fat. Carb choices: 2.

Cornmeal Waffles with Blueberry Compote

Cut waffles into sticks for fun and to make the single waffle serving look generous.

SERVINGS 8 (½ of a 6-inch waffle and 3 tablespoons blueberry compote each)
CARB. PER SERVING 31 g or 28 g

¾ cup all-purpose flour
½ cup cornmeal
2 tablespoons packed brown sugar*
1 teaspoon baking powder
¼ teaspoon salt
1 cup buttermilk
½ cup fat-free milk
3 tablespoons canola oil
2 egg yolks
½ teaspoon vanilla
2 egg whites
1 recipe Blueberry Compote (below)

1. In a large bowl, combine flour, cornmeal, brown sugar, baking powder, and salt.
2. In a medium bowl, combine buttermilk, milk, oil, egg yolks, and vanilla. Whisk to combine. Whisk mixture into flour mixture until just combined (do not overmix).
3. In a large bowl, beat egg whites with an electric mixer on medium-high speed until soft peaks form. Fold egg whites gently into batter.
4. Pour about ¾ cup batter into grids of a preheated, well-greased waffle baker. Close lid quickly; do not open until done. Bake according to manufacturer's directions. Repeat with remaining batter. Serve warm with Blueberry Compote.

BLUEBERRY COMPOTE: In a medium saucepan, bring 1 cup apple juice and 1 tablespoon lemon juice to boiling. Reduce heat and simmer, uncovered, for 8 to 10 minutes or until reduced by half. Stir in 2 cups fresh blueberries, ½ teaspoon finely shredded lemon peel, and ⅛ teaspoon ground cinnamon. Return to boiling; reduce heat. Simmer, uncovered, for 5 minutes more.

***SUGAR SUBSTITUTES:** Choose from Sweet'N Low Brown or Sugar Twin Granulated Brown. Follow package directions to use product amount equivalent to 2 tablespoons brown sugar.

PER SERVING: 204 cal., 7 g total fat (1 g sat. fat), 54 mg chol., 176 mg sodium, 31 g carb., 2 g fiber, 5 g pro. Exchanges: 1 starch, 1 carb., 1.5 fat. Carb choices: 2.

PER SERVING WITH SUBSTITUTE: Same as above, except 191 cal., 28 g carb.

Spiced Oatmeal Pancakes
with Sautéed Apples

Spiced Oatmeal Pancakes with Sautéed Apples

Choose tart cooking apples to make the topping.

SERVINGS 8 (4 mini pancakes, ¼ cup apple mixture, and 2 tablespoons syrup each)

CARB. PER SERVING 30 g

½ cup regular (not quick-cooking) rolled oats
¾ cup white whole wheat flour
1½ teaspoons brown sugar
1½ teaspoons baking powder
¼ teaspoon apple pie spice
1 cup fat-free milk
⅓ cup refrigerated or frozen egg product, thawed
2 tablespoons canola oil
1 recipe Sautéed Apples (right)
1 cup sugar-free maple-flavor syrup, warmed

1. Place rolled oats in a blender or food processor. Cover and blend or process until very fine, resembling flour. In a large bowl, combine ground oats, flour, brown sugar, baking powder, apple pie spice, and dash *salt*.

2. In a medium bowl, combine milk, egg product, and oil. Add to flour mixture and whisk just until combined (mixture should be lumpy).

3. For each pancake, pour about 1 tablespoon batter onto a hot, lightly greased griddle or heavy skillet. Cook over medium heat for 1 to 2 minutes on each side or until pancakes are golden brown, turning to second side when pancakes have bubbly surfaces and edges are slightly dry. Serve warm with Sautéed Apples and maple syrup.

SAUTÉED APPLES: In a large skillet, cook 2 cored, sliced cooking apples in 2 teaspoons hot canola oil over medium-high heat until apples are golden brown. Sprinkle with ¼ teaspoon apple pie spice.

PER SERVING: 175 cal., 5 g total fat (0 g sat. fat), 1 mg chol., 169 mg sodium, 30 g carb., 3 g fiber, 5 g pro. Exchanges: 1.5 starch, 0.5 carb., 1 fat. Carb choices: 2.

QUICK TIP ◖
Top each serving with
one type of fresh berry or
use a combo of all three—
blueberries, raspberries,
and blackberries.

Spiced Apple
Berry Oatmeal

Spiced Apple Berry Oatmeal

*A sprinkling of toasted pecans adds crunch
to this wholesome morning meal.*

SERVINGS 6 (¾ cup each)

CARB. PER SERVING 34 g

- 2 cups water
- 1¾ cups apple juice
- 1 cup steel-cut oats
- 1 medium apple, cored and chopped
- ½ teaspoon apple pie spice
- ¼ teaspoon salt
- ½ cup fresh blueberries, raspberries, or blackberries
- 1 cup fat-free milk
- ¼ cup chopped pecans or almonds, toasted (optional)

1. In a large saucepan, bring the water and apple juice to boiling. Stir in oats, apple, apple pie spice, and salt. Return mixture to a simmer; reduce heat. Simmer, uncovered, stirring occasionally, about 30 minutes or until desired consistency and oats are tender. Top each serving with berries. Serve with milk and, if desired, pecans.

PER SERVING: 164 cal., 2 g total fat (0 g sat. fat), 1 mg chol., 120 mg sodium, 34 g carb., 4 g fiber, 6 g pro. Exchanges: 0.5 fruit, 1.5 starch. Carb choices: 2.

Mix-and-Match
Banana Berry
Smoothie

Mix-and-Match Banana Berry Smoothie

*Frozen berries are a good option to the fresh
in this creamy, fruit-filled drinkable breakfast.*

SERVINGS 4 (1 cup smoothie, 1 tablespoon granola, and 1 tablespoon additional berries each)

CARB. PER SERVING 34 g

- 1 medium banana, cut up
- 1 cup fresh blueberries, raspberries, blackberries, and/or strawberries
- 1 cup frozen unsweetened peach slices
- ½ cup pomegranate, cherry, blueberry, or cranberry juice
- ½ cup plain or vanilla low-fat soymilk
- 1 cup ice cubes
- ¼ cup low-fat granola
- ¼ cup fresh blueberries, raspberries, blackberries, and/or strawberries

1. In a blender, combine banana, 1 cup berries, peaches, fruit juice, and soymilk. Cover and blend until smooth. With the motor running, add ice cubes, one at a time, through the opening in the lid until combined and slushy. Top each serving with 1 tablespoon each of the granola and the additional berries.

PER SERVING: 145 cal., 1 g total fat (0 g sat. fat), 0 mg chol., 32 mg sodium, 34 g carb., 3 g fiber, 2 g pro. Exchanges: 1.5 fruit, 0.5 carb. Carb choices: 2.

good-for-you
snacks

Filling in between hearty meals with a nutritious snack is a great way to keep your blood glucose levels in check. Make yourself one of these flavorful munchies when you need a little something to nibble on. You may be surprised that something so healthful tastes so good.

Caponata

If you have extra, use a bit of this Italian-style relish as a sandwich spread.

SERVINGS 6 (½ cup mixture and 6 pita crisps each)
CARB. PER SERVING 28 g

- 1 medium eggplant, halved lengthwise
- 1 medium red sweet pepper, halved and seeded
- 1 medium red onion, cut into wedges
- 2 cloves garlic
-    Olive oil nonstick cooking spray
- 2 medium roma tomatoes, chopped
- 2 tablespoons red wine vinegar
- 2 teaspoons capers, drained
- 1 teaspoon honey
- ½ teaspoon Italian seasoning, crushed
- 1 recipe Pita Crisps (below)

1. Preheat oven to 450°F. Line a baking sheet with foil. Place the eggplant, cut sides up, on the baking sheet. Place sweet pepper halves, cut sides down, on baking sheet. Place onion wedges and garlic on baking sheet. Lightly coat vegetables with cooking spray. Roast, uncovered, about 20 minutes or until vegetables are tender and sweet pepper skin is lightly charred. Place vegetables in a bowl; cover and let stand for 10 minutes.
2. Remove and discard skins from eggplant and sweet pepper. Chop vegetables or place vegetables in a food processor and pulse with several on/off turns until chopped.
3. In a large bowl, combine roasted vegetables, tomatoes, vinegar, capers, honey, and Italian seasoning. Serve Caponata with Pita Crisps.
PITA CRISPS: Preheat oven to 400°F. Cut 3 whole wheat pita bread rounds in half horizontally. Cut each half into 6 wedges. Place wedges on a baking sheet. Lightly coat wedges with cooking spray. Bake about 6 minutes or until lightly browned and crisp.
PER SERVING: 132 cal., 1 g total fat (0 g sat. fat), 0 mg chol., 204 mg sodium, 28 g carb., 7 g fiber, 5 g pro. Exchanges: 1 vegetable, 1.5 starch. Carb choices: 2.

Rosemary
White Bean Dip

Rosemary White Bean Dip

*If you need to monitor your sodium intake, substitute
1¾ cups cooked cannellini beans for the canned variety.*
SERVINGS 11 (2 tablespoons each)
CARB. PER SERVING 6 g

- 1 15-ounce can no-salt-added cannellini beans (white kidney beans), rinsed and drained
- 2 tablespoons lemon juice
- 2 tablespoons olive oil
- 1 tablespoon snipped fresh parsley
- 1 teaspoon snipped fresh rosemary
- 2 cloves garlic
- ⅛ teaspoon black pepper
- ⅓ cup chopped pitted ripe olives
  Fresh parsley sprigs (optional)
  Assorted vegetable dippers

1. In a food processor, combine beans, lemon juice, olive oil, snipped parsley, rosemary, garlic, and pepper. Cover and process until just smooth. Stir in olives.
2. To serve, garnish with parsley sprigs, if desired, and serve with vegetable dippers.
PER SERVING: 58 cal., 3 g total fat (0 g sat. fat), 0 mg chol., 48 mg sodium, 6 g carb., 2 g fiber, 2 g pro. Exchanges: 0.5 starch, 0.5 fat. Carb choices: 0.5.

Roasted Poblano Guacamole

*A poblano may seem quite large in comparison to other
fresh chile peppers, but it is also mild in flavor.*
SERVINGS 4 (⅓ cup guacamole and 9 tortilla chips each)
CARB. PER SERVING 27 g

- 1 medium fresh poblano chile pepper
- ½ of a medium sweet onion, cut into ½-inch slices
- 2 small avocados, halved, seeded, and peeled
- 2 tablespoons lime juice
- ½ teaspoon ground cumin
- ¼ teaspoon salt
- 1 recipe Spiced Tortilla Chips (below)

1. Preheat oven to 425°F. Halve poblano; remove seeds and membranes (see tip, page 127). Place onion slices and poblano pepper, cut sides down, on a foil-lined baking sheet. Roast about 20 minutes or until poblano skin and onion are lightly charred. Wrap the pepper in the foil; let stand for 20 to 30 minutes or until cool enough to handle. Peel skin off pepper. Chop poblano and onion.
2. In a medium bowl, mash avocados. Stir in poblano, onion, lime juice, cumin, and salt.
3. Serve guacamole with Spiced Tortilla Chips.
SPICED TORTILLA CHIPS: Preheat to 400°F. Cut six 6-inch corn tortillas into 6 wedges each. Place wedges on a baking sheet. Coat lightly with nonstick cooking spray. Sprinkle with ¼ teaspoon chili powder. Bake for 8 to 10 minutes or until crisp and edges are lightly browned.
PER SERVING: 188 cal., 8 g total fat (1 g sat. fat), 0 mg chol., 174 mg sodium, 27 g carb., 6 g fiber, 4 g pro. Exchanges: 2 starch, 1 fat. Carb choices: 2.

Lima Bean Hummus

*Store this creamy dip in the refrigerator
and give it a quick stir before serving.*
SERVINGS 8 (¼ cup hummus and 6 pita wedges each)
CARB. PER SERVING 25 g

- 1 10-ounce package frozen Fordhook lima beans
- 1 6-ounce carton plain low-fat yogurt
- 2 medium shallots, peeled and coarsely chopped (¼ cup)
- 2 tablespoons lemon juice
- 1 tablespoon honey
- 1 tablespoon chopped fresh chives
- 2 cloves garlic

Lima Bean Hummus

½ teaspoon black pepper
¼ teaspoon salt
3 whole grain pita bread rounds
Nonstick cooking spray

1. In a medium saucepan, cook lima beans in a small amount of boiling water for 10 minutes; drain.
2. In a food processor, combine lima beans, yogurt, shallots, lemon juice, honey, chives, garlic, pepper, and salt. Cover and process until smooth.

3. Preheat oven to 400°F. Cut pita bread rounds in half horizontally. Cut each half into eight wedges. Place wedges on a baking sheet. Lightly coat wedges with cooking spray. Bake about 6 minutes or until lightly browned and crisp.
4. Serve hummus with pita crisps.
PER SERVING: 129 cal., 1 g total fat (0 g sat. fat), 1 mg chol., 237 mg sodium, 25 g carb., 4 g fiber, 6 g pro. Exchanges: 1 vegetable, 1.5 starch. Carb choices: 2.

Sweet Potato Wedges
with Honey Mustard
Dipping Sauce

Watermelon, Mango,
and Jicama Salsa

Black Bean Salsa

Smart Snacking

Healthful snacks can boost energy
and prevent overeating at meals. Use
these strategies when you feel the
urge to munch.

1. **Seek out foods** that are
    naturally high in fiber, such
    as vegetables and fruits
    with the peel on, if edible.

2. **When choosing crackers,**
    cereals, and bread
    products, go with the whole
    grain variety.

3. **Stick with lower-fat
    options** when nibbling on
    yogurt, cheese, and other
    dairy products.

4. **Pair protein-rich lean
    meat** or lower-fat dairy
    products with complex-
    carbohydrate-containing
    foods such as cereals,
    crackers, and tortillas.

5. **Instead of mindlessly
    nibbling** from a box, pour
    your snack into a measuring
    cup to ensure you're eating
    a single serving.

6. **Eat slowly,** allowing
    yourself to savor the snack
    and make it more satisfying.

Black Bean Salsa

Not only is this salsa the perfect dipper, it also makes a terrific topper. Spoon it over grilled pork, chicken, or salmon.

SERVINGS 10 (⅓ cup salsa and 1 ounce baked tortilla chips each)

CARB. PER SERVING 8 g

- 1 15-ounce can black beans, rinsed and drained
- 1½ cups chopped and seeded cucumber (1 medium)
- ½ cup chopped tomato (1 medium)
- ½ cup sliced green onions (4)
- ¼ cup lime juice
- 1 tablespoon snipped fresh cilantro
- 1 tablespoon olive oil
- ½ teaspoon ground cumin
- ⅛ teaspoon salt
- ⅛ teaspoon cayenne pepper
  Baked tortilla chips

1. In a medium bowl, combine beans, cucumber, tomato, green onions, lime juice, cilantro, oil, cumin, salt, and cayenne pepper. Cover and chill for 4 to 24 hours.

2. Serve salsa with tortilla chips.

PER SERVING: 47 cal., 2 g total fat (0 g sat. fat), 0 mg chol., 136 mg sodium, 8 g carb., 2 g fiber, 3 g pro. Exchanges: 0.5 starch, 0.5 fat. Carb choices: 0.5.

Watermelon, Mango, and Jicama Salsa

This exotic salsa makes 24 servings for a simple and sassy party appetizer.

SERVINGS 24 (¼ cup salsa and 1 ounce baked tortilla chips each)

CARB. PER SERVING 28 g

- 3 cups chopped, seeded watermelon
- 1½ cups peeled and chopped jicama
- 1 cup peeled, pitted, and chopped mango
- 2 tablespoons chopped green onion (1)
- 1 medium fresh jalapeño chile pepper, seeded and finely chopped*
- 1 tablespoon snipped fresh cilantro
- 1 tablespoon lime juice
- ⅛ teaspoon cayenne pepper
  Baked tortilla chips

1. In a medium bowl, combine watermelon, jicama, mango, green onion, jalapeño pepper, cilantro, lime juice, and cayenne pepper. If desired, cover and chill for up to 24 hours.

2. Serve salsa with tortilla chips.

*TEST KITCHEN TIP: Because chile peppers contain volatile oils that can burn your skin and eyes, avoid direct contact with chiles as much as possible. When working with chile peppers, wear plastic or rubber gloves. If your bare hands do touch the chile peppers, wash your hands and nails well with soap and warm water.

PER SERVING: 126 cal., 1 g total fat (0 g sat. fat), 0 mg chol., 201 mg sodium, 28 g carb., 2 g fiber, 3 g pro. Exchanges: 1 starch, 1 carb. Carb choices: 2.

Sweet Potato Wedges with Honey Mustard Dipping Sauce

For a complete meal, pair this hearty snack with slices of roasted turkey breast and a fresh green salad.

SERVINGS 4 (7 or 8 potato wedges and 2 teaspoons sauce each)

CARB. PER SERVING 29 g

- 1½ pounds sweet potatoes, peeled and cut lengthwise into ½-inch-thick wedges
- 1 cup water
- 1 tablespoon olive oil
- ½ teaspoon paprika
- ⅛ teaspoon salt
- 1 recipe Honey Mustard Dipping Sauce *(below)*

1. Preheat broiler. In a 2-quart microwave-safe baking dish, combine sweet potatoes and the water. Cover with vented plastic wrap. Microwave on 100 percent power (high) for 6 to 8 minutes or until nearly tender, rearranging once halfway through cooking. Drain well.

2. Brush sweet potatoes with olive oil. Sprinkle sweet potatoes with paprika and salt.

3. Place sweet potatoes on the greased unheated rack of a broiler pan. Broil 4 inches from the heat for 4 minutes, turning once halfway through broiling.

4. Serve sweet potato wedges with Honey Mustard Dipping Sauce.

HONEY MUSTARD DIPPING SAUCE: In a small bowl, combine 1 tablespoon Dijon-style mustard and 1 tablespoon honey.

PER SERVING: 156 cal., 3 g total fat (0 g sat. fat), 0 mg chol., 232 mg sodium, 29 g carb., 4 g fiber, 2 g pro. Exchanges: 2 starch. Carb choices: 2.

Sweet Yogurt
Fruit Dip

Celery with Confetti Cream Cheese

*Use a rubber spatula to fold and stir
the chopped vegetables into the cream cheese.*

SERVINGS 6 (¼ cup dip and 2 celery stalks each)

CARB. PER SERVING 6 g

- 1 8-ounce container whipped cream cheese
- ¼ cup finely chopped carrot
- ¼ cup finely chopped roma tomato
- 1 tablespoon finely chopped Kalamata olives
- 1 tablespoon chopped fresh basil
- ½ teaspoon finely shredded lemon peel
- ¼ teaspoon cracked black pepper
- 12 stalks celery

1. In a mixing bowl, beat cream cheese with an electric mixer on medium to high speed for 30 seconds. Stir in carrot, tomato, olives, basil, lemon peel, and pepper.
2. Serve dip with celery sticks.

PER SERVING: 90 cal., 6 g total fat (4 g sat. fat), 18 mg chol., 261 mg sodium, 6 g carb., 2 g fiber, 4 g pro. Exchanges: 1 vegetable, 1 fat. Carb choices: 0.5.

Sweet Yogurt Fruit Dip

*If you need to cut up the fruit ahead,
brush the apple and pear slices with a little
lemon juice to keep them from browning.*

SERVINGS 6 (2 tablespoons dip and ½ cup fruit each)

CARB. PER SERVING 14 g

- 1 6- to 7-ounce carton plain low-fat Greek yogurt
- 1 tablespoon maple syrup
- ¼ teaspoon ground cinnamon
- ⅛ teaspoon ground nutmeg
  Dash ground cloves
- 1 medium apple, cored and cut into wedges
- 1 medium pear, cored and cut into wedges
- 1 cup strawberries

1. In a small bowl, combine yogurt, maple syrup, cinnamon, nutmeg, and cloves. If desired, sprinkle with additional ground cinnamon.
2. Serve dip with apple wedges, pear wedges, and whole strawberries.

PER SERVING: 67 cal., 1 g total fat (0 g sat. fat), 1 mg chol., 10 mg sodium, 14 g carb., 2 g fiber, 3 g pro. Exchanges: 0.5 fruit, 0.5 carb. Carb choices: 1.

Turkey-Vegetable "Sushi"

Look for slices of turkey without rips or tears.

SERVINGS 8 (three 1-inch slices each)

CARB. PER SERVING 2 g

- ½ of an 8-ounce package reduced-fat cream cheese (Neufchâtel), softened
- 8 slices deli roasted turkey
- 2 teaspoons snipped fresh dillweed or ½ teaspoon dried dillweed
- 1 medium carrot, coarsely shredded
- ½ cup coarsely shredded zucchini
- ½ cup finely chopped red sweet pepper

1. Carefully spread cream cheese onto each slice of turkey. Sprinkle with dillweed and top with vegetables. Tightly roll up each turkey slice. Cover and chill rolls for 1 hour or until ready to serve. Cut rolls crosswise into 1-inch slices.

PER SERVING: 51 cal., 3 g total fat (2 g sat. fat), 15 mg chol., 154 mg sodium, 2 g carb., 0 g fiber, 3 g pro. Exchanges: 0.5 lean meat, 0.5 fat. Carb choices: 0.

Turkey-Vegetable "Sushi"

Cinnamon Popcorn

Fiery Snack Mix

Cinnamon Popcorn

A spritz of butter-flavor nonstick cooking spray takes the place of a drizzle of butter and saves you from lots of fat.

SERVINGS 4 (2 cups each)

CARB. PER SERVING 15 g or 13 g

- 8 cups popped popcorn
- 2 teaspoons sugar*
- ½ teaspoon ground cinnamon
  Butter-flavor nonstick cooking spray

1. Preheat oven to 350°F. Spread popcorn in a shallow roasting pan. In a small bowl, combine sugar and cinnamon. Lightly coat popcorn with cooking spray; toss to coat evenly. Sprinkle popcorn with sugar-cinnamon mixture; toss again to coat evenly. Bake about 5 minutes or just until crisp. Store in an airtight container for up 24 hours.

*****SUGAR SUBSTITUTES:** Choose from Splenda granular, Equal Spoonful or packets, or Sweet'N Low bulk or packets. Follow package directions to use product amount equivalent to 2 teaspoons sugar.

PER SERVING: 72 cal., 1 g total fat (0 g sat. fat), 0 mg chol., 1 mg sodium, 15 g carb., 2 g fiber, 2 g pro. Exchanges: 1 starch. Carb choices: 1.

PER SERVING WITH SUBSTITUTE: Same as above, except 63 cal., 13 g carb.

Fiery Snack Mix

Crisp mixed vegetable sticks come in a mix of potato, tomato, and spinach flavors. Look for them in the chip aisle.

SERVINGS 20 (½ cup each)

CARB. PER SERVING 13 g

- 4 cups crisp mixed vegetable sticks
- 2 cups round toasted oat cereal
- 2 cups bite-size corn square cereal
- 1¾ cups pretzel sticks
- ½ cup whole almonds
- 1 teaspoon packed brown sugar*
- 1 teaspoon paprika
- ½ teaspoon ground ancho or pasilla chile pepper or chili powder
- ½ teaspoon ground cumin
- ¼ teaspoon cayenne pepper
- ¼ teaspoon salt
  Olive oil nonstick cooking spray

1. Preheat oven to 300°F. In a roasting pan, combine vegetable sticks, cereals, pretzel sticks, and almonds. In a small bowl, combine brown sugar, paprika, ancho chile pepper, cumin, cayenne pepper, and salt. Lightly coat cereal mixture with cooking spray; toss to coat evenly. Sprinkle cereal mixture with spice mixture; toss again to coat evenly.

2. Bake for 18 to 20 minutes or until toasted, stirring twice. Spread mixture on a large piece of foil to cool. Store in an airtight container for up to 1 week.

*SUGAR SUBSTITUTES: Choose from Sweet'N Low Brown or Sugar Twin Granulated Brown. Follow package directions to use product amount equivalent to 1 teaspoon brown sugar.

PER SERVING: 92 cal., 3 g total fat (0 g sat. fat), 0 mg chol., 214 mg sodium, 13 g carb., 1 g fiber, 2 g pro. Exchanges: 1 starch, 0.5 fat. Carb choices: 1.

PER SERVING WITH SUBSTITUTE: Same as above, except 91 cal.

Watermelon-Kiwi Pops

When shopping for kiwifruits, select ones that yield to gentle pressure. If the fruit is not quite ripe, let it stand at room temperature for a day or two.

SERVINGS 8 (1 pop each)
CARB. PER SERVING 17 g or 14 g

¼ cup water
2 tablespoons sugar*
2 cups seedless watermelon cubes
8 5-ounce paper cups
8 wooden frozen dessert sticks
8 kiwifruits, peeled and cut up

1. In a small bowl, stir together the water and sugar until sugar is dissolved. In a blender, combine watermelon cubes and 1 tablespoon of the sugar-water mixture. Cover and blend until very smooth. Divide mixture among paper cups. Cover tops with foil. Cut a slit in the center of the foil on each cup; insert a wooden stick in each slit. Place cups on a small baking sheet. Freeze for 1 to 2 hours or until thick and slushy.

2. In a blender, combine cut-up kiwifruits and the remaining sugar-water mixture. Cover and blend until very smooth. Remove foil from paper cups. Pour kiwifruit mixture evenly over watermelon layer in cups. Freeze for at least 4 hours or until completely solid.

3. To serve, peel away the paper cups.

*SUGAR SUBSTITUTES: Choose from Splenda granular, Equal Spoonful or packets, or Sweet'N Low bulk or packets. Follow package directions to use product amount equivalent to 2 tablespoons sugar.

PER POP: 70 cal., 0 g total fat, 0 mg chol., 3 mg sodium, 17 g carb., 2 g fiber, 1 g pro. Exchanges: 1 fruit. Carb choices: 1.

PER POP WITH SUBSTITUTE: Same as above, except 59 cal., 14 g carb.

PINEAPPLE-BLUEBERRY POPS: Prepare as directed, except substitute 2 cups cut-up fresh pineapple for the watermelon and 2 cups fresh blueberries for the kiwifruits.

PER POP: 52 cal., 0 g total fat, 0 mg chol., 1 mg sodium, 13 g carb., 1 g fiber, 0 g pro. Exchanges: 1 fruit. Carb choices: 1.

PER POP WITH SUBSTITUTE: Same as above, except 42 cal., 11 g carb.

MANGO-RASPBERRY POPS: Prepare as directed, except substitute 2 cups cut-up fresh mango for the watermelon and 2 cups fresh raspberries for the kiwifruits. (If desired, after blending raspberry mixture, pass through a fine-mesh sieve to remove seeds.)

PER POP: 55 cal., 0 g total fat, 0 mg chol., 1 mg sodium, 14 g carb., 3 g fiber, 1 g pro. Exchanges: 1 fruit. Carb choices: 1.

PER POP WITH SUBSTITUTE: Same as above, except 44 cal., 11 g carb.

Jiggly Fruit Blocks

*When the partially set mixture is the consistency of
unbeaten egg whites, it's time to add
the mandarin oranges and pineapple tidbits.*

SERVINGS 8 (about 14 cubes each)

CARB. PER SERVING 22 g

3 cups orange juice

4 envelopes unflavored gelatin

1 cup cold pineapple juice

1 11-ounce can mandarin oranges, drained

1 8-ounce can pineapple tidbits (juice pack), drained

1. In a small saucepan, bring orange juice just to boiling.

2. In a large bowl, sprinkle gelatin over cold pineapple juice. Let stand for 1 minute. Add orange juice and stir about 5 minutes or until gelatin is dissolved. Pour into a 3-quart rectangular baking dish.

3. Chill about 30 minutes or until partially set. Stir in drained mandarin oranges and pineapple.

4. Chill for 3 to 4 hours or until firm. Cut into 1-inch cubes to serve.

PER SERVING: 137 cal., 0 g total fat, 0 mg chol., 31 mg sodium, 22 g carb., 1 g fiber, 13 g pro. Exchanges: 1 fruit, 0.5 carb., 1.5 lean meat. Carb choices: 1.5.

Jiggly Fruit Blocks

Peanut Butter and
Banana Pita Bites

Peanut Butter and Banana Pita Bites

To make a single serving of this quick snack, use half
a pita round, 2 teaspoons peanut butter spread,
a few chocolate pieces, and a couple of banana slices.

SERVINGS 12 (1 pita bite each)
CARB. PER SERVING 17 g

- 6 small (about 3 inches) whole wheat or whole grain pita bread rounds
- ½ cup reduced-fat peanut butter spread
- 2 tablespoons miniature semisweet chocolate pieces
- 2 small bananas, peeled and sliced

1. Cut pita breads in half horizontally. Spread peanut butter on cut sides of pitas; sprinkle with chocolate pieces. Top with banana slices.

PER SERVING: 122 cal., 5 g total fat (1 g sat. fat), 0 mg chol., 150 mg sodium, 17 g carb., 2 g fiber, 4 g pro. Exchanges: 1 starch, 1 fat. Carb choices: 1.

Speedy Pizza Rounds

When baked before topping, flat sandwich rolls make
a crispy crust.

SERVINGS 8 (1 mini pizza each)
CARB. PER SERVING 13 g

- 4 whole grain white flat sandwich rolls, split
- ½ cup no-salt-added tomato sauce
- 1 teaspoon Italian seasoning, crushed
- ¼ teaspoon crushed red pepper
- 3 ounces thinly sliced smoked turkey sausage
- ½ cup chopped yellow or red sweet pepper
- ¾ cup shredded part-skim mozzarella cheese (3 ounces)

1. Preheat oven to 400°F. Place roll halves, cut sides up, on a large baking sheet. Bake for 5 minutes. Meanwhile, stir together tomato sauce, Italian seasoning, and crushed red pepper.
2. Spread rolls with sauce mixture. Top with sausage and sweet pepper. Sprinkle with cheese. Bake about 8 minutes more or until cheese melts.

PER SERVING: 105 cal., 4 g total fat (1 g sat. fat), 14 mg chol., 255 mg sodium, 13 g carb., 3 g fiber, 8 g pro. Exchanges: 1 starch, 1 medium-fat meat. Carb choices: 1.

▶ QUICK TIP

If you like the flavor combo of peanut butter and jelly, use a few fresh strawberry slices or fresh whole raspberries in place of the banana slices.

delightful
desserts

We all deserve a little something sweet from time to time. If you make wise choices, you can indulge in dessert, even with diabetes. From fruit crisps and cream tarts to frosted cakes and layered bars, all of these recipes are perfect picks—each lightened and made more healthful for you.

Country Apple Tart

If you have apple pie spice on hand, use it instead of the cinnamon, ginger, nutmeg, and cloves.

SERVINGS 10 (1 wedge each)
CARB. PER SERVING 23 g

- 1 recipe Oat Pastry (below)
- 1 tablespoon all-purpose flour
- ½ teaspoon ground cinnamon
- ¼ teaspoon ground ginger
- ⅛ teaspoon ground nutmeg
- Dash ground cloves
- 3 large red-skin cooking apples (such as Braeburn, Jonathan, or Rome), cored and sliced
- ¼ cup pure maple syrup
- 2 tablespoons coarsely chopped pecans
- 1 tablespoon regular rolled oats
- Fat-free milk

1. Preheat oven to 375°F. Line a baking sheet with foil; sprinkle lightly with flour. Place Oat Pastry on foil. Slightly flatten dough ball. Using a rolling pin, roll dough from center to edge into a 12-inch circle. Set aside.

2. In a large bowl, stir together the 1 tablespoon flour, the cinnamon, ginger, nutmeg, and cloves. Add apple slices and maple syrup. Toss gently to coat. Mound apple mixture in center of pastry circle, leaving a 2-inch border around the edge. Fold border up over apples, pleating dough as needed. Sprinkle apples with pecans and oats. Brush pastry lightly with milk.

3. Bake for 55 to 60 minutes or until apples are tender. If necessary to prevent overbrowning, cover tart with foil for the last 10 to 15 minutes of baking. Cool for 30 minutes and serve warm. (Or cool completely.)

OAT PASTRY: In a medium bowl, stir together ¾ cup all-purpose flour, ½ cup oat flour or whole wheat flour, 2 tablespoons flaxseed meal, and ¼ teaspoon salt. Using a pastry blender, cut in ⅓ cup chilled vegetable oil spread until pieces are pea size. Sprinkle 1 tablespoon cold water over part of the flour mixture; gently toss with a fork. Push moistened dough to the side of the bowl. Repeat moistening flour mixture, using 1 tablespoon cold water at a time, until all flour mixture is moistened (3 to 4 tablespoons cold water total). Shape dough into a ball.

PER SERVING: 158 cal., 7 g total fat (2 g sat. fat), 0 mg chol., 108 mg sodium, 23 g carb., 2 g fiber, 2 g pro. Exchanges: 0.5 fruit, 1 carb., 1 fat. Carb choices: 1.5.

Plum Galettes

The pastry is tender, so work with care when folding and pleating it around the plums.

SERVINGS 8 (½ of a galette each)
CARB. PER SERVING 26 g or 25 g

- 2 ounces tub-style low-fat whipped cream cheese
- 2 tablespoons refrigerated or frozen egg product, thawed, or 1 egg yolk
- 2 tablespoons low-sugar orange marmalade
- ½ teaspoon ground ginger
- 1 recipe Browned Butter Pastry (below)
- 4 medium plums, pitted and sliced ¼ inch thick
- 2 tablespoons almonds or walnuts, chopped
  Fat-free milk
- 4 teaspoons honey

1. Preheat oven to 375°F. Line a baking sheet with parchment paper; set aside. In a medium bowl, beat cream cheese with an electric mixer on medium to high speed for 30 seconds. Beat in egg product, orange marmalade, and ginger.

2. Prepare Browned Butter Pastry. Divide pastry dough into four portions. On a lightly floured surface, roll each dough portion to a 7-inch circle. Top each portion with some of the cream cheese mixture, leaving a 1-inch border. Top with plum slices and almonds. Fold border up over filling, pleating pastry as needed. Place galettes on prepared baking sheet. Brush tops and sides of crust with milk.

3. Bake about 30 minutes or until crust is golden brown. Serve warm or cool. Drizzle with honey.

BROWNED BUTTER PASTRY: In a small saucepan, heat and stir 2 tablespoons butter over medium heat until light brown; set aside to cool slightly. In a medium bowl, stir together 1¼ cups all-purpose flour, 1 tablespoon granulated sugar,* and ¼ teaspoon salt. Using a pastry blender, cut in 2 tablespoons shortening and the browned butter until mixture resembles crumbs. Sprinkle 1 tablespoon cold water over part of the mixture; toss gently with a fork. Push moistened dough to side of bowl. Repeat moistening flour mixture, using 1 tablespoon cold water at a time, until all of the flour mixture is moistened (2 to 3 tablespoons total). Form dough into a ball.

*SUGAR SUBSTITUTES: Choose from Splenda Sugar Blend for Baking, Equal Sugar Lite, or Sun Crystals Granulated Blend. Follow package directions to use product amount equivalent to 1 tablespoon sugar.

PER SERVING: 187 cal., 8 g total fat (3 g sat. fat), 11 mg chol., 136 mg sodium, 26 g carb., 1 g fiber, 4 g pro. Exchanges: 0.5 fruit, 1 starch, 0.5 carb., 1.5 fat. Carb choices: 2.

PER SERVING WITH SUBSTITUTE: Same as above, except, 185 cal., 25 g carb. Exchanges: 0 carb. Carb choices: 1.5.

Plum Galettes

Lemon Tart with
Ginger-Oat Crust

Lemon Tart with Ginger-Oat Crust

You'll need two lemons to get enough finely shredded peel and juice for this sure-to-please dessert.

SERVINGS 12 (1 wedge each)
CARB. PER SERVING 25 g or 16 g

Nonstick cooking spray
1 recipe Ginger-Oat Crust (below right)
2 egg yolks or ¼ cup refrigerated or frozen egg product, thawed
⅔ cup sugar*
2 tablespoons cornstarch
1 tablespoon finely shredded lemon peel
6 tablespoons lemon juice
6 tablespoons water
¼ cup vegetable oil spread
½ cup light sour cream
Lemon slices, lime slices, and/or orange slices (optional)

1. Preheat oven to 350°F. Coat a 9-inch tart pan with removable side with cooking spray. Using your damp fingers, press Ginger-Oat Crust dough onto bottom and up the side of the prepared tart pan. Line crust with a double thickness of foil that has been lightly coated on the bottom with cooking spray. Bake for 8 minutes. Carefully remove foil. Bake for 5 to 7 minutes more or until crust is lightly browned. Cool completely on a wire rack.
2. In a small bowl, use a fork to lightly beat egg yolks; set aside. In a medium saucepan, stir together sugar and cornstarch. Stir in lemon peel, lemon juice, and the water. Cook and stir over medium heat until thickened and bubbly. Stir half of the lemon mixture into egg yolks. Add egg mixture to lemon mixture in saucepan. Cook and stir over medium heat until mixture comes to a gentle boil. Cook and stir for 2 minutes more. Remove from heat. Whisk in vegetable oil spread until well mixed. Cover surface of the cooked lemon mixture with plastic wrap. Let stand at room temperature for 15 minutes. Whisk in sour cream until well mixed.
3. Pour lemon mixture into cooled tart crust. Cover loosely and chill at least 1 hour before serving. Remove side of pan to serve. If desired, top with lemon, lime, and/or orange slices.

GINGER-OAT CRUST: In a medium bowl, beat ¼ cup softened butter with an electric mixer on medium to high speed for 30 seconds. Add 2 tablespoons packed brown sugar.* Beat until combined, scraping bowl occasionally. Beat in 1 egg white and ½ teaspoon vanilla until combined. Beat in ⅓ cup all-purpose flour. Stir in ½ cup ground gingersnaps (8 to 9 gingersnaps), ½ cup quick-cooking rolled oats, and ⅛ teaspoon ground ginger.

*SUGAR SUBSTITUTES: Choose Splenda Sugar Blend for Baking to substitute for the ⅔ cup sugar. Choose from Sweet'N Low Brown or Sugar Twin Granulated Brown to substitute for the brown sugar. Follow package directions to use product amounts equivalent to ⅔ cup sugar or 2 tablespoons brown sugar.

PER SERVING: 186 cal., 9 g total fat (4 g sat. fat), 48 mg chol., 101 mg sodium, 25 g carb., 1 g fiber, 2 g pro. Exchanges: 1 starch, 0.5 carb., 1.5 fat. Carb choices: 1.5.
PER SERVING WITH SUBSTITUTE: Same as above, except 160 cal., 16 g carb. Exchanges: 0 carb. Carb choices: 1.

QUICK TIP

Humidity makes meringues sticky, so it's best to bake them on a dry day. You can wrap the baked shells in foil and freeze them for up to 6 months.

Vanilla Meringue Tarts

Banana Split
Ice Cream Pie

Vanilla Meringue Tarts

Crispy meringue shells, rich vanilla filling, and in-season fresh fruits combine to make a company-special dessert.

SERVINGS 10 (1 filled meringue shell each)
CARB. PER SERVING 23 g or 17 g

1 recipe Meringue Shells (below)
⅓ cup sugar*
2 tablespoons cornstarch
2¼ cups low-fat milk
¼ cup refrigerated or frozen egg product, thawed, or 1 egg, lightly beaten
1 tablespoon vegetable oil spread
1½ teaspoons vanilla
1 cup fresh whole or sliced berries

1. Prepare Meringue Shells. Meanwhile, for filling: In a medium saucepan, combine sugar and cornstarch. Gradually stir in milk. Cook and stir over medium heat until thickened and bubbly; reduce heat. Cook and stir for 2 minutes more. Remove from heat. Gradually stir about 1 cup of the hot milk mixture into egg. Add egg mixture to milk mixture in pan. Bring to a gentle boil; reduce heat. Cook and whisk for 2 minutes more. Remove from heat. Stir in vegetable oil spread and vanilla. Place saucepan in a very large bowl half-filled with ice water. Whisk filling constantly for 2 minutes to cool quickly. Transfer filling to a medium bowl. Cover surface of filling with plastic wrap. Chill 2 to 24 hours.
2. Spoon filling into Meringue Shells. Serve at once or cover and chill for up to 30 minutes before serving. Top individual servings with berries.
MERINGUE SHELLS: Preheat oven to 250°F. Cover one or two large baking sheets with parchment paper. Draw ten 2½-inch circles on the paper. Set aside. In a medium bowl, combine 2 egg whites, ½ teaspoon vanilla, ¼ teaspoon cream of tartar, and ⅛ teaspoon salt. Beat with an electric mixer on medium speed until soft peaks form (tips curl). Gradually add ½ cup sugar,* about 1 tablespoon at a time, beating on high speed until stiff peaks form (tips stand straight). Spoon mixture into a pastry bag fitted with an open star tip. Pipe mixture in a spiral pattern over the circles on paper, piping the side of each circle up to a height of 1¼ inches. Bake about 1¼ hours or until meringues appear dry and are firm when lightly touched. Cool meringues on paper on a wire rack. Peel from paper; transfer to a serving platter.
*SUGAR SUBSTITUTES: Choose from Splenda granular or Sweet'N Low bulk or packets to substitute for the sugar in filling. Follow package directions to use product amount equivalent to ⅓ cup sugar. We do not recommend sugar substitutes for the Meringue Shells.
PER SERVING: 117 cal., 2 g total fat (1 g sat. fat), 3 mg chol., 85 mg sodium, 23 g carb., 1 g fiber, 3 g pro. Exchanges: 1.5 carb., 0.5 fat. Carb choices: 1.5.
PER SERVING WITH SUBSTITUTE: Same as above, except 95 cal., 17 g carb. Exchanges: 1 carb. Carb choices: 1.

Banana Split Ice Cream Pie

Create a different dessert each time you make this recipe by changing the flavors of low-fat or light ice cream. Also pictured on the cover.

SERVINGS 10 (1 wedge each)
CARB. PER SERVING 27 g

1 purchased reduced-fat graham cracker crumb pie shell
2 tablespoons refrigerated or frozen egg product, thawed, or 1 egg white, lightly beaten
1½ cups low-fat or light chocolate ice cream, softened
1½ cups low-fat or light vanilla ice cream, softened
1 large banana, sliced
1 cup sliced fresh strawberries
2 tablespoons light chocolate-flavor syrup
⅔ cup frozen light whipped dessert topping, thawed (optional)

1. Preheat oven to 375°F. Brush pie shell with egg. Bake for 5 minutes. Cool on a wire rack. Spread chocolate ice cream in the bottom of the cooled pie shell. Spread vanilla ice cream evenly over chocolate ice cream. Cover and freeze for at least 4 hours or up to 1 week.
2. To serve, arrange banana and strawberry slices over ice cream layers. Drizzle with chocolate syrup. Cut into wedges to serve. If desired, top each serving with whipped topping.
PER SERVING: 167 cal., 5 g total fat (2 g sat. fat), 6 mg chol., 115 mg sodium, 27 g carb., 1 g fiber, 3 g pro. Exchanges: 2 carb., 0.5 fat. Carb choices: 2.

Nectarine
Blueberry Crisp

Berry-Topped Cheesecake

*A pretzel-and-almond crust topped with
a creamy filling that's studded with fresh fruit—
now that's a cheesecake like no other!*

SERVINGS 12 (1 wedge each)

CARB. PER SERVING 14 g

1½ cups small pretzel twists (2 ounces; about 33)
  2 tablespoons sliced almonds, toasted
  3 tablespoons butter, melted
  ⅓ cup water
  1 envelope unflavored gelatin
1½ 8-ounce tubs light cream cheese, softened
  1 8-ounce carton light sour cream
  ¼ cup powdered sugar
  ½ teaspoon almond extract
  ½ of an 8-ounce container frozen light whipped dessert
     topping, thawed
  1 cup quartered or halved fresh strawberries
  1 cup fresh blackberries or blueberries

1. Preheat oven to 350°F. For crust: In a food processor,
combine pretzels and sliced almonds; cover and process
until finely crushed. Add butter; cover and process until
combined. Press pretzel mixture on the bottom of an
8- or 9-inch springform pan. Bake for 8 to 10 minutes or
until lightly browned. Cool on a wire rack.
2. For filling: Place the water in a small saucepan;
sprinkle with gelatin (do not stir). Let stand for
5 minutes to soften. Cook and stir over low heat until
gelatin dissolves; set aside to cool slightly.
3. In a large bowl, combine cream cheese, sour cream,
powdered sugar, and almond extract; beat with an
electric mixer on medium speed until smooth.
Add gelatin mixture; beat until combined. Fold in
whipped topping.
4. Spread half of the filling evenly over cooled crust.
Top with half of the strawberries and half of the
blackberries. Spread the remaining cream cheese
mixture over berries. Cover and chill cheesecake for 4 to
24 hours or until set. Run a long sharp knife around edge
of cheesecake to loosen; remove side of pan. Cut
cheesecake into wedges. Top individual servings with
the remaining strawberries and blackberries.
PER SERVING: 176 cal., 11 g total fat (7 g sat. fat), 28 mg chol.,
236 mg sodium, 14 g carb., 1 g fiber, 6 g pro. Exchanges:
1 carb., 2 fat. Carb choices: 1.

Nectarine Blueberry Crisp

*Peaches and nectarines can be used interchangeably. If
using peaches, remove the fuzzy peels before slicing.*

SERVINGS 8 (about ⅔ cup each)

CARB. PER SERVING 27 g or 22 g

  4 cups sliced fresh nectarines
  5 tablespoons packed brown sugar*
  ¼ cup whole wheat flour or all-purpose flour
  ½ teaspoon ground cinnamon
  1 cup fresh or frozen unsweetened blueberries or
     blackberries, thawed
  ⅔ cup quick-cooking rolled oats
  2 tablespoons butter, cut up
  ⅓ cup chopped pistachios or walnuts

1. Preheat oven to 375°F. For fruit filling: In a large bowl,
combine nectarine slices, 3 tablespoons of the brown
sugar, 2 tablespoons of the flour, and the cinnamon. Add
blueberries and ¼ cup *water*; toss to combine. Spoon
mixture into a 2-quart square baking dish.
2. For topping: In a medium bowl, stir together oats,
remaining 2 tablespoons brown sugar, and remaining
2 tablespoons flour. Using a pastry blender, cut in the
butter until mixture is crumbly. Sprinkle topping onto
fruit in dish. Top with nuts.
3. Bake for 35 to 40 minutes or until the fruit filling is
bubbly and topping is lightly browned. Cool slightly on a
wire rack; serve warm.
*SUGAR SUBSTITUTE: Choose Splenda Brown Sugar Blend.
Follow package directions to use product amount
equivalent to 5 tablespoons brown sugar.
PER SERVING: 166 cal., 6 g total fat (2 g sat. fat), 8 mg chol.,
24 mg sodium, 27 g carb., 3 g fiber, 3 g pro. Exchanges:
0.5 fruit, 1 starch, 0.5 carb., 1 fat. Carb choices: 2.
PER SERVING WITH SUBSTITUTE: Same as above, except 152 cal.,
22 g carb., 22 mg sodium. Exchanges: 0 carb. Carb
choices: 1.5.

Grilled Plum and Strawberry Skewers with Sweet Mint Pesto

This subtly sweet mint, basil, and pine nut pesto is a sensational partner for juicy grilled fruit. Another time, serve the pesto as a dip for a fresh fruit platter.

SERVINGS 4 (2 skewers and 1 tablespoon pesto each)
CARB. PER SERVING 12 g

- ⅔ cup lightly packed fresh mint leaves
- ¼ cup lightly packed fresh basil leaves
- 3 tablespoons pine nuts, toasted
- ½ teaspoon finely shredded orange peel
- 3 tablespoons orange juice
- Dash salt
- 4 plums, pitted and each cut into six wedges (24 wedges total)
- 8 large strawberries
- Nonstick cooking spray

1. For pesto: In a blender or food processor, combine mint, basil, pine nuts, orange peel, orange juice, and salt. Cover and blend or process until smooth, stopping and scraping side as needed. Set aside.

2. Thread plum wedges and strawberries on eight 6-inch-long skewers.* Lightly coat fruit with cooking spray. For a charcoal grill, place skewers on the grill rack directly over medium coals. Grill, uncovered, for 3 to 4 minutes or until heated through and grill marks are visible, turning occasionally to brown evenly. (For a gas grill, preheat grill. Reduce heat to medium. Place skewers on grill rack over heat. Cover and grill as above.)

3. Serve skewers with pesto.

*TEST KITCHEN TIP: If using wooden skewers, soak skewers in enough water to cover for at least 30 minutes before grilling.

PER SERVING: 85 cal., 4 g total fat (1 g sat. fat), 0 mg chol., 36 mg sodium, 12 g carb., 1 g fiber, 3 g pro. Exchanges: 1 fruit, 0.5 fat. Carb choices: 1.

Grilled Plum and Strawberry
Skewers with Sweet Mint Pesto

May Basket Cupcakes

To create captivating May baskets, wrap a wide strip of decorative paper around each cupcake, holding it in place with double-stick tape. Then attach narrow strips of plain paper for the basket handles.

SERVINGS 12 (1 cupcake each)
CARB. PER SERVING 30 g or 23 g

Nonstick cooking spray
1⅔ cups all-purpose flour
1½ teaspoons finely shredded lime peel
1¼ teaspoons baking powder
½ teaspoon baking soda
⅛ teaspoon salt
¼ cup butter, softened
¾ cup sugar*
½ cup refrigerated or frozen egg product, thawed, or 2 eggs
⅔ cup light sour cream
2 tablespoons fat-free milk
1½ cups sliced or coarsely chopped fresh strawberries, kiwifruit, pineapple, and/or whole fresh raspberries or blueberries
1 cup frozen light whipped dessert topping, thawed
2 tablespoons coconut chips, lightly toasted (optional)

May Basket Cupcakes

1. Preheat oven to 350°F. Line twelve 2½-inch muffin cups with paper bake cups. Coat paper bake cups with cooking spray; set aside. In a medium bowl, combine flour, lime peel, baking powder, baking soda, and salt; set aside.

2. In a large bowl, beat butter with an electric mixer on medium speed for 30 seconds. Gradually add sugar, beating until light and fluffy. Beat in eggs. In a small bowl, combine sour cream and milk. Alternately add flour mixture and sour cream mixture to egg mixture, beating on low speed after each addition just until combined.

3. Spoon batter evenly into prepared muffin cups, filling each ⅔ to ¾ full. Bake for 18 to 20 minutes or until a toothpick inserted near the centers comes out clean. Cool in cups on a wire rack for 5 minutes. Remove cupcakes from pans. Cool completely on wire rack.

4. Using a small knife, cut out a shallow area in the top of each cupcake. Save scraps for another use, such as for fruit parfaits. Fill cupcake tops with fruit, whipped topping, and, if desired, coconut chips.

*SUGAR SUBSTITUTES: Choose Splenda Sugar Blend for Baking. Follow package directions to use product amount equivalent to ¾ cup sugar.

PER SERVING: 186 cal., 6 g total fat, (4 g sat. fat), 14 mg chol., 157 mg sodium, 30 g carb., 1 g fiber, 3 g pro. Exchanges: 2 carb., 1 fat. Carb choices: 2.

PER SERVING WITH SUBSTITUTE: Same as above, except 167 cal., 23 g carb. Exchanges: 1.5 carb. Carb choices: 1.5.

Lemon Poppy Seed Snack Cake

Use clean beaters and a clean bowl when beating the egg whites. Any trace of fat will prevent the egg whites from whipping properly.

SERVINGS 10 (1 slice each)
CARB. PER SERVING 27 g or 18 g

Nonstick cooking spray
1 cup all-purpose flour
1 tablespoon poppy seeds
1 teaspoon baking powder
¼ teaspoon baking soda
⅛ teaspoon salt
⅔ cup granulated sugar*
2 egg yolks
3 tablespoons canola oil
⅓ cup lemon-flavor low-fat yogurt
2 teaspoons finely shredded lemon peel
2 egg whites
1 recipe Lemon Glaze (page 143)

Lemon Poppy Seed Snack Cake

1. Preheat oven to 350°F. Lightly coat an 8×1½-inch round cake pan with cooking spray; set aside. In a small bowl, stir together flour, poppy seeds, baking powder, baking soda, and salt.

2. In a large mixing bowl, combine sugar, egg yolks, and oil. Beat with an electric mixer on high speed for 2 minutes. Add yogurt and lemon peel; beat until combined. Add flour mixture; beat until just combined.

3. Thoroughly wash beaters. In a medium mixing bowl, beat egg whites until stiff peaks form (tips stand straight). Stir one-third of the egg whites into batter to lighten. Fold in remaining egg whites. Spread batter in prepared pan.

4. Bake about 30 minutes or until a toothpick inserted near the center comes out clean.

5. Cool in pan on a wire rack for 10 minutes. Use tines of a fork to pierce cake. Slowly drizzle Lemon Glaze over cake. Cool completely. Invert to remove from pan; turn cake top side up.

LEMON GLAZE: In a small bowl, stir together 3 tablespoons lemon juice and 2 tablespoons powdered sugar.*

*****SUGAR SUBSTITUTES:** Choose from Splenda Sugar Blend for Baking or Sun Crystals Granulated Blend for the ⅔ cup granulated sugar. Choose from Splenda granular, Equal Spoonful or packets, or Sweet'N Low bulk or packets for the 2 tablespoons powdered sugar. Follow package directions to use product amounts equivalent to ⅔ cup granulated sugar or 2 tablespoons powdered sugar.

PER SERVING: 167 cal., 6 g total fat (1 g sat. fat), 42 mg chol., 115 mg sodium, 27 g carb., 1 g fiber, 3 g pro. Exchanges: 1 starch, 1 carb., 1 fat. Carb choices: 2.

PER SERVING WITH SUBSTITUTE: Same as above, except 142 cal., 18 g carb. Exchanges: 0 carb. Carb choices: 1.

▶ QUICK TIP
Be sure to lightly grease and flour the pans so you can remove the cakes easily. Loosen around the edges with a knife and then invert the cakes onto wire racks.

Carrot Cake with
Fluffy Cream
Cheese Frosting

Carrot Cake with Fluffy Cream Cheese Frosting

If you make the towers, save cake scraps and layer with light whipped dessert topping to make parfaits.

SERVINGS 14 to 16 (1 slice each)
CARB. PER SERVING 34 g or 25 g

- 1½ cups all-purpose flour
- ⅔ cup flaxseed meal
- 2 teaspoons baking powder
- 1 teaspoon pumpkin pie pice
- ½ teaspoon baking soda
- ¼ teaspoon salt
- 3 cups finely shredded carrots (about 6 medium)
- 1 cup refrigerated or frozen egg product, thawed, or 4 eggs, lightly beaten
- ½ cup granulated sugar*
- ½ cup packed brown sugar*
- ½ cup canola oil
- 1 recipe Fluffy Cream Cheese Frosting (below)

1. Preheat oven to 350°F. Grease and lightly flour two 8×1½- or 9×1½-inch round cake pans. Set aside.
2. In a large bowl, stir together flour, flaxseed meal, baking powder, pumpkin pie spice, baking soda, and salt; set aside. In another large bowl, combine carrots, eggs, sugars, and oil. Add egg mixture all at once to flour mixture. Stir until combined. Spoon batter into prepared pans, spreading evenly.
3. Bake for 25 to 30 minutes for 8-inch pans or 20 to 25 minutes for 9-inch pans or until a toothpick inserted near the centers comes out clean. Cool cakes in pans on wire racks for 10 minutes. Invert cakes onto racks. Cool.
4. Place one cake on a platter. Top with half of the Fluffy Cream Cheese Frosting. Place the second cake layer on top of the frosting; spread with the remaining frosting. If desired, garnish with additional shredded carrot.
FLUFFY CREAM CHEESE FROSTING: In a medium bowl, beat 2 ounces softened reduced-fat cream cheese (Neufchâtel) with an electric mixer on medium to high speed until smooth. Beat in ½ teaspoon vanilla. Gradually add ¼ cup powdered sugar, beating until smooth. Thaw 1½ cups frozen light whipped dessert topping. Fold about ½ cup of the topping into cream cheese mixture. Fold in remaining topping.
CARROT CAKE TOWERS: Prepare batter as directed through Step 2, except grease and lightly flour one 15×10×1-inch pan; line bottom of pan with waxed paper. Grease and lightly flour the waxed paper. Bake for 25 to 30 minutes or until a toothpick inserted near the center comes out clean. Cool cake in pan on a wire rack for 10 minutes. Invert onto wire rack. Cool completely. Transfer cake to a large cutting board. Using a 2-inch round cutter, make cutouts in the cake, leaving as little space as possible between cutouts. You should get 28 to 32 cutouts. For each serving, place one cake cutout on a serving plate. Spread or pipe about 1 tablespoon Fluffy Cream Cheese Frosting on top of cake round. Top with a second cake round and about 1 tablespoon additional frosting
***SUGAR SUBSTITUTES:** Choose Splenda Sugar Blend for Baking for the granulated sugar and Splenda Brown Sugar Blend for the brown sugar. Follow package directions to use product amounts equivalent to ½ cup granulated sugar and ½ cup brown sugar.
PER SERVING: 254 cal., 11 g total fat (2 g sat. fat), 3 mg chol., 188 mg sodium, 34 g carb., 3 g fiber, 5 g pro. Exchanges: 2 carb., 2 fat. Carb choices: 2.
PER SERVING WITH SUBSTITUTE: Same as above, except 231 cal., 25 g carb. Exchanges: 1.5 carb. Carb choices: 1.5.

Grown-Up S'mores

Rosemary is the surprise ingredient in these toasty morsels.

SERVINGS 6 (1 s'more each)
CARB. PER SERVING 16 g

- 6 graham cracker squares
- 1 1.45-ounce bar dark chocolate, divided into 6 portions
- 1 teaspoon finely shredded orange peel
- 1 teaspoon snipped fresh rosemary
- 6 large marshmallows
- 6 fresh raspberries

1. Place graham crackers in a single layer on a platter. Top each with a portion of chocolate; set aside. Combine orange peel and rosemary; set aside. Lightly coat a long metal skewer with *nonstick cooking spray.* Thread marshmallows onto skewer, leaving ½ inch between each.
2. For a charcoal grill, using an oven mitt, hold marshmallow skewer just above grill rack directly over medium coals about 2 minutes or until marshmallows are soft and lightly toasted, turning occasionally. (For a gas grill, preheat grill. Reduce heat to medium. Using an oven mitt, hold marshmallow skewer just above grill rack over heat. Grill as above, leaving grill uncovered.)
3. Use a fork to push one marshmallow onto each chocolate-topped graham cracker. Sprinkle with orange peel mixture; top each with a raspberry.
PER SERVING: 91 cal., 3 g total fat (1 g sat. fat), 0 mg chol., 57 mg sodium, 16 g carb., 1 g fiber, 1 g pro. Exchanges: 1 carb., 0.5 fat. Carb choices: 1.

To make drizzling easy, transfer the melted chocolate to a heavy resealable plastic bag and snip the corner.

No-Bake Apricot-
Almond Balls

No-Bake Apricot-Almond Balls

Use slightly wet hands to pack the fruit, nut, and cereal mixture together into balls.

SERVINGS 18 (1 ball each)
CARB. PER SERVING 9 g

⅓ cup creamy peanut butter
¼ cup vegetable oil spread
2 tablespoons honey
¼ teaspoon almond extract
2 cups rice and wheat cereal flakes, crushed slightly
⅓ cup finely snipped dried apricots
2 tablespoons finely chopped toasted almonds
¼ teaspoon ground ginger
2 ounces bittersweet or semisweet chocolate, chopped
¼ teaspoon shortening

1. In a medium saucepan, combine peanut butter, vegetable oil spread, honey, and almond extract. Cook over low heat just until melted and nearly smooth, whisking constantly. Stir in cereal, apricots, almonds, and ginger until well mixed. Using slightly wet hands or a 1-ounce scoop, shape mixture into balls. Let stand on a waxed paper-lined baking sheet about 15 minutes or until firm.
2. In a small saucepan, heat and stir chocolate and shortening over low heat until melted. Drizzle balls with chocolate. Chill about 15 minutes or until chocolate is set. Store in an airtight container in the refrigerator.
PER SERVING: 93 cal., 6 g total fat (2 g sat. fat), 0 mg chol., 65 mg sodium, 9 g carb., 1 g fiber, 2 g pro. Exchanges: 0.5 starch, 1 fat. Carb choices: 0.5.

Chocolate Chunk Cherry Cookies

Satisfy your chocolate craving yet stick to your diabetes meal plan with these chewy, chocolate-loaded cookies.

SERVINGS 28 (1 cookie each)
CARB. PER SERVING 14 g or 10 g

¼ cup vegetable oil spread
⅓ cup packed brown sugar*
⅓ cup granulated sugar*
½ teaspoon baking soda
⅛ teaspoon salt
¼ cup refrigerated or frozen egg product, thawed, or 1 egg, lightly beaten
2 tablespoons unsweetened cocoa powder
1 teaspoon vanilla

²⁄₃ cup all-purpose flour
²⁄₃ cup rolled oats
¼ cup flaxseed meal
4 ounces dark chocolate, chopped
2 ounces white baking chocolate, chopped
½ cup dried tart cherries, coarsely chopped

1. Preheat oven to 350°F. In a large mixing bowl, beat vegetable oil spread with an electric mixer on medium to high speed for 30 seconds. Add brown sugar, granulated sugar, baking soda, and salt. Beat until well mixed, scraping bowl occasionally. Beat in egg, cocoa powder, and vanilla until combined. Beat in flour. Using a wooden spoon, stir in rolled oats and flaxseed meal. Stir in 3 ounces of the dark chocolate, 2 tablespoons of the white chocolate, and ⅓ cup of the cherries.

2. Drop dough by rounded teaspoons 2 inches apart onto ungreased cookie sheets. Top with remaining dark chocolate, white chocolate, and cherries. Bake for 8 to 10 minutes or until edges are set. Let cookies cool on cookie sheets for 1 minute. Transfer cookies to wire racks; let cool.

*SUGAR SUBSTITUTES: Choose from Sugar Twin Granulated Brown or Sweet'N Low Brown for the brown sugar. Choose Splenda Sugar Blend for Baking for the granulated sugar. Follow package directions to use product amounts equivalent to ⅓ cup brown or granulated sugar.

TO STORE: Layer cookies between waxed paper in an airtight container; cover. Store at room temperature for up to 5 days or freeze for up to 1 month.

PER SERVING: 84 cal., 4 g total fat (2 g sat. fat), 0 mg chol., 53 mg sodium, 14 g carb., 1 g fiber, 1 g pro. Exchanges: 1 carb., 0.5 fat. Carb choices: 1.

PER SERVING WITH SUBSTITUTES: Same as above, except 70 cal., 10 g carb. Exchanges: 0.5 carb. Carb choices: 0.5.

Fruited Oatmeal Cookies

Full of fruits and nuts, these spiced bites make a great snack.

SERVINGS 48 (1 cookie each)
CARB. PER SERVING 17 g or 13 g

---

2 cups rolled oats
Nonstick cooking spray
½ cup butter, softened
1½ cups packed brown sugar*
¾ teaspoon baking soda
¼ teaspoon salt

Fruited Oatmeal Cookies

¼ teaspoon ground allspice
1 6-ounce carton plain low-fat yogurt
½ cup refrigerated or frozen egg product, thawed, or 2 eggs, lightly beaten
1 teaspoon vanilla
2¼ cups all-purpose flour
¼ cup snipped dried apricots
¼ cup currants
¼ cup chopped walnuts, toasted

1. Preheat oven to 375°F. Spread oats in a shallow baking pan. Bake about 10 minutes or until toasted, stirring once; set aside. Lightly coat a cookie sheet with cooking spray; set aside.

2. In a large mixing bowl, beat butter for 30 seconds. Add brown sugar, baking soda, salt, and allspice; beat until combined. Beat in yogurt, eggs, and vanilla. Beat in as much of the flour as you can with the mixer. Using a wooden spoon, stir in oats, apricots, currants, walnuts, and any remaining flour. Drop dough by rounded teaspoons 2 inches apart on prepared cookie sheet.

3. Bake for 9 to 11 minutes or until edges and bottoms are browned. Transfer cookies to a wire rack; let cool.

*SUGAR SUBSTITUTE: Choose Splenda Brown Sugar Blend. Follow package directions to use product amount equivalent to 1½ cups brown sugar.

TO STORE: Place cookies in an airtight container; cover. Store at room temperature up to 3 days or freeze up to 2 months.

PER SERVING: 101 cal., 3 g total fat (1 g sat. fat), 5 mg chol., 55 mg sodium, 17 g carb., 1 g fiber, 2 g pro. Exchanges: 0.5 starch, 0.5 carb., 0.5 fat. Carb choices: 1.

PER SERVING WITH SUBSTITUTE: Same as above, except 90 cal., 13 g carb.

Layered Brownies

4. Meanwhile, in a medium bowl, whisk together the remaining ½ cup egg product or 2 eggs, the granulated sugar, and oil. Stir in the remaining ½ cup flour, the cocoa powder, and baking powder. Stir in semisweet chocolate pieces. Pour evenly over partially baked crust. If necessary, gently spread with a metal spatula. Stir nuts and the 2 tablespoons oats into the reserved oat mixture (mixture may be a little soft). Crumble over the top of the mixture in the baking pan.

5. Bake for 13 to 15 minutes or until the top is puffed and set. Cool completely in pan on a wire rack. Using the edges of the foil, lift the uncut brownies out of the pan; cut into bars.

*SUGAR SUBSTITUTES: Choose Splenda Brown Sugar Blend for the brown sugar. Choose from Splenda granular or Sweet'N Low bulk or packets for the granulated sugar. Follow package directions to use product amounts equivalent to ⅔ cup brown sugar or ¼ cup granulated sugar.

TO STORE: Layer brownies between waxed paper in an airtight container; cover. Store in the refrigerator for up to 5 days or freeze for up to 3 months.

PER SERVING: 163 cal., 8 g total fat (2 g sat. fat), 0 mg chol., 75 mg sodium, 21 g carb., 1 g fiber, 3 g pro. Exchanges: 1.5 carb., 1.5 fat. Carb choices: 1.5.

PER SERVING WITH SUBSTITUTES: Same as above, except 145 cal., 16 g carb. Exchanges: 1 carb. Carb choices: 1.

Layered Brownies

Lining the baking pan with foil makes lifting the uncut baked brownies from the pan easy.

SERVINGS 24 (1 brownie each)
CARB. PER SERVING 21 g or 16 g

- ⅔ cup packed brown sugar*
- ⅔ cup vegetable oil spread
- ¼ teaspoon baking soda
- ¾ cup refrigerated or frozen egg product, thawed, or 3 eggs, lightly beaten
- 2 cups all-purpose flour
- 1½ cups quick-cooking rolled oats
- ¼ cup granulated sugar*
- ¼ cup canola oil
- 3 tablespoons unsweetened cocoa powder
- ½ teaspoon baking powder
- 2 tablespoons miniature semisweet chocolate pieces
- 2 tablespoons chopped walnuts
- 2 tablespoons quick-cooking rolled oats

1. Preheat oven to 350°F. Line a 9×9×2-inch baking pan with foil, extending foil up over the edges of the pan. Lightly grease the foil. Set aside.

2. For crust: In a large mixing bowl, beat brown sugar, vegetable oil spread, and baking soda with an electric mixer on medium speed until well mixed, scraping bowl occasionally. Beat in ¼ cup of the egg product or one of the eggs. Beat in 1½ cups of the flour. Stir in the 1½ cups oats.

3. Set aside ½ cup of the oat mixture. Spread the remaining oat mixture into the bottom of the prepared pan. Bake about 12 minutes or just until crust is set.

Apple Spice Bars

An oaty shortbreadlike mixture is used for the crust and the crumb topping.

SERVINGS 16 (1 bar each)
CARB. PER SERVING 30 g or 24 g

- 1½ cups all-purpose flour
- ½ cup quick cooking oats
- ⅓ cup granulated sugar*
- ½ teaspoon baking powder
- ¼ teaspoon salt
- ½ cup vegetable oil spread
- ¼ cup refrigerated or frozen egg product, thawed, or 1 egg, lightly beaten
- 5 medium cooking apples, peeled if desired, cored, and chopped (5 cups)
- ½ cup dried cherries
- 2 tablespoons lemon juice
- 3 tablespoons packed brown sugar*
- 2 tablespoons all-purpose flour

1 teaspoon ground cinnamon
½ teaspoon ground ginger
¼ teaspoon ground cloves

1. Preheat oven to 350°F. In a large bowl, combine the 1½ cups flour, the oats, granulated sugar, baking powder, and salt. Cut in vegetable oil spread until mixture resembles coarse crumbs. Stir in egg. Press half of the mixture into a 9×9×2-inch baking pan.
2. In a large bowl, combine apples, dried cherries, and lemon juice. Add brown sugar, the 2 tablespoons flour, the cinnamon, ginger, and cloves; toss to combine. Layer apple mixture evenly over the crust. Sprinkle with remaining flour mixture.

3. Bake about 50 minutes or until topping is lightly browned and apples are tender. Cool slightly; serve warm. Cut into bars to serve.

*SUGAR SUBSTITUTES: Choose from Splenda granular, Equal Spoonful or packets, or Sweet'N Low bulk or packets for the granulated sugar. Choose from Sweet'N Low Brown or Sugar Twin Granulated Brown for the brown sugar. Follow package directions to use product amounts equivalent to ⅓ cup granulated sugar and 3 tablespoons brown sugar.

PER SERVING: 167 cal., 4 g total fat (1 g sat. fat), 0 mg chol., 100 mg sodium, 30 g carb., 2 g fiber, 2 g pro. Exchanges: 0.5 fruit, 1 starch, 0.5 carb., 0.5 fat. Carb choices: 2.
PER SERVING WITH SUBSTITUTES: Same as above, except 143 cal., 24 g carb. Exchanges: 0 carb. Carb choices: 1.5.

Apple Spice Bars

Tri-Colored Sherbet

This easy recipe lets you serve a sophisticated trio of white chocolate, blackberry, and raspberry-rhubarb sherbets all at once. For the best flavor, be sure to use a premium white chocolate for the white chocolate sherbet.

SERVINGS 18 (½ cup [3 small scoops] each)
CARB. PER SERVING 24 g

- 1 cup sugar*
- 1 envelope unflavored gelatin
- 1 12-ounce can evaporated fat-free milk
- ¾ cup fresh or frozen sliced unsweetened rhubarb**
- ¾ cup fresh raspberries
- 1½ cups fresh blackberries
- 1 16-ounce carton light sour cream
- 6 ounces white chocolate (with cocoa butter), chopped
- 1 8-ounce package reduced-fat cream cheese (Neufchâtel), cubed
- 1 cup fat-free milk

1. In a medium saucepan, combine sugar and unflavored gelatin. Stir in evaporated milk. Cook and stir until sugar and gelatin dissolve. Remove from heat.
2. Place rhubarb and raspberries in a large bowl. Place blackberries in another large bowl. Divide hot sugar mixture between the two bowls of fruit. Let stand for 5 minutes. Using a potato masher, mash fruit in each bowl. Spoon half of the sour cream into fruit in each bowl; stir until well mixed. Pour fruit mixtures into two separate 2-quart square baking dishes or 2-quart shallow freezer containers. Cover and freeze about 5 hours or until mixtures are firm but not totally frozen, stirring occasionally so mixtures freeze evenly.
3. Meanwhile, in the same medium saucepan, heat white chocolate over low heat until melted and smooth, stirring frequently. Gradually add cream cheese, stirring until well mixed. Gradually stir in milk until smooth. Pour mixture into another 2-quart square baking dish or 2-quart shallow freezer container. Cover and freeze for 3 to 4 hours or until firm but not totally frozen, stirring occasionally so mixture freezes evenly.
4. For each frozen mixture, break up mixture and transfer to a large food processor or large chilled bowl. Cover and process until smooth but not melted. Or if using the large bowl, beat with an electric mixer on medium speed until smooth and fluffy but not melted. Spread mixtures back into the 2-quart baking dishes or freezer containers, keeping mixtures separate. Cover and freeze for 2 to 3 hours or until mixtures are frozen.

Let stand at room temperature for 20 minutes before serving. Using a tiny scoop, place a scoop of each frozen mixture into dessert dishes.

SUGAR SUBSTITUTES: We do not recommend sugar substitutes for this recipe.
****TEST KITCHEN TIP:*** If using frozen rhubarb, measure while frozen. Thaw; do not drain.

PER SERVING: 198 cal., 9 g total fat (6 g sat. fat), 21 mg chol., 109 mg sodium, 24 g carb., 1 g fiber, 6 g pro. Exchanges: 1.5 carb., 1.5 fat. Carb choices: 1.5.

Banana Buster Pops

Everyone will love this dressed-up version of frozen bananas. It includes peanut butter, chocolate, and peanuts.

SERVINGS 4 (1 pop each)
CARB. PER SERVING 18 g

- 4 teaspoons peanut butter
- 1 large banana, cut into 12 equal slices
- 4 6- to 8-inch white sucker sticks or wooden skewers
- 2 ounces milk chocolate or semisweet chocolate, melted
- 2 tablespoons finely chopped unsalted dry-roasted or cocktail peanuts

1. Line a baking sheet with waxed paper; set aside. Spoon ½ teaspoon of the peanut butter onto each of eight of the banana slices. Place four of the peanut butter-topped banana slices on the remaining four peanut butter-topped slices to make four stacks of two banana slices with peanut butter between and peanut butter on top. Place one of the remaining banana slices on top of each stack. Push a sucker stick or skewer all the way through the center of each banana stack.
2. Place melted chocolate in a shallow dish. Place peanuts in another shallow dish. Roll each banana stack in the melted chocolate. Use a thin metal spatula to help spread the chocolate into a thin, even layer over the stacks. Immediately roll in peanuts. Place on prepared baking sheet.
3. Freeze banana pops about 30 minutes or until firm. Serve straight from the freezer.

PER SERVING: 165 cal., 9 g total fat (4 g sat. fat), 3 mg chol., 38 mg sodium, 18 g carb., 2 g fiber, 4 g pro. Exchanges: 0.5 fruit, 0.5 carb., 0.5 high-fat meat, 1 fat. Carb choices: 1.

Tri-Colored Sherbet

Fruit Desserts

When you are craving a little something sweet, dish up one of these quick fresh-fruit fix-ups.

1. **Dip dry, clean fresh strawberries** in melted bittersweet chocolate.

2. **Top mixed berries** with a spoonful of plain low-fat Greek yogurt.

3. **Sprinkle a grilled wedge of fresh pineapple** with a little toasted coconut.

4. **Crumble a crisp gingersnap cookie** over fresh peach or nectarine slices.

5. **Spread a little peanut butter** on a lengthwise half of banana; sprinkle with a few crushed peanuts and a few miniature semisweet chocolate pieces.

6. **Swirl some whipped cream cheese** on a graham cracker and top with a few orange segments.

7. **Top a bowl of mixed fruit** with a small scoop of fruit sorbet.

Banana
Buster Pops

Dark Chocolate-Orange Pudding
recipe on page 153

Watermelon-Berry Granita

You can change the color of this icy refresher
by varying the berries you use. All blueberries with
the watermelon will give a purplish red ice.
Add all strawberries for a vivid red hue.

SERVINGS 10 (¾ cup each)

CARB. PER SERVING 14 g or 8 g

¾ cup water
⅓ cup sugar*
3 cups seeded watermelon cubes
2 cups blueberries and/or halved strawberries
   Snipped fresh lemon balm or mint (optional)
   Fresh raspberries and/or blueberries (optional)
   Fresh lemon balm or mint sprigs (optional)

1. In a small saucepan, combine the water and sugar (if using); bring to boiling, stirring until sugar is dissolved. Boil gently, uncovered, for 2 minutes. Remove from heat; cool slightly. If using a sugar substitute, combine water and sugar substitute in a small bowl; stir to dissolve. Do not heat.

2. Meanwhile, in a blender or food processor, combine watermelon and berries. Cover and blend or process until nearly smooth. Add the sugar mixture; blend or process until smooth. Transfer to a 3-quart rectangular baking dish. Cover and freeze about 2½ hours or until almost solid.

3. Remove mixture from freezer. Using a fork, break up the frozen mixture until almost smooth but not melted. Cover and freeze for 1 hour more.** Break up the frozen mixture with a fork and serve in paper cups or shallow bowls. If desired, garnish each serving with additional raspberries and/or blueberries and lemon balm sprigs.

*****SUGAR SUBSTITUTES:** Choose from Splenda granular, Equal Spoonful or packets, or Sweet'N Low bulk or packets. Follow package directions to use product amount equivalent to ⅓ cup sugar.

****TEST KITCHEN TIP:** If mixture is frozen longer than the final hour, let it stand at room temperature about 20 minutes before breaking up mixture with a fork and serving.

PER SERVING: 56 cal., 0 g total fat, 0 mg chol., 1 mg sodium, 14 g carb., 1 g fiber, 0 g pro. Exchanges: 0.5 fruit, 0.5 carb. Carb choices: 1.

PER SERVING WITH SUBSTITUTE: Same as above, except: 33 cal., 8 g carb. Exchanges: 0 carb. Carb choices: 0.5.

Dark Chocolate-Orange Pudding

A combination of cocoa powder and dark chocolate gives this creamy pudding loads of chocolate flavor. Pictured on page 151.

SERVINGS 5 (about ½ cup each)
CARB. PER SERVING 30 g

- ⅓ cup sugar*
- 2 tablespoons cornstarch
- 2 tablespoons unsweetened cocoa powder
- 2¼ cups fat-free milk
- ¼ cup refrigerated or frozen egg product, thawed, or 1 egg, lightly beaten
- 2 ounces dark chocolate, finely chopped
- 1 tablespoon vegetable oil spread
- 1 teaspoon vanilla
- 1 teaspoon finely shredded orange peel
  Kumquat, orange, or clementine slices (optional)
- ⅓ cup frozen light whipped dessert topping, thawed (optional)

1. In a medium saucepan, combine sugar, cornstarch, and cocoa powder. Gradually stir in milk. Cook and stir over medium heat until thickened and bubbly; reduce heat. Cook and stir for 2 minutes more. Remove from heat. Gradually stir about ¼ cup of the hot milk mixture into egg. Gradually stir in another ¼ cup of the milk mixture into egg. Add egg mixture and chocolate to the remaining milk mixture in saucepan. Bring to a gentle boil, whisking constantly; reduce heat. Cook and whisk for 2 minutes more. Remove from heat.

2. Whisk in vegetable oil spread, vanilla, and orange peel. Place saucepan in a very large bowl half-filled with ice water. Whisk pudding constantly for 2 minutes to cool quickly. Transfer pudding to a medium bowl. Cover surface of pudding with plastic wrap. Chill in the refrigerator for 2 to 24 hours.

3. Spoon pudding into dessert dishes. If desired, garnish with kumquat slices and/or whipped dessert topping.

*****SUGAR SUBSTITUTES:** We do not recommend sugar substitutes for this recipe.

PER SERVING: 196 cal., 6 g total fat (3 g sat. fat), 2 mg chol., 102 mg sodium, 30 g carb., 1 g fiber, 6 g pro. Exchanges: 1 milk, 1.5 carb., 1 fat. Carb choices: 2.

Blackberry-Banana Lemon Trifles

No matter what type of fresh berries you choose, this no-fuss, four-ingredient dessert makes a scrumptious ending to any meal.

SERVINGS 2 (1 trifle each)
CARB. PER SERVING 35 g

- 2 3.75-ounce containers lemon- or vanilla-flavor* sugar-free reduced-calorie ready-to-eat pudding
- 1 small banana, sliced
- ½ cup fresh blackberries, blueberries, raspberries, or sliced strawberries
- 1 100-calorie pack shortbread cookies, coarsely broken

1. Divide one of the containers of pudding between two 8-ounce straight-side glasses, spooning pudding evenly into glasses. Top pudding in glasses with half of the banana slices, half of the blackberries, and half of the cookies. Repeat layers with the remaining pudding, banana, berries, and cookies.

*****TEST KITCHEN TIP:** If using vanilla pudding, stir ¼ teaspoon finely shredded lemon peel into each of the containers of pudding.

PER SERVING: 165 cal., 3 g total fat (2 g sat. fat), 0 mg chol., 236 mg sodium, 35 g carb., 3 g fiber, 2 g pro. Exchanges: 1 fruit, 1 carb., 0.5 fat. Carb choices: 2.

Blackberry-Banana Lemon Trifles

recipe index

metric information

The charts on this page provide a guide for converting measurements from the U.S. customary system, which is used throughout this book, to the metric system.

Product Differences

Most of the ingredients called for in the recipes in this book are available in most countries. However, some are known by different names. Here are some common American ingredients and their possible counterparts:

* All-purpose flour is enriched, bleached or unbleached white household flour. When self-rising flour is used in place of all-purpose flour in a recipe that calls for leavening, omit the leavening agent (baking soda or baking powder) and salt.
* Baking soda is bicarbonate of soda.
* Cornstarch is cornflour.
* Golden raisins are sultanas.
* Light-colored corn syrup is golden syrup.
* Powdered sugar is icing sugar.
* Sugar (white) is granulated, fine granulated, or castor sugar.
* Vanilla or vanilla extract is vanilla essence.

Volume and Weight

The United States traditionally uses cup measures for liquid and solid ingredients. The chart below shows the approximate imperial and metric equivalents. If you are accustomed to weighing solid ingredients, the following approximate equivalents will be helpful.

* 1 cup butter, castor sugar, or rice = 8 ounces = ½ pound = 250 grams
* 1 cup flour = 4 ounces = ¼ pound = 125 grams
* 1 cup icing sugar = 5 ounces = 150 grams

Canadian and U.S. volume for a cup measure is 8 fluid ounces (237 ml), but the standard metric equivalent is 250 ml.

1 British imperial cup is 10 fluid ounces.

In Australia, 1 tablespoon equals 20 ml, and there are 4 teaspoons in the Australian tablespoon.

Spoon measures are used for smaller amounts of ingredients. Although the size of the tablespoon varies slightly in different countries, for practical purposes and for recipes in this book, a straight substitution is all that's necessary. Measurements made using cups or spoons always should be level unless stated otherwise.

Common Weight Range Replacements

Imperial / U.S.	Metric
½ ounce	15 g
1 ounce	25 g or 30 g
4 ounces (¼ pound)	115 g or 125 g
8 ounces (½ pound)	225 g or 250 g
16 ounces (1 pound)	450 g or 500 g
1¼ pounds	625 g
1½ pounds	750 g
2 pounds or 2¼ pounds	1,000 g or 1 Kg

Oven Temperature Equivalents

Fahrenheit Setting	Celsius Setting*	Gas Setting
300°F	150°C	Gas Mark 2 (very low)
325°F	160°C	Gas Mark 3 (low)
350°F	180°C	Gas Mark 4 (moderate)
375°F	190°C	Gas Mark 5 (moderate)
400°F	200°C	Gas Mark 6 (hot)
425°F	220°C	Gas Mark 7 (hot)
450°F	230°C	Gas Mark 8 (very hot)
475°F	240°C	Gas Mark 9 (very hot)
500°F	260°C	Gas Mark 10 (extremely hot)
Broil	Broil	Grill

*Electric and gas ovens may be calibrated using celsius. However, for an electric oven, increase celsius setting 10 to 20 degrees when cooking above 160°C. For convection or forced air ovens (gas or electric), lower the temperature setting 25°F/10°C when cooking at all heat levels.

Baking Pan Sizes

Imperial / U.S.	Metric
9×1½-inch round cake pan	22- or 23×4-cm (1.5 L)
9×1½-inch pie plate	22- or 23×4-cm (1 L)
8×8×2-inch square cake pan	20×5-cm (2 L)
9×9×2-inch square cake pan	22- or 23×4.5-cm (2.5 L)
11×7×1½-inch baking pan	28×17×4-cm (2 L)
2-quart rectangular baking pan	30×19×4.5-cm (3 L)
13×9×2-inch baking pan	34×22×4.5-cm (3.5 L)
15×10×1-inch jelly roll pan	40×25×2-cm
9×5×3-inch loaf pan	23×13×8-cm (2 L)
2-quart casserole	2 L

U.S. / Standard Metric Equivalents

⅛ teaspoon = 0.5 ml	
¼ teaspoon = 1 ml	
½ teaspoon = 2 ml	
1 teaspoon = 5 ml	
1 tablespoon = 15 ml	
2 tablespoons = 25 ml	
¼ cup = 2 fluid ounces = 50 ml	
⅓ cup = 3 fluid ounces = 75 ml	
½ cup = 4 fluid ounces = 125 ml	
⅔ cup = 5 fluid ounces = 150 ml	
¾ cup = 6 fluid ounces = 175 ml	
1 cup = 8 fluid ounces = 250 ml	
2 cups = 1 pint = 500 ml	
1 quart = 1 litre